Lacan in the End Time

C000200970

This book explores themes around the Father, His absence in modern society and the decline of mental health. The nature of this decline can be uniquely psychoanalytically theorised, in both the corresponding ferocity of the *internal* object and exposure to the Real.

The first part of this book underlines what psychoanalysis and psi-sciences continue to overlook: who now provides what Lacan called the "narrow footbridge" between anxiety and death? What terror(ism) must replace the father? How can reality be stabilised once more? The second part follows the atomised world as it turns towards extremism and utopian dreams: in Ireland via Hanaghan's radical psychoanalysis; in Levinasian ethics; in Gnostic belief in an evil world; and in the clinic of the death drive. The conclusion turns finally to the God *beyond* God, and the overwhelming evidence for God's presence in the world.

Lacan in the End Times will be of interest to psychoanalysts, psychotherapists, counsellors, social workers, and scholars in critical theory, philosophy, cultural theory, literary theory, and theology.

Rob Weatherill is practising and supervisory analyst in Dublin, Ireland, a member of two psychoanalytic groups (IFPP (Irish Forum for Psychoanalytic Psychotherapy) and ICP (Irish Council for Psychotherapy)) and a founding member of APPI (Association for Psychoanalysis and Psychotherapy in Ireland). He has a master's degree in psychotherapy from St. Vincent's University Hospital as well as a European Certificate in Psychotherapy. He taught psychoanalysis in post-graduate courses at University College Dublin, Trinity College Dublin and the Milltown Institute of Philosophy and Theology. He currently convenes two supervision groups that meet fortnightly. He has published five books internationally and edited one other.

Lacan in the End Times

In the Name of the Absent Father

Rob Weatherill

Routledge
Taylor & Francis Group

LONDON AND NEW YORK

Cover image: the fish mosaic (Christian symbol) dating from the second half of the 4th century in the Cathedral Basilica of the Assumption of Mary, a Roman Catholic basilica in the Istrian town of Poreč, Croatia. © Getty Images

First published 2023
by Routledge
4 Park Square, Milton Park, Abingdon, Oxon OX14 4RN

and by Routledge
605 Third Avenue, New York, NY 10158

Routledge is an imprint of the Taylor & Francis Group, an informa business

British Library Cataloguing-in-Publication Data
A catalogue record for this book is available from the British Library

Library of Congress Cataloging-in-Publication Data
Names: Weatherill, Rob, author.
Title: Lacan in the end times: in the name of the absent father/Rob Weatherill.
Description: Abingdon, Oxon; New York, NY: Routledge, 2023. | Includes bibliographical references and index. |
Identifiers: LCCN 2022014132 (print) | LCCN 2022014133 (ebook) | ISBN 9781032125268 (hbk) | ISBN 9781032125275 (pbk) | ISBN 9781003225010 (ebk)
Subjects: LCSH: Fathers–Psychology. | Reality–Political aspects. | Symbolism (Psychology) | Lacan, Jacques, 1901-1981.
Classification: LCC HQ756 .W39 2023 (print) | LCC HQ756 (ebook) | DDC 150.19/5092–dc23/eng/20220517
LC record available at https://lccn.loc.gov/2022014132
LC ebook record available at https://lccn.loc.gov/2022014133

ISBN: 9781032125268 (hbk)
ISBN: 9781032125275 (pbk)
ISBN: 9781003225010 (ebk)

DOI: 10.4324/9781003225010

Typeset in Bembo
by Deanta Global Publishing Services, Chennai, India

To my sons Ben and John and my father Norman.

Contents

Acknowledgements   viii
Preface   ix

PART I   1

1 Do You Believe in Reality?   3

2 Where Have All the Fathers Gone?   22

3 Loving the Father into Life   44

4 Being (not) in the World without a Father   64

PART II   81

5 The Mystical Origin of Psychoanalysis in Ireland   83

6 Hanaghan Returns   106

7 Is it Righteous to Be?   121

8 Tired to Death in an Evil World   143

9 The Irreducible Datum   175

PART III   191

10 The Evidence   193

Index   227

Acknowledgements

Some sections of this book have been derived in part from material recently published, or from talks recently given. **Chapter 1** is based on a talk of the same title given at the Congress of The Irish Forum for Psychoanalytic Psychotherapy: "The Subject is 'Dreaming'" in Dublin on 9 November 2019. **Chapter 2** is based in part on the keynote address of that title given to the annual Congress of the Association of Psychoanalytic Psychotherapy in Dun Laoghaire, Ireland on 10 November 2018. This presentation was one of a series that day to mark the launch of the book *The Anti-Oedipus Complex. Lacan, Critical Theory and Postmodernism*. This paper was later published in *Lacunae. APPI International Journal for Lacanian Psychoanalysis*. June 2019. *Issue 18*: 9–35. A version of this paper formed the basis of a talk given at the Percy French Summer School in July 2021. **Chapter 4** is a longer version of a paper published in *Lacunae. APPI International Journal for Lacanian Psychoanalysis*. July 2018. *Issue16*: 64–90. **Chapter 5** and 6 are longer version of the two papers that first appeared in *Lacunae. APPI International Journal for Lacanian Psychoanalysis*. June 2021. *Issue 22*: 128–153 and 163–189. **Chapter 9** is partly based on a paper of that title in *Sitegeist*. Summer 2019. *Issue 14:* 24–44.

A book like this can only be written with the help, challenge, open discussion, and disagreement with colleagues and friends. The ideas expressed in the book are entirely compiled and choreographed by the author and are the responsibility of the author alone, unless otherwise made clear by reference to others. With that proviso, I would like to appreciate many friends and colleagues whose support and encouragement I have always greatly valued.

Preface

In Ireland, there is a chain of convenience stores in petrol stations called *On the Run*.[1] Indeed! We must hit the ground running or, indeed, not even hit the ground at all, because post-Heidegger *there is no ground* – cosmological, epistemological, psychological, ontological, or ethical. There is no place to stand still or rest. Long gone are the old notions of presence, objectivity and will to power.

Our most treasured possession is called a "mobile", presumably because it enables us to be just that, in touch with anywhere in the world – *stay connected and be mobile*! The mobile is addictive and with the Metaverse, a quantum jump, both potentially immersive and addictive.

No time to think, all is in ceaseless movement in the gig economy. Across the world there are mass migrations fleeing war, persecution, climate change, and now pandemics. Many people are forced to leave their homes. Eighty million people worldwide have been forcibly displaced, not including the recent war in Ukraine.[2]

The subject's pursuit of meaning is generally incapacitating and should be suspended.

This is the first sentence of a PhD thesis.[3] At one time to find meaning was considered enlightening. Now, to find meaning is deemed incapacitating and even narcissistic. It limits mobility and this is bad for the globalist, universalist, transhuman economy. The psychotic is caught by too many meanings, while the neurotic is caught by too narrow a meaning which restricts life. Should we prefer meaninglessness? Is meaning code for tradition and old ways and therefore must be suspended? Post-Lacan, meaning becomes an impossible enigma: 'We are enjoyed by our thoughts'.[4] Ours is a post-interpretive era, beyond meaning!

The modern subject must be light, ephemeral, fleeting, nomadic – a subject "from anywhere".[5] The subject "from somewhere", with his illusion of meaning*ful* rootedness in family or community and *so on, should be suspended*. A college education normally serves to achieve the transition to the anywhere required, mandated especially today by globalisation: mobility *not* rootedness. And increasingly the mobilisation required is TOTAL. So the universities have taken their proselytising message of anywhereness out into the community.

All the "from somewhere" have to transition to "from anywhere". The pandemic has vastly accelerated the cyborg revolution as we have all been forced to be virtual from anywhere, to work remotely, avoid contact, remain in our bubbles.

A mega-process, in train since the industrial revolution, moves to the end point of hyper-individualism, with isolated subjects suitably hollowed-out, *de*-meaned and *de*-racinated, disconnected from religion, family, nation, and *so on*, even their own gender and, quite soon, their own bodies, as we approach the trans- or post-human total immersion.

The notion of progress, of unimagined freedom, the motor of liberalism in all its forms, now unites more or less everyone, left and right. It has very rapidly become the new orthodoxy. Social justice meets transnational corporations meets big tech meets NGOs (non-governmental organisations) meets world government, all essentially united in the old globalist project of the rational scientific management of humanity on the basis of equality, post-America, post-the West.

But, what now of privacy and freedom? Imperilled like never before? We are about to surrender freedom for safety and security. Freedom or intimate inescapable surveillance? There will be no escape?

The ambitious aim of this book is to assess what these tectonic shifts might mean and already mean for the ailing ephemeral subject attempting to adjust to, indeed comply with – **compliance is key** – measured quantitively to determine social credit scores. You do not have a choice?

The modest job (!) here is to register loss within the maelstrom, drawing on, necessarily only, the tiniest fraction of the wisdom of the world. The amazing thing still strikes one, as Levinas says, 'Within this world, it appears that the opening of certain books can cause the abrupt invasion of truths from outside',[6] he has in mind Jewish truth, but also Christian truth, or what Boris Gunjevic calls 'the thrilling romance of radical orthodoxy'[7] – the *only* mirror in which to see, to illumine, the contemporary? Opening certain books can bring an abundance of joy, truth, and freedom!

On each page, I want to register **loss**, aware that much contemporary language necessarily fails this task of representing the Real. Critics, mostly the young, will say, *what* loss! What are you measuring "loss" against? And, where is this loss? I see only gain! The reader will judge. Mention the words Jewish or Christian, by the way, and understandably because of endemic corruption in the Church and past violence, people will turn away. And they will turn away too because of ongoing anti-Christian propaganda and persecution across the world.

However, *underground* Christianity remains such a threat and arguably represents the only substantial resistance to the juggernaut of globalism and post-humanism now gathering pace and led inexorably by China. And, turning away, let us be very clear, means turning your back on two millennia of the most serious thinking that would genuinely liberate you. Maybe, that's what you are doing: not turning your back on a Christian fairy tale, as the atheists have it, but turning your back on that serious thinking.

Writing a book in these times one is on very shaky ground, in danger of disappearing or just being "cancelled". De(con)struction has (over)done its work. Like the trick of pulling off the tablecloth leaving the cups, plates and utensils in place. The removal of the (Symbolic) fabric is the univocal vocation of the endless modernising process – the stripping of the world of its underpinning cloth, its very spiritual substance. Now, at this *late* stage of modernity we are smashing the cups, plates, and turning over the tables, like Christ, with increasing ferocity, such is the apocalyptic rage of frustration generated by the wrong answers to the wrong questions. The result? Antagonism without end. Leveraging gender, ethnic, class cleavages. Recall, the *bonlieus* burning in French cities, the "peace lines" in Belfast, the burning and looting in American cities during 2020. And this is just the first world. Now we have the Afghani terror superstate as well as Somalia, Ethiopia and Ukraine.

As Ihab Hussan commented a generation ago apropos the postmodern,

> Everywhere now we observe societies riven by the double and coeval process of planetisation and retribalisation, totalitarianism and terror, fanatic faith and radical disbelief. Everywhere we meet, in mutant or displaced forms, that conjunctive/disjunctive technological rage which affects postmodern discourse.[8]

Chairman Mao knew precisely how to de-mean subjects, how to "liberate" the subject from the incapacitating meaning of the "Four Olds" – ideals, culture, customs, habits. He may be coming back.

> In a very short time … several hundred million peasants will rise up like a mighty storm. Like a hurricane, a force so swift and violent that no power, however great, will be able to hold it back. They will smash all the trammels that bind them … sweep all the imperialists, warlords, corrupt officials, local tyrants and evil gentry into their graves.[9]

And so it happened. From 1958 to 1962, his Great Leap Forward led to the deaths of up to 45 million people – easily making it the biggest episode of mass murder ever recorded.[10] The photograph accompanying this article shows not triumphant peasants but a huddled heap of suffering humanity. This crime has never been accounted for and therefore is bound to be repeated. Maybe "liberation" this time round will be absolute safety, security and equality.

What is the link between these massive world events and psychoanalysis? Analysis proceeds one-by-one; and analysis is a cure through love. It must always resist the corrupting power of the political and *the personal as political*.

The register of the Symbolic does not belong to anyone, but to all. Yet, our medium, our praxis, seems to have become irredeemably atheistic. There is no centre, no point of orientation, no quilting point. Archimedes says, 'Give me a fulcrum, and I will shake the world'.[11] However, the world is undoubtedly shaking with intense feelings, and we always feel duty-bound to say that it is working out well, it is working out for the best.

Even as we accelerate towards the end point. After several centuries we approach the Singularity(!)[12] which, according to Stephen Hawkins and others, will lead to our demise as a species.

In this time of epochal uncertainty, the book offers **ten** chapters. The first chapter deals with the question of reality and its disappearance/reversal/undoing, and the next three chapters deal with the disappearance of specific "realities" – "the father" on the one hand and "the child" on the other. In the second part of the book we look at some examples of apocalypticism and messianism, the amazing lost story of Christian psychoanalysis in Ireland, the question of our "right to be" in the world, God's tiredness and withdrawal, modern Gnostic heresy, the (Freudian) death drive and, in conclusion, the lightning strike of the Incarnation/Resurrection and the joyous gift of freedom and free association.

Underpinning the whole book is the question that is rarely heard being asked these days! **How is it going *without* the Father?**

★★★

Notes

1 *On the Run* is a flagship convenience store brand developed by ExxonMobil, used at Exxon and Mobil stations in the United States, BP and Mobil in Australia and at Esso and Mobil stations internationally.
2 www.unhcr.org/en-ie/figures-at-a-glance.html.
3 Urban, W. 2014.
4 Solano-Suarez, E. in Voruz, V. and Wolf, B. (Eds) 2007, p. 98.
5 Goodhart, D. 2017.
6 In Hand, S. 1989, p. 191.
7 In Žižek, S. and Gunjevic, B. 2012.
8 Hussan, I. 1992, p. 204.
9 Mao, T.-T. 1966, p. 119. See further Weatherill, R. 2017, chapter 9.
10 Somin, I. 2016.
11 Cited in Weil, S. 1951, p. 47.
12 Kurzweil, R. 2005.

References

Goodhart, D. 2017. *The Road to Somewhere: The Populist Revolt and the Future of Politics*. London: C Hurst & Co Publishers Ltd.
Hand, S. 1989. *The Levinas Reader*. Oxford and Cambridge, MA: Blackwell.
Hussan, I. 1992. "Pluralism in postmodern perspective". In Jencks, C. (Eds.) 1992 *The Post-Modern Reader*. New York and London: St. Martin's Press and Academy Edition, pp. 40–72.

Jencks, C 1992, *The Post-Modern Reader*. New York and London: St. Martin's Press and Academy Editions.

Kurzweil, R. 2005. *The Singularity is Near*. New York: Penguin Putnam Inc.

Mao, T.-T. 1966. *Quotations From Chaiman Mao*. Peking: Foreign Languages Press.

Solano-Suarez, E. in Voruz, V., Wolf, B. (Eds.) 2007. *The Later Lacan. An Introduction*. New York: The State University of New York Press.

Somin, I. 2016. "Remembering the Biggest Mass Murder in the History of the World". *The Washington Post*. https://www.washingtonpost.com/news/volokh-conspiracy/wp/2016/08/03/giving-historys-greatest-mass-murderer-his-due/

Urban, W. 2014. "Sexuated Topology and the Suspension of Meaning: A Non-hermeneutical Phenomenological Approach to Textual Analysis. https://yorkspace.library.yorku.ca/xmlui/handle/10315/27706

Weatherill, R. 2017. *The Anti-Oedipus Complex. Lacan, Critical Theory and Postmodernism*. London and New York: Routledge.

Weil, S. 1951. *Waiting for God*. New York and London: Harper Perennial Modern Classics, 2009.

Zizek, S., Gunjevic, B. 2012. *God in Pain*. New York: Seven Stories Press.

Part I

1   Do You Believe in Reality?

This chapter explores the question of reality versus phantasy in psychoanalysis and in postmodern theory generally. Should we privilege reality? Is reality now just a matter of belief? For the psychoanalyst, reality is indeed stranger than fiction. Psychoanalysis has been accused of covering up the reality of sexual abuse and, more recently, rape culture. The loss of reality leads to a sense of injustice and insecurity among potential victims. This chapter follows a number of psychoanalytic theorists, such as Winnicott from *Playing and Reality*, Bion's explication of the dispersal of reality in the "paranoid-schizoid" (PS) position and the rigid "realities" of the borderline in Rosenfeld and Meltzer. The register of the Real in Lacan is considered in relation to *The Matrix*. And, as Baudrillard asserts that *nothing exists* bar appearances, the discussion moves to performative "realities", simulations, and fake news, and the widespread crisis of legitimacy. Who can be believed? The themes developed here are returned to throughout this book.

'Do you believe in reality?' a person (a potential patient) shouts down the phone. '**Do you believe in reality**? Because my previous analyst did not', she continues. 'My younger sister died when I was five and my analyst never directly referred to this tragedy'.

The analyst was thinking that Kleinian analysis focusses so much on the internal world of early childhood that the apparent neglect of her sister's death is entirely possible.

Is reality a matter of *belief*? Surely not. Reality is out there; it is out there to be observed and we can set the dream, even the daydream, against reality. At least that's how things used to be. Now it is hard to be so certain. It is an understatement, but reality these days is hotly contested.

Freud was the first analyst who seemed to abandon reality when he retracted his Seduction Theory in 1897. This caused quite a hoo-ha nearly a century later when Masson published his book, *The Assault on Truth: Freud's Suppression of the Seduction Theory* in 1984. This was at the time when the first reports of sexual **abuse** were reaching the media. Abuse was just beginning to become

DOI: 10.4324/9781003225010-2

a new reality! Paedophilia was technically legal up until 1983 in the UK. The Paedophile Information Exchange (PIE) was a pro-paedophile activist group which was affiliated to the National Council for Civil Liberties (NCCL) in the UK. It was at the margin of the sexual revolution, to be sure, but tolerated nevertheless. Back in the late 60s, a number of key figures on the Left in France, Sartre, de Beauvoir, Derrida, Barthes, Foucault, Aragon, Deleuze, Guattari, Dolto, Lyotard, controversially approved of sex with children, signing petitions, 'demanding decriminalisation of paedophilia and the right to do with one's body what one liked opposing the culturally constructed frontier that separates children from adults'.[1] How times change. How reality changes.

Around that time, the story was told of how an Irish priest would visit a prestigious Catholic girls' boarding school every Sunday and take just one of the senior girls out for lunch at the nearby hotel. They returned much later to a chorus of delighted nuns who flattered the priest promising to see him again next week. The girls never told each other what had happened to them after the sumptuous meal.[2]

For Masson and others, many others, Freud was covering up the reality of sexual abuse that his female patients were reporting. Apparently Freud could not believe that so many of his patients had been sexually interfered with in childhood. As we might say today, Freud – the man, the bourgeois male – was covering up, protecting psychoanalysis, protecting the patriarchy. Outside psychoanalytic circles this view has held: if you say you were abused, you were abused, period. *Believe the victim.* More recently, a one-time significant figure in Lacanian psychoanalysis goes further than Masson suggesting that psychoanalysis not only covered up abuse but also justified rape culture.[3]

But the big contribution that psychoanalysis has made here is likely to be lost – that is the dimension of the subject's Oedipal **dreaming** – the strong desire to gain the love of her father, an intense dream she never truly gives up. As George Bataille has emphasised, it is of the nature of the erotic to be about fusion – a fusion of bodies, so the possibilities of misunderstandings here abound: my father's playing with me, bathing me, tossing me up in the air, reading a night-time story – ah! But was that abuse? Surely that **was** abuse? He denies it; oh yes! He would wouldn't he! And *so on.* Add to this mix a notion of predatory, toxic masculinity and the Oedipal dream becomes "a reality" for which the father must be blamed. *LISTEN, YOU WERE ABUSED; YOU ARE INNOCENT.* And the whole psychoanalytically informed question of the child's (forbidden shameful) desire is lost. The great irony is that the child/adult today has nowhere to go with her secrets as no one will believe her. We are back in pre-Freudian times.

And, for the record, Freud did not deny that sexual abuse occurs. He acknowledged that the excessive libido released by the abuse overwhelms the ego and can lead to psychosis. Furthermore, he added that *every* infant is sexually stimulated by the bodily care it gets as a baby during changing and feeding.[4]

Thus, psychoanalysis stresses the **primacy** of the internal or psychical world, the world of wish fulfilment, the world of phantasy stretching from daydreaming to night dreaming all of which subtly colour our perception of reality. So, in 1911, Freud published a paper on the pleasure principle and the reality principle; the pleasure principle governing the internal world and the reality principle the external world. Our access to reality is limited by the pleasure principle, as the id tries to dominate the scene with illusions of mastery, egocentricity, and sexual conquest.

And this is best observed in transference and dreams of transference love (or hate). And here Freud acknowledges that the wish-fulfilling dreams of love and reality are really hard to disentangle. Having insisted that transference love must be analysed for the dream longing persisting from early childhood that it is, and not acted upon or gratified in any way by the analyst, at the end of this paper Freud concedes the apparent "genuineness" of transference love! 'If it seems so lacking in normality, this is sufficiently explained by the fact that being in love in ordinary life, outside analysis, is also more similar to abnormal than normal mental phenomena'.[5]

At the beginning of life, **Winnicott** stressed the provision of "primary illusionment"[6] created by 100 per cent "primary maternal preoccupation" leading to, throughout life, the possible shelter from reality offered by the so-called "transitional space"[7] where the subject can continue to dream and be creative inside her own bubble. However, Winnicott is clear, the phantasy-dream *must have brakes* and these come in the shape of the survival of the object – out there in reality – after the phantasied destructive attack. As Winnicott put it rather poetically, the infant "kills" the other who survives its phantasied attacks, therefore reality is separate and distinct from phantasy. I kill you; you survive, therefore you are real and outside my omnipotent control and therefore I can begin to believe in reality *out there*, which is a liberation.[8]

To be stuck in your dream is madness. Take, for instance, the phantasy of killing the other and the other *actually* dies (through illness, separation, drug addiction, and *so on*), this is a disaster as my phantasy now seems omnipotent – that is has **no** brakes. And, this *is* a disaster for many young children whose rage now knows no bounds. This is why the analyst must survive destructive attacks (from disturbed patients) in order that the patient can begin to believe that the analyst is real – out there – and not under his crazy perverse omnipotent control. This is how reality OUT THERE is established, as against one's subjective dreaming.

When T.S. Eliot says, as everyone knows, we cannot bear very much reality, **Wilfred Bion** would concur when he does not automatically disparage the so-called Kleinian "paranoid-schizoid" (PS) position in favour of the "depressive position". The former position fragments reality in order to disperse feelings so that not too much feeling can accumulate in any one place as it were. That would lead to a depression. Thus the PS position makes life bearable without becoming overtly psychotic. With this "normal" dreaming state, we can continue to live a tolerable life because of the dispersal and deferral of meaning that is potentially too intense. This has something in common with Lacan's notion of 'the passion for ignorance',[9] a persistent avoidance of truth, an active dynamic of negation. People say, apropos news, '*Don't tell me! Don't* *tell me! I know it's bad, but I don't wanna know!*' In the depressive position, on the contrary, all the fragments of reality tend to come together to create a depressive crisis – an appalling awareness of the Real of suffering and the causes of suffering either in the world or in psychical reality, or both.

However, it is worth noting that the persistence of the PS position leads to a kind of colourless reality – a reality devoid of meaning and a loss of interest in reality or truth, which ultimately is not good for mental health.

And there is a particularly bad dream that must be mentioned and it can give some people little or no rest. I wrote about this in my book *Cultural Collapse* under the heading "The Empty Self" because it is essentially an empty dream.[10] It is the dream of failure, or as we would say today – being a "loser", being a "weirdo" or being "toxic". Here the victim seems to live not with a life-giving partner but with a death-dealing internal object that continually denigrates the ego and threatens desertion. Freud said as much in section 5 of *The Ego and the Id*. He is referring to the fear of death in depression, 'the ego gives itself up because it feels itself hated and persecuted by the superego, instead of loved'. 'It sees itself deserted by all protecting forces and lets itself die'.[11]

Herbert Rosenfeld speaks of the self being trapped in a rigid character structure which is psychotic, infantile, narcissistic, and omnipotent, that remains all powerful and 'which not only pulls him away towards death, but infantilizes him and prevents him from growing up, by keeping him away from [living] objects who could help him to achieve growth and development'.[12] Furthermore, this structural configuration 'poses as an ideal friend and helper'.[13] Imprisoned in this way, damaged personalities believe that they will at least be free from pain and anxiety, but at the price of being terrified of change, clinging to the persecutory imago (the archaic superego) rather than facing the extreme anxiety that would be induced by any sort of breaking away. That is why these narcissistic, borderline, or schizoid personalities are so difficult to treat therapeutically.

In a similar vein, this time in relation to perversion, Donald Meltzer suggests that,

> an illusion of safety is promulgated by the omniscience of the destructive part and perpetuated by the sense of omnipotence generated by the perversion or addictive activity involved. The tyrannical, addictive bad part is dreaded [because] … the essential hold over the submissive part of the self is by way of the dread of loss of protection against terror.[14]

Here then appears a parallel self that imprisons the subject allegedly for their own safety and protection.

Recall Freud saying:

> No stronger impression arises from the resistances during the work of analysis that of there being a force [the death drive] which is defending itself by every possible means against recovery and which is absolutely resolved to hold on to illness and suffering.[15]

Thus, here we have a dream of resistance *par excellence*, a deadly resistance against life and its openness and generosity. The psychotic compound of envy, greed, omnipotence, and narcissism acts as a parallel self, allegedly "protecting" the subject against impingement. Any possibility of improvement or amelioration that inevitably raises anxiety levels is struck out or destroyed internally. The ire of this "internal mafia gang" as Rosenfeld refers to it must not be raised. Only compliance brings full protection against change and against life. This is a common dream of control that often manifests in the analytic session as contempt towards others which can pass unnoticed. In the more extreme cases life cannot progress beyond the minimal.

This dystopian dream is illustrated by Rob Doyle in a short story aptly called "No Man's Land". The narrator, in his twenties, in the middle of mental torment, has dropped out of college. He finally leaves his room and his Xbox and has taken to walking in the vast wasteland of the Ballymount industrial estate on the outskirts of Dublin. 'Between the clusters of buildings … realms of unearthly silence … high metal railings … shapeless swathes of long and withered grass … a place beyond the world … There in the Ballymount estate, it took little imagination to believe that the catastrophe had already happened'. He avoids all human contact, until he comes across an older man in faded clothes who offers him a smoke and a can of Dutch Gold. The older man says:

> 'What do you know about Nietzsche?' 'Not much', comes the reply, 'God is dead … Nietzsche didn't see *this* coming … he didn't know how bad it would get … he held out hope for some kind of breakthrough … There is no father. There is no appeal', the abject man opines.

Is this Doyle's dystopia, a phantasy born of destructive narcissism or is this really reality? A world where there is no father. Is there no reality beyond phantasy to which one can appeal? If we take postmodern theorists seriously, do you believe in reality? Maybe, this is a dream appropriate to the times, a dream of invulnerability and radical autonomy, necessary to survive. A dream of something NOT nothing. I am f***ing something, NOT NOTHING.

Referent

What characterises the postmodern is the absence, the radical absence, of any agreed reality. Or, even reality itself.

Derrida: 'There never was any perception';[16]
Deleuze: 'Every perception is hallucinatory'.[17]
Nietzsche: 'There are no facts only interpretations'.[18]
Baudrillard: 'Appearances … the traces of the continuity of nothing'.[19]
Lacan: 'There is nothing outside the text'.

If I say that *I* am "speaking as a woman", then that is what I am. I am defined by this text (not the sort of real body I have as *there is no referent*). If I forget my password, I cannot gain access to the world online; I do not exist without this piece of arbitrary text.

Is this not illustrated when we phone a public utility, more often than not, we are speaking to a voice-activated system, with no hope of speaking to a real person. For example, you have some pressing and immediate problem with a utility. Eventually, personal help is at hand, but unfortunately the call centre person cannot sort out your issue after all. In desperation, as you are about to abort the call, the assistant says: 'Is there anything else I can help you with today?' Or, take for example when you are playing back your phone messages, 'There are *no* messages. To listen to your messages, press one'.

Or, on your computer, 'Keyboard unavailable. Press any key'.

When the van driver in Ken Loach's recent film, *I, Daniel Blake* (2016) wanted time off to visit the doctor, he was told that the algorithm that continuously monitored his driving performance does not allow for sickness, unless he can provide a replacement driver. This man therefore is not real, he cannot get sick as he is defined by an algorithm.

If prospective presidential candidate Elizabeth Warren says that she is Cherokee Indian, then maybe she is – that's the way she *feels* even though her DNA is less than 1 per cent Native American. But surely DNA is the ultimate text, consisting of just four letters arranged in unique patterns – the code that is said to define how long we will live, genetic diseases, and *so on*. We might find all our answers to our lives in this code. We are biological machines regulated by this code. Just text. And if I am Nobel prizewinner Tim Hunt who on one occasion makes a silly joke publicly about women, then *that* defines him and no one remembers his pioneering work on the mechanism of cell division and cancer.

Speaking of non-existent truth, Nietzsche says: 'truths are illusions … we have forgotten that they are illusions, metaphors which have become worn by frequent use and have lost all sensuous vigor, coins which, having lost their stamp, are now regarded as metal and no longer as coins'.[20] And **my** dream – people say this is my dream house … my dream holiday … my dream partner. Whatever it is: THIS IS *MY* DREAM. Don't spoil my dream even if it bears very little relation to reality.

Baudrillard explains our problem with reality:

> The main objection to reality is its propensity to submit unconditionally to every hypothesis you can make about it. With this its most abject conformism, it discourages the liveliest minds. You can subject it … to the most cruel torments, the most obscene provocations, the most paradoxical insinuations. It submits to everything with unrelenting servility.[21]

Thus, it is not necessarily the destructive narcissism of these patients that destroys the world in phantasy and denudes it of content, but post-Nietzschean theorists into the bargain who have moved from the one-time margins of academia confined to critical theory departments in universities, into the mainstream.

However, with reality and truth disappearing and the inevitably precipitous anxiety that ensues but is not acknowledged as such, we witness proliferations of *hyper*reality in its place. Such is the desolation felt by these patients, they feel bound to push to the event horizon, to the ultimate point of destruction and hyper-feeling carried along by the singular purity of the (death) drive.

Rob Doyle circles this horizon when writing the aptly named, *Threshold*, with drugs, abjection, and transcendental states. 'For years I have travelled to far flung places, lingering for short or long spells before drifting on, with no purpose whatsoever – had gone to these places, even, *because* no one would bother me'.[22] However, he acknowledges that writers like Cioran, Bataille, and Schopenhauer encourage despair. He has the gift of writing and maybe there is a turning point.

The status of the hyperreal bears investigation. How does it relate to the allegedly non-existent real. It is a *forcing* of the Real, a violence done to it by making it really appear so that you cannot possibly miss it. These are the "cruel torments" and the "obscene provocations". It is –*in your face*! Everything is overdone, over-hyped, and it is increasing all the time. It is meticulous in its revelations. Nothing is left out or left to chance. It becomes indoctrination.

Baudrillard's well-known triad formulation will help to better situate this hyper-phenomenon. Baudrillard is building on the work of Pierre Klossowski and Gilles Deleuze. Nietzsche had already declared his aim to show: 'How the "True World" Finally Became a Fable'.[23] The aim was to reverse the Platonic hierarchy between essence and appearance, the true from the false, when, as today, anyone could claim to be a *real* even hyperreal this or that, with sufficient sophistry and rhetoric.

The Baudrillardian triad – Illusion, Real, Simulation.[24] 1) Illusion plays (*ludere*) to appearances, the world before we appear, the glimpse of strangeness and beauty or horror. It has the aura quality of an original.

2) The Real in the Baudrillardian sense, rather than the Lacanian Real, is the "cut", the application of science and analytic knowing, the pixilation of appearances, gaining control over the otherness of the world, which is no longer playful. The Real is the real-*isation* via experiment and classification leading to, for example, the butterfly pinned to the board, the flowers pressed, named and preserved in the herbarium, the animals kept in perfect conditions in the zoo, recreational sex with health, protection and full consent of both parties (preferably written consent).

3) The third stage is the full exploitation of earlier realisations, with the possibility of endless, interminable Simulations, like the miniatures in art gallery shops – tea towels, scarves, pencil sharpeners, scrolls, prints, cards, etc., all with images of the masterpiece. *The original might as well never have existed.*

The Lacanian triad – Symbolic, Imaginary, Real – is now distorted as the Symbolic cedes ground to the Imaginary, the image being worth a thousand words. With the ubiquity of the camera phone, all is subsumed by the *hyperreal*, an accelerated and aggravated form of the Real which effortlessly dominates all human concerns, leaving nothing hidden, demanding the transparency and forcing of everything, with multiple copies.

As Baudrillard says, '"Objective" reality was always in some way a critical reality: it carried out its own defence. In the face of extreme reality [simulation, hyperreal] we are, by contrast, defenceless'. Further on, his interlocutor says,

> It's terrifying, this kind of nuclear winter that is spreading over theory and the world, which eliminates at birth the slightest trace of life. If out of panic, illusion has been eliminated, the traces of illusion must be wiped out. We are confronted with the pluperfect crime.[25]

You could argue that the Imaginary register for Lacan was a fight between equals: my image versus myself. With the hyperreal, by contrast, the "myself" 'submits to everything with unrelenting servility', there is no equality – the image is the Master. The slave all but disappears. The effects on mental health cannot be estimated.

The proliferation of screens has made us terrified to disappear, not to be "liked", not to be "followed". We have all become victims of the virtual self and its glamour and its fear of missing out and fear of disappearing. Everything seems governed by this hyperreal dream of narcissistic self-promotion and its imminent failure as it sucks the life out of us with its demand for our continuous attention – the person stopped on the pavement or in the road staring at their screen.

This dream of all dreams has taken over reality which, as Baudrillard says, has 'submitted unconditionally'. Our real has become our *hyper*real dream of ourselves. And we have been reduced to tech-slaves queuing around the block for the latest iPhone. And this dream grants every wish with an app. And we grovel for the love of the other. The danger here is of a backlash (ever-present): that my perfected image that I am feeding, the image of the other (me), which always is being compared with the perfected image of the other other – my friends my rivals – will turns its gaze back towards me on THIS side of the screen with smirking contempt – you slave, you worthless piece of sh★t, why don't you end it all? and *so on*. The risk is of a terrifying loss of self-esteem, condemned as we could by *our* dream image. And, the more the screens are laughing and punching the air in celebration of this or that, the more the mortal danger is that we might cease to join in the laughter of the crowd, heaven forbid! In a moment of honesty, in a moment of difference, we might not want to laugh and cheer along with the other. Then you're DEAD. It all hangs on a fragile thread. And then, as Molly Russell[26] found, there are websites that show you how to make a noose. Yes, this hyper-simulation mainly affects young women who increasingly will alter their bodies surgically to create the dream image.

What is to be done in this extreme bifurcation of self and hyper-imaging? Baudrillard tells us – it is to rediscover the power of absence; *learn how to disappear*.[27] I would add that if we do not learn how to disappear in life, what used to be a normal phenomenon of mere privacy in pre-internet times, then the fragile distraught subject may feel condemned to act out disappearance by suicide.

At this point, we might recall the phenomenon of "cutters" (mostly women who experience an urge to cut themselves with razors or otherwise hurt themselves), strictly correlative to the dominance of the hyperreal on social media. Cutting stands for a desperate strategy **to return to the Real of the body**. As such, cutting is to be contrasted with the standard tattoo inscriptions (signifiers) on the body, which guarantee the subject's inclusion in the symbolic order, albeit in a literal way, like a slave or an inmate. However, with the cutters, the problem is the opposite one, namely the assertion of the Real itself. Far from being suicidal, far from signalling a desire for self-annihilation, cutting is a radical attempt to (re)gain a stronghold in reality, or to firmly ground our ego in our bodily reality, *against the unbearable anxiety of perceiving oneself as non-existing*. The standard report of cutters is that, after seeing the warm blood flowing out of the self-inflicted wound, they feel alive again, firmly rooted in reality. So, although, of course, cutting is a pathological phenomenon, it is nonetheless a pathological attempt at regaining some kind of normalcy, at avoiding breakdown.[28]

The choreographed perfection enabled by image capture, with apps to doctor flaws in the skin and modify body shape to conform to an extreme ideal of slimness, deprives the subject of any malignancy. 'Edit your photos to perfection with this fast, powerful, and easy photo editor! Remove pimples, smooth wrinkles, even out skin tone, whiten teeth, and more to get the perfect photo every time'.[29]

What happens to the "remainder" outside the hyperreal image? How does the young girl deal with her malignancy totally removed from her ideal image (Ideal Ego).

In today's market, we find a whole series of products and activities deprived of their malignant properties: coffee without caffeine, cream without fat, beer without alcohol, butter without cholesterol, meat without the animal, even a virus without symptoms. Famously, "Guinness Clear", Guinness without Guinness, that is, 100 per cent water in a Guinness glass, allegedly to encourage responsible drinking! Baudrillard himself "invented" powdered water: to reconstitute, just add water! And there's even 'fake news you can trust'.[30]

You don't just go shopping you have a shopping *experience*. You don't just go to the toilet; you have to press a smiley face as you leave. You don't just get ill, you are "fragile", and you are "on a journey". (Non) meetings over Zoom. "Stay apart to stay close". Disincarnation and disembodiment, as a preparation for the fully post-human.

Virtual reality simply *generalises* this procedure of offering a product deprived of its substance, its materiality, its body, its humanity. In the same way decaffeinated coffee smells and tastes like real coffee. Virtual reality is experienced as reality without being real. However, at the end of this process of virtualisation, we have no choice but to accept that reality is its own best semblance. And there is NO choice, there are *only* semblances, simulations. We have moved seamlessly from the representational (with a referent) to the operational. The operational runs itself alone – *without people*.[31]

As Noailles and Baudrillard observe, 'If the reflected form disappeared, it would no longer be possible even to smash the mirror. Are we talking about the disappearance of another order here, an extermination?'[32]

★★★

We may not die from some external catastrophe but from banality, the banality of simulated seriousness or virtue signalling. Not being able to speak in any way about deep things, with no adequate language, and not even being at all aware of the loss of depth. Here is a clip from a programme on Irish radio, Newstalk.[33] The subject up for discussion at the book club is Viktor Frankl's *Man's Search for Meaning*. It was clear that the panel had not read this deeply thoughtful book on Frankl's experience of the Holocaust and his development of a variant of existential psychoanalysis, "Logotherapy". Also noted was the squeamishness and ignorance about the Holocaust itself.

It grabbed me, you know. Oh my God! Wow! It actually happened.

At the time I was reading it, the Australian bush fires were happening and I felt there was already a negative tone to the world. And I said to my husband, if we can come out of this blatant disregard for human life, maybe we can come out of anything. It was horrendous just to think that that was normal life for people at that time.

You know, you grow up with the Holocaust, you grow up with that word, but I didn't really know what it was. But it grabbed me when I started reading it. Yeah! Wow. *This actually happened*! I was hooked. At the end of the day it is a self-help book, and I wanted to see how he remained positive.

And you know when he talks about having a purpose, it's so hard now with everything that's going on. This book is so old, but it still has relevance today.

He was a doctor, caring for people, and then he might step away and look at the sunset or something and we are talking high barbed-wire fences and the like, but *still* he'd find joy and humour.

We all have something that can lift our spirits.

Yeah. We all have "highs" and "lows" and he does talk about suffering and I think it's really important as it is all part of the rich tapestry.

He had that mindset, you know, for resilience. You know what, he says you have to go through this to come out the other side. He didn't put any deadlines on it. But you learn a lot in the down days.

Stay in the NOW; the past has gone.

When they got out, they suffered *more*!

And he mentions his Jewish faith and they are waiting for the promised land.

We have to have those hooks in our lives.

You know it put our last book in the shade. I think I'd give this one an "eight".

No. I'd be closer to a "ten". Man's search for meaning, or *woman's* search for meaning – you need to get it, get a copy and give it to your children and your friends. No, really. You must. I mean it.

It's a lovely book …

No, it's really true, there's so much goodness in it.

As John Caputo says, 'If you do not have religion, then the only searching you do takes place in a shopping mall',[34] or online simulation.

The mirror, the video, the screen, and subjective elimination, 'The self is not a fixed, organic thing, but a dramatic effect that emerges from a performance [simulation],' says Jia Tolentino, 'The internet adds a host of other, nightmarish metaphorical structures: the mirror, the echo, the panopticon'.[35]

For those born directly into postmodernity with "truth" and "reality" free of the referent, free of what we used to call "depth" and where that space is left entirely *empty*. The generation of the hyperreal who want everything, feel entitled to everything – the kudos of the rat race, the hyper-socialisation of the big city, and yet also the simple life that comes from families and real relationships. And the well-nigh impossible sacrifice inherent in choosing, in making a choice! As journalist Gavin Haynes quipped, 'You cannot live the rest of a life everywhere, with everyone, one to one, always and forever'.[36]

Cyber operational takeover

If reality does not exist, or if it bends to our wishes, or it is in the eye of the beholder because there is no longer any referent; if there are only subjective, illusory versions of reality, and *so on*, then surely the empty field, the vacated space, is ripe for propaganda without end.

Every so-called "reality" is just someone's biased narrative, their conspiracy, their agenda, and *so on*. To be safe to be tentative, one had better put most things in parenthesis.

Rather than leading to a new kind of utopia of radical openness with the other without prejudice, it leads to quite the reverse. Everyone is potentially under suspicion. Are we not now in the same position as Herr K? 'Someone must have slandered Josef K., for one morning, *without having done anything truly wrong*, he was arrested'.[37] And according to his translator's introduction, Breon Mitchell says, 'Over the course of a year, Josef K. gradually weakens in his struggle with the mysterious forces that surround him. His true trial begins with the first sentence and ends only with his death'.[38]

Everyone is potentially under formal bureaucratic suspicion and it increases day by day, without this ever being made explicit. To do the simplest application online, we are obliged to fill in large forms with personal data with proof of this and proof of that. Young people are au fait with this intrusion and give no thought about these "mysterious forces" that bespeak iron conformity. Older people who can remember the given respect of informal relationships, conducted in person and in generosity of spirit with no state or corporate bureaucratic involvement, are variously disturbed, saddened, and even humiliated. Sensing their helplessness, they use humour, knowing that resistance is pointless. And humour is as far from the System as it is possible still to get.

Back in 1986, Ronald Reagan said – 'the nine worst words in the English language! *I am from the Government and I'm here to help!*' Thirty-five years later *global* governance together with world corporations are ever closer to overwhelming us, right in our homes, **and here to help**, with their *High Tech Dystopia*. As Naomi Klein warns,

> The future that it is being rushed into being since our past weeks of physical isolation, not as the painful necessity to save lives, but as a living laboratory for a permanent and highly profitable no touch future. For the privileged, almost everything is home delivered. It is the future that employs far fewer teachers, doctors, and drivers, accepts no cash or credit cards under the guise of virus control. It claims to be run on artificial intelligence but is actually held together by tens of millions of anonymous workers, tucked away in warehouses, data centres, content moderation mills, electronic switch shops, lithium mines, industrial farms, meat processing plants, and prisons, where they are left, unprotected from disease and hyper-exploitation. A shimmering screen to hide the millions of oppressed people to secure it. Eric Schmitt is at the centre of the new Shock Doctrine. At the heart of this version is a seamless integration of government with a handful of silicon valley giants with public schools, hospitals, doctors offices, police and military all outsourcing at a high cost many of their core functions to private tech companies.[39]

CEO of Steer Tech Anuja Sonalker says, 'There has been a distinct warming up to human-less, contactless technology … *Humans are biohazards, machines are not*'.[40]

Approaching Orwell, making crystal clear the removal of the referent:

> Do You realise that the past, starting from yesterday, has been actually abolished? … Every record has been destroyed or falsified, every book rewritten, every picture has been repainted, every statue and street building has been renamed, every date has been altered. And the process is continuing day by day and minute by minute. History has stopped. Nothing exists except an endless present in which the Party is always right.[41]

A political prisoner in a Chinese labour camp goes up to the librarian and says I want to check out a book on democracy. He slips a piece of paper under the glass and the librarian looks at the title of the book, punches some characters into the computer. The librarian replies, we don't have the book, but we do have the author.

Before the 2020 election in America, Biden mistakenly said that his campaign has assembled the 'most extensive and inclusive voter fraud organization in the history of American politics'.[42] Biden did not notice his mistake. It was later claimed that this was a slip.

> Barack Obama: If we do not have the capacity to distinguish what's true from what's false, then by definition the marketplace of ideas doesn't work. And, by definition, our democracy doesn't work. We are entering into an "epistemological crisis", in which our society is losing its handle on something called truth.[43]

Next to a sign with truth labels pointing in different directions, the *New York Times* begs Biden to appoint a "**reality czar**". Reality is now the predictable "reality" of officialdom.[44]

Hoisted by their own petard, postmodernists have created so many "realities" that are not real, they now find themselves in this bind! My God! Where is reality when you need it? Reality is what we say it is! We are going to control reality to save democracy – controlling the narrative. Basically, it's the alt-Right that is spoiling reality for the rest of us and their "extremism" must be controlled, these "domestic terrorists".[45] Bring on the Facebook whistleblower, Frances Haughen. Haughen is no normal whistleblower, at risk of obliteration by colleagues. She is funded by billionaire Pierre Omidyar and feted around the world giving the MSM the message they want to hear – Facebook incites hate! Facebook incites hate! The aim will be to bring it into the orbit of government control, so that it will control the hate coming from the Right.

And the new name for Facebook is Meta as in Metaverse. The internet is no longer *out there*, with us "using" it on this side of the screen. Soon it will engulf and surround us.

If we follow French historian Georges Bensoussan:

> There is a new language aimed at obscuring reality behind words that mean the exact opposite of what they are saying. The new language wants the listener to doubt his own opinions and so be persuaded that the perceptions of the party, the organization, the elite – that this new "public opinion" – is really just common sense.[46]

According to tech company founder Heywood Floyd, the so-called "Disintegration Directive", also known as the "Decomposition Directive" (officially *Richtlinie* 1/76 or the *Zersetzung* in German), was the approach that the East German secret police (the *Stasi*) took from 1976 onwards to crush dissent. This was less severe and therefore less controversial than the earlier prison and Gulag methods.[47] 'The goal was to destroy dissidents and potential dissidents socially and emotionally without resorting to arrest and imprisonment'. The Stasi "disintegrated" their target's private life, their careers, and family life by spreading false rumours. The victim becomes so preoccupied with the turmoil generated that they have no will to fight the State.

Floyd concludes:

> At this point, I think the parallels with the cancel culture of the modern West are obvious. To be clear, I'm not suggesting that the U.S. or other western governments are using these methods (yet). But I am suggesting that private groups and movements are doing so.[48]

Well-known philosopher Alisdair MacIntyre framed this loss wholesale of reality under the heading of "emotivism". 'To a large degree people now think, talk and act as if emotivism were true, no matter what their avowed theoretical standpoint maybe. Emotivism has become embodied in our culture ... this marks a degeneration, a grave cultural loss'.[49] In a chapter in *After Virtue*, aptly named "Nietzsche or Aristotle", he recognises the contemporary celebration of Nietzsche's take-down of inner moral sentiment or categorical imperatives, and *so on*, in favour of 'autonomous moral subjects ... *let will replace reason*'.[50] No more slave moralities!

The field is thus wide open for a variety of forms of *subjectivism* – feelings first – hysteria, seduction, psychotisation, dark forces unleashed without restraint. The Bolshevik revolutionary Nikolai Bukharin famously described the human person as a concentrated collection of social influences united in a small unit, as the skin of a sausage is filled with sausage meat.[51] However, today's fluid world might be represented better by "a soup" in which all fixed categories are being actively dissolved and blended with gender at the top of the list. All moral categories, norms, customs are abolished lest judgement arising might injure another. As Frank Furedi says, 'the crusade against binary thinking is principally driven by the desire to abolish moral judgement. Unfortunately, non-judgementalism already enjoys widespread institutional support in Western societies'.[52]

However, at the same time as so-called non-judgementalism comes *extreme* judgementalism fuelled by social media, which I prefer to call social *im*-media. The media in general fails to live up to its name. There is no distance from the Real, no mediation as such. Or, as Ricky Gervais calls social media, the toilet of the world. Instead of re-presenting the Real, it presents it (shit) directly, immediately, violently. Instead of de-monstrating the Real it monstrates. The Real *becomes a monster*.

People cite **The Matrix**, where the main character Neo is offered the choice between a red pill and a blue pill by rebel leader Morpheus. Morpheus in Greek mythology is the God of dreams. Humans are unknowingly imprisoned in the utopian dreamworld of the computer-generated matrix. Thus the subject is indeed dreaming. The red pill represents an uncertain future as it frees Neo from the enslaving control of the machine-generated dreamworld and allows him to escape into the real world of chaos and suffering. Living the truth of reality is harsher and much more difficult. On the other hand, the blue pill represents a beautiful prison of the dream pleasure-principle oriented world. It would lead him back to ignorance, living in comfort without want or fear within the simulated reality of *The Matrix*. Truth or pleasure? Neo chooses the red pill the pill that will bring truth.

Needless to say, the postmodernists variously denounce this reading of the story as naively simplistic. They would say axiomatically that the revealed so-called "reality" is just another fiction masquerading as reality.[53]

No, instead, we should follow the postmodern philosopher of hermeneutics Gianni Vattimo, helpfully summarised by Andrzej Kobyliński?

> Instead of reacting to the disintegration of reality with attempts to restore identity and belonging, one should rather perceive nihilism as an opportunity for emancipation. To discover the world as a conflict of interpretations also means to acknowledge oneself as heir of the tradition of weakening the strong structures of being in every dimension of existence. If we are uncomfortable today, it is not because we are nihilists, but rather because we are not nihilistic enough, because *we are unable to live the experience of the disintegration of being through and through*. This is the root of all the feelings of frustration and being lost that we call alienation.[54]

Vattimo's ethically oriented "weak thought" (*pensiero debole*) post-Heidegger and Nietzsche, understands philosophy should abandon claims to foundationalism, allow a weakening of thinking in a world that apparently needs no absolutes.[55] Vattimo thanked God he was an atheist. Doubtless, he was a philosopher for globalisation. But, as we have emphasised, there is a problem living with the disintegration of being. Someone spots the weakness in *pensiero debole*, and wants to impose *their* narrative. Never more so than now, since 2016. The strongest elbows out the weakest, whatever it takes. And the strongest now is big tech, which Paul Virilio predicted, following Einstein, 'the first bomb was the atomic bomb, the second one is the information bomb'.[56]

With no referent *any* narrative is possible and can be *made* credible by instantaneous repetition in the media. The 'disintegration of being through and through' is not liberating and expansive, but factional and enslaving, quickly becoming more like intense ideological warfare – Syria for the past decade, Lybia post-Gaddafi, Somalia, American cities during 2020, and *so on*.

Hermeneutic nihilism is a step too far for psychoanalysis, as it becomes a clinic of the death drive. This is a controversial point as we will see.[57] Instead, the task of the analytic treatment is interpretively combating these various resistance dreams, in order to tease out the truth of the subject's position in the symbolic world and wake up to, let us call it, the real illusion of reality. That is, one has to "create" a credible reality as a baseline, as it were, so as to create an orientation point – a story of origin, like the death of your sister when you were aged 5 and your symbolic world collapsed.

A well-known dream that Freud recounts comes to mind. A father has cared for his sick child for days and nights on end. After the child has died, the father falls asleep in the next room, leaving the door open so that he can see into the room where the child's body is laid out. He later dreams that his beloved child is alive and standing by his bed. Grasping him by the arm, the child says, '*Father, don't you see I'm burning*?' The child's body has indeed been partly set alight by a candle as the old man who was charged with staying by the dead body in the next room has also fallen asleep. The father eventually awakes from his dream and rushes to the dead body, but not before the wish that his beloved child is *still alive* is fulfilled in the dream. As Freud says,

> for the sake of fulfillment of this wish the father prolonged his sleep by one moment. The dream was preferred to a waking reflection [he probably could have seen the burning body] because it was able to show the child as once more alive.[58]

Freud comments more generally that we prefer to continue dreaming and sleeping, rather than wake up. '"Let the dream go on" – such was his motive – "or I shall have to wake up". In every other dream, just as in this one, the wish to sleep lends its support to the unconscious wish'.[59] We dream in order to continue sleeping. Freud says, 'All dreams are dreams of convenience: they serve the purpose of prolonging sleep instead of waking up. Dreams are the guardians of sleep not its disturbers'.[60]

But like Neo we should choose the red pill, to seek truth over pleasure, except that now this is nearly impossible in the virtual world and its total seductive power.

Is this not the reason why people, mostly young men, went in their thousands to hear Jordan Peterson in Dublin last year? Peterson speaks to young men, in particular, with his wake-up call to responsibility – wake up to what is going on around you. His message is sombre: the world is malevolent; there is suffering out there. RESPOND TO IT. 'Incarnate the spirit of the Logos'.[61]

A father is needed to stabilise the world. A father is needed to *believe* in reality. The urgent appeal is to the Father – *can't you see* …

Father.
Belief.
Reality.

Notes

1 Žižek, S. 2017, p. 221.
2 Personal communication.
3 Schneiderman, S. 2021. *Had Enough Therapy?* http://stuartschneiderman.blogspot.com.
4 Reference should also be made to Weatherill, R. 2011, chapters 1 and 5 for a more detailed exposition of the importance of psychoanalysis in relation to abuse.
5 Freud, S. 1915 [1914], p. 168.
6 Winnicott, D. 1971, p. 11.
7 Ibid., pp. 1–25.
8 Ibid., p. 88ff.
9 Lacan, J. 1972–1973, p. 110.
10 Weatherill, R. 1994, pp. 135–153.

11 Freud, S. SE 19, p. 58.
12 Rosenfeld, H. 1987, p. 113.
13 Ibid., p. 132.
14 Meltzer, D. 1973, pp. 105–106.
15 Freud, S. SE 23, p. 242.
16 Derrida, J. 1973, p. 103.
17 Deleuze, G. 1993, p. 93.
18 Nietzsche, F. 1883–1888, section 481.
19 Baudrillard, J. 1995, p. 1.
20 Nietzsche, F cited in Guess, R. and Speirs, R. 1999, pp. 39–53.
21 Baudrillard, J. 1995, p. 3.
22 Doyle, R. 2020, p. 179.
23 Nietzsche, F. 1889, pp. 485–486.
24 Baudrillard, J. and Noailles, E. 2005, pp. 43–58.
25 Ibid., p. 23.
26 Molly Russell was just 14 when she took her own life in 2017. After she died her family found graphic posts about suicide and self-harm on her Instagram account.
27 Baudrillard, J. 2001, p.100.
28 Derived from Žižek, S. 2006b, p. 103.
29 AirBrush – Best Photo Editor on the App Store.
30 See the Christian satirical website, *Babylon Bee.*
31 A friend who joined the Guinness brewery in Dublin in the early 60s worked with hundreds of others to produce the famous pint. By the new century, it takes just three people to run the whole operation.
32 Baudrillard, J. and Noailles, E. 2005, p. 112.
33 www.newstalk.com/shows/alive-kicking-claire-mckenna-834302 Sunday 16 February 2020.
34 Caputo, J. 2013, p. 49.
35 Tolentino, J. 2019, p. 14.
36 Haynes, G. 2021.
37 Kafka, F. 1925, p. 4, emphasis added.
38 Ibid., p. xxvi.
39 Klein, N. 2020.
40 Anuja Sonalker. www.facebook.com/singularitestech/posts/anuja-sonalker-ceo-of -steer-tech-a-maryland-based-company-selling-self-parking-t/529895134372217/.
41 Orwell, G. 1949, p. 178.
42 Biden speaking on 26 October 2020.
43 Kafka, P. 2020.
44 "How the Biden Administration Can Help Solve Our Reality Crisis".
45 www.whitehouse.gov/briefing-room/statements-releases/2021/06/15/fact-sheet -national-strategy-for-countering-domestic-terrorism/.
46 Bensoussan, G. 2020.
47 Floyd, H. 2021.
48 See also Weatherill, R. 1917, pp. 64–85.
49 MacIntyre, A. 1981, p. 22.
50 Ibid., 114. Emphasis added.
51 See Rowland, T. 2021.
52 Furedi, F. 2021.
53 Žižek, S. 2006a, p. 313.
54 Kobyliński, A. 2008.
55 Vattimo, G. 1988.
56 Armitage, J. (ed) 2002, p. 98.
57 See Chapters 2 and 9.
58 Freud, S. 1900, p. 510.

59 Ibid., p. 571.
60 Ibid., p. 233.
61 Peterson, J. 2018.

References

Armitage, J. (Ed.). 2002. *Virilio Live. Selected Interviews*. London: Sage Publications.

Baudrillard, J. 1995. *The Perfect Crime*. Paris: Éditions Galilée. Trans. Turner, C. London and New York: Verso, 1996.

Baudrillard, J. 2001. *Fragments*. Trans. Turner, C. London and New York: Routledge.

Baudrillard, J., and Noailles, E., 2005. *Exiles from Dialogue*. Paris: Éditions Galilée. Trans. Turner, C. Cambridge: Polity, 2007.

Bensoussan,   G.   2020.   http://hurryupharry.org/2020/02/08/muslim-anti-semitism -islamism-and-terror/ Feb 8th

Caputo, J. 2013. *Truth. Philosophy in Transit*. London: Penguin Books.

Deleuze, G. 1993. *The Fold: Leibniz and the Baroque*. Trans. Tom, C. London: Athlone, 1993.

Derrida, J. 1973. *Speech and Phenomena and Other Essays on Husserl's Theory of Signs*. Northwestern University Press.

Doyle, R. 2020. *Thresholds*. London: Bloomsbury.

Floyd, H.. 21/3/21. https://threadreaderapp.com/thread/1373761707500257280.html

Freud, S. 1900. *The Interpretation of Dreams*. *SE4, 5*.

Freud 1915 [1914] SE. 12. "Observations on Transference Love" pp157–171. SE 12.

Freud, S. n.d.b. SE. 19. The Ego and the Id. Freud, S. 1923 SE 19: 3–108.

Freud, S. n.d.c. SE. 23. Freud, S. 1937. "Analysis Terminable and Interminable" SE 23: 209–254.

Furedi, F. 2021. "The Trans Assault on Freedom". *Spiked-Online*. https://www.spiked -online.com/2021/10/22/the-trans-assault-on-freedom/

Guess, R., Speirs, R. (Eds.). 1999. "On Truth and Lying in a Non-Moral Sense". In *The Birth of Tragedy and Other Writings*. Cambridge and New York: Cambridge University Press.

Haynes, G. 2021. "The Emptiness of the Millennial World". *Unherd*. https://unherd.com /2021/03/do-millennials-have-a-voice/

Kafka, F., 1925. *The Trial*. Trans. Mitchell, B. New York: Schocken Books.

Kafka, P. 2020. "Obama: The Internet is the Single Biggest Threat to Our Democracy". *Vox*. Nov 16. https://www.vox.com/recode/2020/11/16/21570072/obama-internet -threat-democracy-facebook-fox-atlantic

Klein, N. 2020. "How Big Tech Plans to Profit from the Pandemic". *The Guardian*, May 13th. https://www.theguardian.com/news/2020/may/13/naomi-klein-how-big-tech -plans-to-profit-from-coronavirus-pandemic

Kobyliński, A. 2008. "Is Nihilism Our Destiny? The Postmetaphysical Ethics of Gianni Vattimo".   https://www.academia.edu/16176247/Is_Nihilism_Our_Destiny_The _Postmetaphysical_Ethics_of_Gianni_Vattimo?pls=RWLSbr2woN

Lacan, J., 1972–1973. *The Seminar 20. Encore: On Feminine Sexuality, the Limits of Love and Knowledge*. Fink, B. (Ed.). London: W.W. Norton, 1998.

MacIntyre, A. 1981. *After Virtue*. London: Duckworth.

Meltzer, D. 1973. *Sexual States of Mind*. London: Karnac, 1968.

Nietzsche, F. 1883-1888. *The Will to Power.* Trans. Kaufman, W., Hollingdale, R. J. New York: Random House, 1967.

Nietzsche, K. 1889. *Twilight of the Idols.* Trans. Kaufman, W., in *The Portable Nietzsche.* New York: Viking Press, 1954.

Orwell, G. 1949. *Nineteen Eighty-Four.* London: Penguin Classics, 2013.

Peterson, J. 2018. "Jordan Peterson: Truth in the Time of Chaos" https://www.youtube.com/watch?v=EjqXXengN1s

Rosenfeld, H. 1987. *Impasse and Interpretation.* London: Tavistock.

Rowland, T. 2021. "The Truth of Love and the Image of God". *Veritas Amoris Project*, Feb 20th.

Tolentino, J. 2019. *Trick Mirror: Reflections on Self-Delusion.* London and New York: Penguin Random House.

Vattimo, G. 1988. *The End of Modernity: Nihilism and Hermeneutics in Postmodern Culture.* Trans. Snyder J. Baltimore: John Hopkins University Press.

Weatherill. R. 1917. *The Anti-Oedipus Complex. Lacan, Critical Theory and Postmodernism.* London: Routledge

Weatherill. R. 1994. *Cultural Collapse.* London: Free Association Books.

Weatherill. R. 2011. *Forgetting Freud? Is Psychoanalysis in Retreat?* San Francisco: Academica Press.

Winnicott, D. 1971a. *Playing and Reality.* London: Hogarth.

Winnicott, D., 1971b. "Transitional Phenomena and Transitional Space". In Winnicott, D. (Ed.) *Playing and Reality.* London: Hogarth.

Zizek, S. 2006a. *The Parallax View.* Cambridge, MA. MIT Press.

Zizek, S. 2006b. *The Universal Exception.* London and New York: Bloomsbury.

Zizek, S. 2017. *The Courage of Hopelessness.* London and New York: Penguin.

2   Where Have All the Fathers Gone?

> The father, *qua* authority, is a spent force. Psychoanalysis turned its attention to the mother. In the context of the Cultural Revolution, the family became an "ideological conditioning device" (Cooper). This century, social theorists are referring to "Man deserts", with the rise of violent gang culture in cities, and the *psychical* formation of ferocious internal objects that torture the ego. Paraphrasing Freud, *Where the father was, there must the desert come to be*. Note is made about the failure of authorities to curb transnational crime and lawlessness. The loss of the organising principle of the big Other is mirrored by the contemporary Lacanian "clinic of the death drive". Here, the austere analyst undertakes not to help the patient. Instead, the space is left open for the emergence of desire *without the Other*. This revolutionary approach chimes well with atomised, globalised 21st century culture. Against this, Levinas asserts the "Good beyond Being" and that the psyche has a "theological structure".

In a sparklingly clean canteen in a community centre in a poor part of Birmingham, families talk quietly over their sandwiches. At the counter, a fight breaks out between five young men. The cook tries to calm the men down and asks them to leave, but it gets nastier – chairs are thrown, a knife is produced.

'See them? How angry they are', says an older man sitting outside. 'Not one of them ever knew their fathers.'[1]

Ladywood, Birmingham, is one of several UK districts where 70 per cent of children are now raised in households without fathers. An astonishing one million children are growing up in these blighted circumstances, living without a father and rarely even meeting an adult man, according to a recent troubling study of family breakdown by the Centre for Social Justice. Relationships break down fast and frequently. Children of single mothers often end up single mothers themselves. Absent fathers are a common factor among people imprisoned, girls groomed for sex, drug addicts, rioters, self-harmers, and young suicides.[2]

Where have the fathers gone? In psychoanalysis, the question of the father was considered of central importance into the mid-fifties. Lacan said that the

DOI: 10.4324/9781003225010-3

whole Freudian corpus could be summed up by the question: *what is it to be a father?* For Lacan, the father was much more than just a role model. The "In-the-Name-of-the Father" formula implies so much more, approaching the ineffable "Our Father" of the Lord's Prayer. And when Lacan referred to "The-Father-of-the Name",[3] he invoked Genesis. However, Lacanians assert that these are metaphors – the paternal metaphor – something not quite real at all. They are symbols or myths:

> symbols are not elaborations of sensations of reality. What is properly symbolic – and the most primitive of symbols – introduces something else, something entirely different into human reality … The creation of symbols accomplishes the introduction of a new reality into animal reality.[4]

This new reality, 'the introduction of an order, of a mathematical order, whose structure is different from the natural order',[5] is more important than the Real. This "Symbolic register" protects us from the (primal) Father's *jouissance* (as for instance in the near sacrifice of Isaac by Abraham). The "name" is homophonic with *le nom*, the forbidding "No" of the father as Symbolic. Thus with the Symbolic register, law, order, authority come to replace sacrifice. As Lacan says, 'It is in the *name of the father* that we must recognise the support of the symbolic function which, from the dawn of history, has identified his person with the figure of the law'.[6] The father for Lacan is 'a symbolic function to which all group member … are subjected. It provides human beings with an internalized compass of culturally and socially viable principles'.[7] As Lacan underlines, with the Father comes, 'the begetting of soul, the begetting of mind'.[8]

The father, Lacan insists, is the 'the narrow footbridge thanks to which the subject does not feel directly invaded, directly swallowed up by the yawning chasm that opens up as pure and simple confrontation with the anguish of death'.[9] This is key, that by that powerful image of the footbridge provided by the father, **we are shielded from the fall into anxiety on the one side and death on the other.**

Freud declares: the first thing to be loved in this world is the father. 'I cannot think of any need in childhood as strong as the need for a father's protection'.[10] All that is good and the highest in civilisation is derived from, as Freud reminds us, 'the ego-ideal [which] answers to everything that is expected of the higher nature of man. As a substitute for the longing for the father, it contains the germ from which all religions have evolved'.[11] And in his last book, *Moses and Monotheism*, Freud wrote: 'We know that in the mass of mankind there is a powerful need for an authority who can be admired … It is a longing for the father felt by everyone from childhood onwards'.[12]

While it is true to say that all *actual* fathers are less than ideal and that this father-longing (*Vatersehnsucht*) has again the structure of a myth. To invoke the mythic, however, is to underline its eternal importance psychically. However, in these *anti*-Oedipal times the father has long been deemed castrated, a spent force; his rule is over. What we are left with is just the empty husk of Freud's allegedly "defensive idealisation" of the father.

The father (mastery/authority in any form) has long since been castrated, deflated; his rule is over; a spent force. The father has disappeared and Lacan seems duly and strategically to fall in line with the new thinking during the Cultural Revolution of the sixties. He wished to emphasise the father's essential weakness. What Oedipus, Moses, and the Primal Father have in common is that they are part of the Freudian *dream*. As Lacan says, 'What we propose is to analyse the Oedipus complex as being Freud's dream'.[13] For Lacan, unlike Freud, the father does not exist: 'the real father is nothing other than an effect of language'.[14] And if it is axiomatic that the father *is* psychoanalysis, maybe Baudrillard's judgement against Lacan was correct: 'I've always liked Lacan: not at all as constructor of psychoanalysis, but as its destroyer, and precisely under the appearance of doing the opposite'.[15] And the younger Lacanians duly followed suit:

> The belief in the father is a typically neurotic symptom, [merely] a fourth ring within the Borromean structure. Lacan takes his leave from it and starts looking for a new signifier to fulfill the required function, to bind together the three rings.[16]

Not that the other post-Freudian analysts were much better in respect of the father. Their attention turned naturally to the mother, the mother's body, and object relations.[17] Ironically, the very important dramatic Kleinian focus on the fateful early Oedipus and the primitive persecutory superego[18] and the extreme danger foretold there for mental health, makes the *real presence* of the father a matter of life and death. Who else will be able to separate us, will *have the desire* to prise us free from the magnetism of the mother's *jouissance*? Bion's[19] notion of "detoxification" and "metabolising" in relation to "nameless dread" do not quite reach the mark as it misses the mother's *jouissance*. What is needed, according to Levinas for instance, is the father's *election* of the son. The father elects his child; he *chooses* his child. 'The "I" owes its unicity to the paternal eros [desire]'.[20] The son (or daughter) is the unique unexchangeable being through being chosen, through election: 'each son of the father is the unique son, the chosen son'.[21]

And now, more recently, not content with just the castrated father largely out of the picture, there has been much written on the pathology of the patriarchy and indeed masculinity itself. *Nothing less than an outright Oedipal patricide is called for across the board.*

However, we must underline this key psychoanalytic insight.

The Father creates/mediates the world. NO father means NO coherent world, leading to confusion – psychosis or perversion.
More precisely, the Lacanian formula: what is refused in the Symbolic order, in the sense of *Verwerfung*, reappears in the Real.[22]

What is refused is "castration", nothing less than the initiation into the adult world which involves a brush with death and a learning of this entirely new order which Lacan likens to a sophisticated computer whose internal rhythm we must respect.[23] Maybe we should heed Philip K. Dick, 'If you find this world bad, you should see some of the others'.[24]

De-familiarisation

Long before the 1960s' Cultural Revolution, societies had been under-going a process of rapid de-familiarisation in the process of modernisation. Industrialisation needed women to work. In Russia a century ago, Lenin's ideological assault specifically targeted marriage and family. He equated marriage with slavery. He granted easy divorce and abortion in 1920. Divorce was no longer for the rich only. Breaking family bonds enabled women, trapped and isolated on rural farms, to be more easily socialised and indoctrinated. Soviet realist art depicted the new Soviet worker *woman* like a man with broad shoulders. Communism would eliminate the need for families that formed a core resistance against the State. According to Leninist acolyte Alexandra Kollontai, who together with Inessa Armand set up Zhenotdel,[25]

> The housewife may spend all day … cleaning her home, she may wash and iron the linen daily, make every effort to keep her clothing in good order and prepare whatever dishes she pleases and her modest resources allow, and she will still end the day *without having created any values*.[26]

Considering her market value, Kollontai points out that, 'Despite her industry she would not have made anything that could be considered a *commodity*'. Thus, the preserves, the pickles, the wool, the weaving, the candles, the mending, the butter and *so on – all of no value*. Again and again they assert that women's work in the home 'is of no value to the State'. 'It is unproductive'.

Instead, be assured the Communist state will come to the aid of parents. Kollontai continues, 'the old type of family … constitutes the best weapon in the struggle to stifle the desire of the working class for freedom'. The 'narrow and petty' bourgeois family is not capable of creating the "new person". 'Under capitalism marriage was truly a chain of sorrow.' Instead, 'the workers' state will come to replace the family'. Do not worry, relinquish possessiveness, from now on your children are *"our* children", of the great universal proletarian family of workers of the glorious future. As for women who might have been worried that by easy divorce they could lose the "breadwinner" in the family: 'They have not yet understood that a woman must accustom herself to seek and find support in the collective and in society, and not from the individual man'.

When they suggest, 'The family is ceasing *to be necessary either to its members or to the nation as a whole*', are they not ratifying what capitalism in the previous century has already wrought? As Chicago economist James Heckman points out, 'Nobody wants to talk about the family, and the family's the whole story. And it's the whole story about a lot of social and economic issues'.[27]

Without ever asking how *that* social experiment fared, two generations later radical therapist activist David Cooper, who coined the term "Anti-psychiatry", asserted that the bourgeois family should be the key target of the Left: 'The social functioning of the family is as an ideological conditioning device'.[28] From the Left and Right, the family was undermined. During the eighties globalisation caused a further atomisation of life, demanding everyone must fend for themselves in the worldwide marketplace.[29]

As bonds are loosened, *the father is the first to go*, because his spiritual bond with his children is weaker when compared to the power of the mother's *jouissance*. Thus, we have ended up with an *anti*-Oedipal situation,[30] where, with the absence of the father, it became "forbidden to forbid", a slogan of the *soixante-huitards*.[31] Recall the success of *Bowling Alone*,[32] as we move from a "we" society to an "I" society, with the loss of social capital. Family was at the heart of social capital. Collapse of the family hits hardest in the poorest third of the society. There are fewer adults looking out for children, fewer coaches paying attention to kids, fewer neighbours, and a loss of a shared sense of social responsibility for the rearing of children.

Apparently, the progressive ideal for Westerners, the so-called Swedish model,

> was driven by one single, over-arching goal; to sever the traditional, some would say natural, ties between its citizens, be they those that bound children to their parents, workers to their employers, wives to their husbands or the elderly to their families.

Instead, individuals were encouraged – mostly by financial incentive or dis-incentive, but also through legislation, propaganda, and social pressure – to 'take their place in the collective', as one commentator rather ominously put it, 'and become dependent on the government'. But he notes that this can also be truthfully described as liberating Swedish citizens *from each other* allowing them to become autonomous entities. He quotes the Swedish author Henrik Berggren:

> The Swedish system is best understood not in terms of socialism but in terms of Rousseau. Rousseau was an extreme egalitarian and he really hated any kind of dependence – depending on other people destroyed your integrity, your *authenticity* – therefore the ideal situation was one where every citizen was an atom separated from all the other atoms … The Swedish system's logic is that it is dangerous to be dependent on other people, to be beholden to other people. Even to your family.[33]

★★★

A little history: during the two world wars, millions of men died in conflict and it became the norm for children to be brought up by their widowed mothers. One of the key differences then, however, was that extended families played a crucial role in raising a child: grandparents, siblings, aunts, and uncles united to help provide the stable family life missing for so many present-day children.

Back in 1926, millions of British working-class people lived in conditions of *abject* poverty – hunger, poor housing, unemployment, and absence of the breadwinner owing to the carnage of World War I. Nevertheless, even under those conditions, the violent offender rate, per 100,000 of the population, was just 4.4. Today it is over 1,400.[34] In one shocking statistic, David Fraser, who works in the criminal justice system, reveals that there are now 15 times more acts of wounding and endangering life a year than there were in the 1950s.

Criminologist Martin Glynn, who was raised by a single mother, wrote a report called "Dad and Me",[35] which explores the effects of absent fathers today. He has evidence which shows that children abandoned by their fathers are beset by self-loathing and drawn to inappropriate role models such as gang leaders, older lovers, and worse.

As long as 12 years ago, in a discussion on BBC *Newsnight* about a UNICEF report on childhood in Britain, a number of experts and policy makers talked about the breakdown of community. A community worker, Tony Sewell, son of Jamaican immigrants, who had been involved with these communities for two decades asked: 'W*here are the fathers*? Where are the adult males, fathers, uncles, grandfathers who will control the youth?' He says, 'the adults have gone AWOL'.[36] Sewell ran a charity called Generating Genius, which has helped poor black children out of the ghetto and got them into Oxbridge and other Russell Group universities. Talking about knife crime, Sewell says, 'Lack of policing is the answer; not by the police, *but by the parents*, if the kids have any at all'. Sewell asks, 'Why are we making excuses regarding the absence of the fathers from these families?' At least 50 per cent of black children have no dad living at home.

> 'The problem is nobody wants to go there, for political reasons. The police don't want to go there; nor do the social workers, the politicians or the black community itself, which then complains that it is being victimised. *And so it is never, ever addressed*'.[37]

Sewell also blames the myth of the African-Caribbean mum. 'Some black mothers do, indeed, work wonders despite the absence of a father; but not all can, and neither should they be required to. It is a culture that needs to change, for the sake of the children'. Instead, he says,

> Adults now fear children and children fear other children. Children used to have "uncles" and "aunts" in addition to their real relatives who were significant role models – where have all these gone? We should all adopt a child, but people are afraid of being accused of being child abusers.

David Lammy, Labour MP for Tottenham warned, after the London riots, that in areas like his there are 'none of the basic starting presumptions of two adults who want to start a family, raise children together, love them, nourish them and lead them to full independence'. Today, one in four children is brought up by a single parent, compared with one in 14 in 1972. 'The parents are not married and the child has come, frankly, out of casual sex; the father isn't present, and isn't expected to be. There aren't the networks of extended families to make up for it'. He warned that children, without male role models, turn to "hip-hop", "gang culture", and peer groups for their masculinity.

Lammy recalls the loss of his own West Indian father after his taxidermy business failed and his parents separated:

> My most enduring memory was of being pulled towards him as we stood on platform five at King's Cross station. Just two years earlier, on the very same platform, he had told me how proud he was of me for having won a choral scholarship to boarding school in Peterborough. This time was different. Hugging me close, he whispered, 'Take care of Mum, OK?' He was leaving the next day for the United States. Aged 12, I was returning to school. For my father, America held out the promise of a fresh start. He had always been someone I looked up to when he lived with us. He became unimaginably more important the day he left.[38]

Justice Sheehan, who helped establish the Prisoners Rights Organisation in Ireland in the 1970s, became well known for representing vulnerable groups at the fringes of society. Sheehan built one of the biggest criminal defence practices in Dublin. He believes,

> Much of the misery seen in Irish courts is caused by the lack of a father figure in offenders lives. We expect social workers and the HSE [Irish Health Service] to father and mother these children. It's an extraordinarily difficult task. I remember one case. This child, from the west of Ireland, at 13 had been in 40 placements since the age of three, abandoned by his father and intermittently abandoned by his mother. What has happened is that society today has allowed the role of the father to be undermined to our great detriment in human terms but also in financial terms. One of the things that we have to do is encourage young men to be responsible for their children. We have to go back and start at that point. We have allowed the position and the importance of the father to become eroded.[39]

Back in 2008, then Senator Obama told an audience: 'Children who grow up without a father are five times more likely to live in poverty and commit crime; nine times more likely to drop out of schools; and 20 times more likely to end up in prison'.[40] The figure in the US, according to the US Census Bureau, is that 19.7 million children, more than 1 in 4, live without a father in the home (National Fatherhood Initiative, 2017). The figure in Ireland is that 189,000 children live without a father at home.[41]

More recently, Senator Burgess Owens declared that back in the sixties black men led white men in staying married and raising their children. Now,

> we have 70–80% of black fathers desert their families and we are not willing to be honest about that … we cannot be honest about what's going on in our urban communities … There's a reason why out kids are being led into hopelessness. These men will not stay with the mothers of their children and instead will tell them to go get an abortion. We have lost 20m black babies in the last four years. 40% of my race has been exterminated because the men are not willing to protect their own children.

According to a recent report, 'Black women have been experiencing induced abortions at a rate nearly 4 times that of White women for at least 3 decades, and likely much longer'.[42] 'But be aware', continues Owens, 'we're waking up, we're waking up … You're going to see a change back to the productive men that we were when I was growing up'.[43]

Recent research by the ESRI (The Economic and Social Research Institute) in Ireland could not be clearer,

> Family structure emerged as having a significant and consistent relationship with adolescent behaviour, with poorer behaviour across all domains for those in lone-parent families or families that experienced separation during … adolescence. This pattern held even taking account of the socio-economic characteristics of these households and was not fully explained by other factors.[44]

Paula Mayock, Trinity College Dublin (TCD) School of Social Work, speaking on the Pat Kenny programme (RTÉ Radio) recently, has linked homelessness with fatherlessness. One-parent families headed by women make up 60–70 per cent of homelessness. Kenny called it 'the feminisation of homelessness'.[45]

Children in families where a father is actively present at home *do better by every measure*. Even families where there is no father at home within communities where the father is typically present, do better as a whole. Thus, the role of a father is overwhelmingly important. According to Bokoni and Patrick,[46] the rough-and-tumble play that fathers can engage in with their children facilitates psychosomatic integration. Chasing, wrestling and play-fighting, and so forth, where the fathers *set boundaries*, enable the "delay of gratification" so important for emotional development. Children learn to make the proper sacrifices and regulate their drives and in time learn to be adventurous even taking danger in their stride. Children not socialised in this way are more likely to be aggressive, bullying, and excluded from peer groups.

According to Brussioni,

I consider risky play an injury prevention strategy ... Children who have the opportunity to engage with risks in a secure setting with minimal hazards and appropriate supervision learn lessons that will serve them in good stead when they encounter risks in the "real" world.

Compared to mothers, fathers spend a larger percentage of their time playing with their children. Men's approach to caring involves doing activities together and taking kids out to play.

Fathers encourage children to step forth into the world as courageous beings.[47]

Where the Father was, there must the desert come to be

Raise any of these issues with professionals, politicians, and *so on*, and the generally predictable irritated response is,

look the father has gone and he is not coming back!

In private, people sometimes add: and gone with him, a general respect for authority of any kind, the law, knowledge, trust, civility, and the wisdom that comes with age.

The *anti-Oedipus complex* is, to paraphrase Freud – Where the father was, there must the desert come to be. If the Oedipus complex was psychoanalytic approximation for mental stability and ordinary suffering, the *anti*-Oedipus complex, the transvaluation of all values, is freedom for the few but mental instability, self-hate, and suicidal ideation for the many. Maybe, what American chat-show host, Bill Maher, referred to as "emotional haemophiliacs". 'Children swear at their parents – *f*ck you mam*! Parents are pussy whipped by their children. Liberal parents are afraid that parental authority will stunt their creativity'.[48]

However, within psychoanalysis there is still also a sense or an undercurrent that we have lost something very precious – this mystery of the father. In fact, **we seem to be in *two* minds**: 1) bring on the loss with a kind of saintly forbearance and a sigh, a full acceptance that the father is not coming back. Or, 2) a constant repetition of the Name-of-the-Father, a sense of nostalgia at his loss.

Take J.-A. Miller's articulations in this respect:

"the psy"[49] is now being expected to substitute himself for the forebear to assure the transmission of values and continuity between generations. The listening ear of the psy, qualified or not, constitutes the compassionate cushion to the "society of risk" ... the need for personalised attention.[50]

Over and against listening to the suffering other, there is what Miller refers to as the desert of "abstract and anonymous systems" – the State bureaucracy. He gives an impressive list of society's pathologies: detraditionalisation; loss of bearings; disarray of identifications; dehumanisation of desire; violence in the community; suicide among the young; the *passages à l'acte* of the mentally ill. As Miller says, psys are being called upon to constitute or *re*-constitute the social bond which is going through a process of restructuring, 'probably without precedent since the industrial revolution'. Added to this he says psys are asked to, 'assure the transmission of values and continuity between generations'.[51]

While the Name-of-the-Father, or any notion of symbolic authority with the power to transmit a sense of authority and stability between the generations seems irredeemably lost, what fills the vacuum is a universe of perverted *jouissance* that, at best, may be managed/monitored by the law while at the same time endorsing its obscene core – corruption in the police; paedophilia in the Church; the celebration of obscene wealth accumulation; celebrity drug endorsement; scorning of traditional moralities; and *so on*. Thus, it has become impossible to "unmask the law" – to denounce its obscene underside – since there is no foundation from which to denounce or unmask this underside.

To claim that the psys can create the social bond, or can be transmitters of values, or act in place of forebears, is disingenuous. How can the psys ever stand in for the lost father, except as a face-saving expediency for the State authorities and cash-strapped mental health services, but it is entirely unrealistic given the demonstrable empirical need for his continual presence within the family.

Out in the desert

Meantime the front-line services struggle to cope. And we get story after story of desperate parents who cannot control their children. In the extreme, par-amilitaries perform punishment shootings in Northern Ireland on antisocial youth deemed out of control.[52] It is the brutal justice of kneecapping – a shot from a handgun to the knee, elbow, or ankle, i.e. real castration in the place of the prophylaxis of symbolic castration. Likewise, paramilitaries have been used on sink housing estates to "discipline" drug pushers, using so-called "alterna-tive methods".[53] You know you're in trouble when youth stop fearing the leaders of Sinn Fein in your community!

Globally, the situation is quite alarming, the law is becoming less and less effective and all the time finding itself behind the curve of the Real. According to Lynne Owens[54] of the UK's National Crime Agency, all types of transna-tional crime are up: child abuse, modern slavery, human trafficking, cyber-crime, county lines, illicit finance, criminal waste disposal poisoning the groundwater – they are all increasing. Apparently, a report seen by *The Times*[55] has revealed that the Metropolitan police are ignoring about a third of all crime reports, after just one telephone call with the victim. Crimes such as burglary, low-level assault, criminal damage can all be dismissed according to a policy secretly introduced by Scotland Yard last year. They warn that this secretly emboldens criminals. In Britain crimes that end in prosecutions are down to just 7.8 per cent. In Ireland, almost 8,000 reported crimes by more than 3,000 children and young people went unpunished due to serious problems with the

Garda youth referral scheme, the force has confirmed. Serious crimes that were not pursued included one case of rape and one of child neglect.[56]

As part of a series of programmes to mark the end of the millennium, the BBC's John Simpson interviewed the head of Interpol, who acknowledged openly back then that the world's criminal syndicates are beyond the reach of the international and national policing bodies.[57] Since then the growth of the internet and open borders have greatly facilitated international crime.[58]

Then, two decades on, in Biden's America, there are widespread calls from the Democrats, to 'defund the police', or even 'imagine a world without policing', 'dismantling that institution', 'to end policing as we know it', 'to reallocate resources', and *so on*.[59]

Human trafficking is second only to drugs for criminal profitability. And recently we have been told that Ireland is 'easy on trafficking', the worst in Europe.[60] The recent film *Doing Money* was based on the true story of Ana, a student from Romania who was kidnapped on the streets of London in broad daylight on the way home from her cleaning job and forced to become a sex slave in "pop-up brothels" in different cities across Northern Ireland and the Irish Republic. Rejected by her parents back home for now "being a prostitute", she asks: 'do you know what it feels like to be totally alone, totally alone in the whole world when you finally know that nobody's coming?' And it is women who are most at risk. We have had the story here in Ireland that Gardai have not been responding to 999 calls.[61] In the UK rapes are going underinvestigated. And in recent years, several women have been murdered at random on the streets of the capital city.[62]

By comparison, well-known Irish journalist Mary Kenny said recently that when she was just 16 'she felt completely safe on the streets of Dublin during the sixties'.[63] More than half a century later, the contemporary world is an "orphan". As Pope John Paul II reminds us, '[the world] lacks fathers and those who give witness to Fatherhood. There is no true brotherhood without the father'.[64] Indeed, this is the orphan world. And the orphans are unsafe.

There are parts of our big cities where the law does not operate, or it operates *after* the crime. In Frank Berry's *Michael Inside*, young Michael (Dafhyd Flynn) is living with a kindly elderly grandfather, Francis (Lalor Roddy), while his dad is in jail for drug offences. Francis understands the lawless world and the perils lurking round every corner of this rundown Dublin housing estate. Eighteen-year-old Michael, already on probation, is making every effort to stay on the proper path, when he is caught with drugs he was keeping for a friend's older brother. He is sentenced to three months in prison. Once there, he is forced to fight for his life as violence escalates. His grandfather is threatened by the drugs gang to get €2,000 to pay for the confiscated drugs. Michael is released but goes after the gang that is harassing them. He is back inside again on just the day when he is accepted onto a course to study in social care which would have taken him out of this violent underworld. The point here is that the Symbolic father is largely ineffective and so violence escalates with the law only intervening *after* the event. When Michael is briefly back out on the city streets, the grey horizon of the housing estate seems as bleak as the prison he has just been in.

According to Edward Davies of the Centre for Social Justice,

> The thread from fatherless young men to criminality is a conveyor belt that starts young, often with school exclusion, meanders through youth justice, and ends in prison. It's no coincidence that two thirds of our prison population are second generation. Before they first got into trouble, they lost their fathers to incarceration too.[65]

Davies cites the charity Addaction, which deals with drug and alcohol problems among young people. *Pace* Freud, 'They warned a decade ago of an epidemic of "father-hunger". It said this was creating a social time bomb of sub-conscious anger'.

If we follow Mary Eberstadt, in her *First Things* article "The Fury of the Fatherless", commenting on a summer of rage (2020) in the cities in America,

> What is happening to America is an excruciatingly painful truth that life without father, [God, the] Father, and filial piety toward country are not the socially neutral options that contemporary liberalism holds them to be. The sinkhole into which all three have collapsed is now a public hazard. The threefold crisis of paternity is depriving many young people – especially young men – of reasons to live as rational and productive citizens. As the Catholic theologian Deborah Savage put it recently, reflecting on America's youth: 'They have been left alone in a cosmos with nothing to guide them, not even a firm grasp of what constitutes their basic humanity, and no means of finding the way home'.[66]

The contemporary world is an "orphan". This casual, careless, freedom-loving "nobodaddy" culture is not calm or free but **massively enraged, unbound, and uncontained** *jouissance*. Each atom has an electric charge. There is no knowing where the discharge will happen, but happen it does, although it's not yet a chain reaction.

No father.
No God-the-father.
No filial piety.

★★★

The clinic of the death drive

As Terry Eagleton makes clear, our central figure is Nietzsche, but without his tragic vision. Postmodernism is post-tragic.

'Whereas modernism experiences the death of God [the loss of the symbolic father] as a trauma, an affront, as source of anguish as well as a cause for celebration, postmodernism does not experience it at all. There is no God-shaped hole at the centre of the universe, as there is in Kafka, Beckett or even Philip Larkin' ... Post-tragic because, '[t]ragedy involves the possibility of irretrievable loss, whereas for postmodernism *there is nothing momentous missing*'.[67]

In spite of the overwhelming empirical evidence about the importance of the father, J.-A. Miller concurring that *there is nothing momentous missing*, refers to some psychoanalysts 'remaining attached to obsolete beliefs ... and the most ignorant [analysts] and least likable of the lot cry over the Name-of-the-father dreaming of reestablishing its reign'.[68] Note the projective slur from the old Maoist[69] against *those* analysts and never mind his own contradiction with the comments above about the social bond.

Ironically, there may be very much more to cry over with the new authoritarianisms establishing *their* reign, as we will amply illustrate in subsequent chapters.

Let us summarise from the "Project of Declaration of the Principles of Lacanian Practice".[70] According to the introduction to this document, 'for analysts of the [Millerian–Lacanian] school', this declaration is *after* Freud and *after* Lacan. It purports to be an up-to-date defence of psychoanalysis for the new century, the end result of the thorough deconstruction of the Law of the Father:

> Analysis is *not* a dialogue as we [analysts] abstain from re-education, any empathic understanding or identification with the patient ... renounce any pedagogical ideal ... no direction of conscience or spiritual guidance ... no principle of reality, no reality testing ... no notion of a therapeutic alliance with a healthy part of the ego ... nor any function of synthesis or adaptation by the ego.

This approach is radically against Freud: '[t]he ego seeks to bring the influence of the external world to bear upon the id ... to substitute the reality principle for the pleasure principle ... The ego represents what may be called reason and common sense'.[71] And referring to sublimation, Freud states that the uniting and binding effects of Eros, 'helps towards establishing the unity, or tendency to unity, which is particularly characteristic of the ego ... sublimation may take place regularly through the mediation of the ego'.[72] 'The ego is an organization, characterised by a very remarkable trend towards unification, towards synthesis',[73] without which it is impossible to make judgements and be rational.

Of course, Lacan laughs loudly at such egoic suggestions! So-called "synthesis" and so-called "construction". Referring to slips, bungled actions, 'the very text of your existence, they make a grotesque farce of ... the ideal functions of consciousness ... about the person who has to gain control ... *It* dreams, *it* fails and *it* laughs'.[74] At the very least, this "it" is a very perfect "out" for the criminal. No responsibility. Prison doctor, Theodore Dalrymple, would ironically concur, given the title of this recent book: *The Knife Went In*.[75]

Any of the above *human* qualities – empathy, dialogue, reality testing, therapeutic alliance, guidance of any sort, adaptation, education, or engagement – are all now deemed part of a hidden *ideology of social control* (the big Other), a subtle means of controlling the subject's absolute freedom and thus serving to prevent the subject from deciphering that knot of the Real that congealed impasse that *in-sists* in *ex-sistence*, i.e. the death drive that repeats and repeats. Thus, Lacanian psychoanalysis is deemed a clinic of the death drive, that IT (id), that '"irreducible datum" of the unconscious',[76] that is our singular desire, our destiny, our fate. Gradually the various illusions that the Other supports – the desire of the other and our desire for the other's desire – painfully fall away. 'Lacanian practice is guided by the principle of abstinence', where the analyst occupies the position of the *objet a*,[77] a zero position of impotence, a witness no less.

Against Winnicott, but according to WAP (The World Association of Psychoanalysis), 'the analyst does not take enjoyment in his unconscious, the analysand does not take enjoyment in free association'. Indeed, there are to be no "meaningful" interpretations, instead the sessions are to be *a*-semantic, i.e. against proliferations of sense, meaning, insights, and *so on*. There will be no interpretation of the transference repetitions. 'We do not use the counter-transference as an instrument for assessing the unconscious of the patient'.

Nothing can be "helpful". To parody Psalm 23, even though I walk through the valley of the shadow of death, *I am on my own and there is nothing to comfort me*. Me alone; no big Other to guarantee my life in any sense, no father, no symbolic father, no support, no engagement, nothing.

Nothing is the key

Nothing, in the full sense, *can be helpful*, we must concede. As Ana says, being totally alone in the whole world – it makes you grow up. Thus, there is no Socratic "know thyself"; quite the opposite. We are strangers to ourselves. As the poet Georg Trakl writes, 'Something strange is the soul on the earth'.[78] Analysis is a process of estrangement from the (false) self, a shaking of every foundation, a-nihilation. There is no "there there" as Lacan says, no consolation.

Žižek argues the Lacanian position:

> What makes life "worth living" is the very *excess of life*: the awareness that there is something for which we are ready to risk our life (we may call this excess "freedom", "honour", "dignity", "autonomy", etc. or indeed some would call it the death drive in its life negating sense). Only when we are ready to take this risk are we really alive.[79]

Or, as he puts it a few pages later, 'It is crucial … to assert some kind of pri-mordial excess or too-muchness of life itself: human life never coincides with itself; to be fully alive means to be larger than life'.[80]

Quite the antithesis of conformity and adaptation, it says: f**k the other; who cares! Recall, for instance, that Žižek memorably spoke about visiting some ultra-nationalist Serbs in the former Yugoslavia, who shamelessly (i.e. in the absence of the big Other) talked and laughed about their ethnic cleansing, raping, and extreme violence – not for them the petit bourgeois rules of civilised society! This, Žižek recalls, was maybe the best freedom, an "obscene freedom".

The social good

In an atomistic, post-Oedipal culture with broken communities and *so on*, the urgent cultural question should also be about the social good. What happens if everyone tries to assert his freedom, autonomy, etc., this excess of life, good or bad, at the same time? Is this not just entitlement culture? Is this not essentially an elitist notion following the iron Darwinism–Hobbesian law of life from St Matthew: '*For whoever has, to him more* (freedom – honour – dignity – auton-omy – excess) *will be given, and he will have abundance; but whoever does not have, even what he has will be taken away from him*' (Matthew, 12:13).

Those who do not have – those without the father, or without the stable family, without anything familiar, or without means, without education, and *so on* – what little they have will be taken away, the "have-nots". These are not the privileged people, they are the forgotten people, the ones whom the State purports to care for. As Rabbi Jonathan Sachs says, 'A world without morality is good for the successful and the strong but bad for everyone else'. So, when we talk about "freedom – honour – dignity – autonomy" and the glorious *excess* of life – *jouissance* – and we celebrate this freedom, are we not seriously missing something? Is Lacanianism just fine for the elite and for the armchair radicals?

Sloterdijk shares our disillusion:

> In its pretension to co-form a revolutionary subject, politicised psychoa-nalysis failed miserably. So, there are now attempts to shore up a minimal terrain – indeed the terrain of an allegedly pure analysis. The new purists mark themselves off from everything to do with sense-giving, interpreta-tion, construction, life-projects, because this would once again put into play the need to explain people normatively, to develop positive ideas of culture [civilisation], and introduce creative processes.[81]

Steiner refers to the contemporary postmodern as the "after-Word". He says, 'Today, we stand orphaned but free in the place of the a-Logos'.[82]

While it must be conceded (according to the WAP principles), 'Psychoanalysis cannot decide what its aims are in terms of an adaptation of a subject's singular-ity to any norms … or standards of reality', because, 1) the analytic space will be closed down by the analyst's desire to teach and instruct; 2) the analyst cannot know the patient, this emergent enigmatic singularity, strange soul upon the earth; and 3) the analyst cannot act on the basis of her anxiety, i.e. more for her sake than the patient's.

However, *no* engagement, *no* empathy, *no* guidance; only "the postmodern zone of indifference".[83] What can the analysand do but just drone on aimlessly in the void of the analytic silence with the occasional signifier or lapse signalling something maybe? Maybe not. 'Is the patient still speaking?' the supervisor might ask. 'They are continuing to come each week? Well fine! Keep going. See you next week'. Reminiscent surely of the: *is the patient still conscious and breathing? Okay the ambulance is on it way!*

Orphaned but free! Here, the father has gone – the memory of his voice has faded. Good riddance! Is not this deemed the great achievement of modern feminism and de-familiarisation. The end of patriarchy and tradition? How does one assume one's desire in this arid, austere space of the analytic setting of the *no father*? Orphaned but free.

What is missing in this (dis)orientation of the thousand plateaus[84] of new freedom, is the whole question of responsibility. Recall years back when William Richardson dared to suggest that the patient has responsibilities as well as rights to speak and be heard. Was this analyst Richardson still a Lacanian, people asked? Responsibilities to family, to community, to themselves, and *so on*? The question of the social good? Richardson went so far as to add: 'Without an accountable subject [to the other/Other], there is no ethics, and an ethics of psychoanalysis no more than chimera. The whole enterprise would have to be rethought, then – or call itself something else'.[85]

Several years ago, I wondered what an ethics of psychoanalysis would look like from a Kleinian–Levinasian viewpoint sustained by the background of the Platonic Good. Paraphrasing Levinas[86] a little: the Good is not good because we choose it, desire it, and it attracts us, but precisely the opposite. The Good is good because it interrupts ongoing desire and life, redirecting it towards responsibility for the neighbour. It breaks the decadent sacred spell (*jouissance*) to touch the forbidden Thing. The Good is beyond being. The Good renounces any power. It is an anarchy that leaves us free.

How does the Good beyond Being interact with (fallen) beings *per se*, that is, the being of the analyst and analysand. However, Levinas refers not to an interaction which implies some sort of equality, but rather the irruption of a "brilliant light".[87] I formulated just ten principles:

1) At the core of psychoanalytic psychotherapy is the safeguarding of the analysand's freedom.
2) The analytic situation is a presentation in silence (never shown, stated, or represented) of goodness in which both the analysand and the analyst participate. This goodness is infinite and beyond knowing.
3) It is "participation in" rather than "possession of", which correlates with Bion's "without memory or desire", as it cuts across and undermines the

analyst's omnipotence, always present in some degree because the analyst is a desiring subject. However, if the analyst or therapist tries to become the Good, or presents himself in any way as master of this goodness, the whole project will be doomed.

4) The psychoanalytic understanding of human desire inevitably means that analysis is there to be destroyed in phantasy. But it is important that the process survive in reality, so that it can be destroyed again and again á la Winnicott.[88]

5) The goodness of the analytic situation must be "dosed", measured out (this is a question of technique), otherwise it would induce regression and psychosis, a danger inherent in some more active post-Freudian psychotherapies. Therefore, analysis takes time. The ego will shield itself from truth with hatred (subjectivity) so that it can maintain its domination.

6) Analysands hate the increase in emotional knowledge (alpha-function) that analysis ushers in, and claim that they are getting worse, while they may be gaining a capacity to bear feelings and be more alive – the depressive position. Unless these feelings are held, they may quickly revert to beta elements again. There is a danger of psychotic breakdown.

7) The background of an unstated goodness is the only basis upon which any analysis can proceed. Without this faith in presence behind the absent-presence of the analyst, nothing can be said and nothing would be worth destroying.

8) The goodness must remain background. If there is an attempt to introduce it into discourse, then someone will want to possess it. This is the problem identified already, with therapy and therapy culture: the forcing and commercial promotion of goodness.

9) Unless the analyst has some acknowledged or unacknowledged faith in this goodness, he will not be able to bear failure, and will resort to cynicism, power, or manipulation.

10) The ego is in danger of being burst open by the Good – dispossessed, uprooted, exposed, and ashamed. How can it recover? We are unfree to choose the Good, no one chooses it voluntarily, and there is no time to choose, as such, because it chooses us, although no one is enslaved by it.[89]

To a Protestant–atheistic–postmodern–Millerian orientation, we need the ultimate Nietzschean–Stoical courage – proud to face life alone, *amor fati* in face of the void, whatever the risk of the backfire, reaction, *ressentiment*, and mental illness. Maybe freedom for the few. The Radical Orthodox position,[90] on the face of it, seems less arduous, because it is connected and embedded and thus emboldened by the Good beyond and within being. However, to sustain commitment to the other, to family, to a set of values, to the increasingly broken community, and not least to faith in a world that rejects faith requires sustained courage. At the extreme it involves "detachment", loss of ego, kenosis, affliction, dying to life – in short, "the Cross" in anticipation of prodigality, donation, and joy.

Assuming one's history in responsibility (to the other) should be precisely the psychoanalytic goal. Recall – witnessing, on the edge of strangeness, meaninglessness, and death, in the manner of a vigil, fully awake but anticipating death – is only fully possible *in the light of the Good*. As Levinas makes clear, 'Goodness gives to subjectivity its irreducible signification'.[91] We need Simone Weil's unshakeable conviction that, 'come what may, the universe is full'.[92]

Notes

1   Alibhai-Brown, J. 2013.
2   Ibid.
3   Lacan, J. 1974–1975, pp. 101–102.
4   Lacan, J. 1963, pp. 44–45.
5   Lacan, J. 1955–1956, p. 320.
6   Lacan, J. 1963, p. 67.
7   Vanheule, S. 2011, p. 61.
8   Lacan, J. 1955–1956, pp. 212–213.
9   Lacan, J. 1958–1959. Session of 7/1/59.
10 Freud. S. 1930, p. 72.
11 Freud, S. 1923, p. 37.
12 Freud, S. 1939, p. 109.
13 Lacan, J. 1969–1970, p. 117.
14 Ibid., p. 127.
15 In Gane, M. 1993, p. 59.
16 Verhaeghe, P. and Declercq, F. 2002, in Thurston, T (ed) 2002, p. 71.
17 Etchegoyen, A. 2001.
18 Klein, M. 1928.
19 Bion, W. 1962.
20 Levinas, E. 1961, p. 278.
21 Levinas, E. 1961, p. 279.
22 Lacan, J. 1955–1956, p. 13.
23 Ibid., p. 12.
24 Dick, P. 1977.
25 Zhenotdel was devoted to improving the conditions of women's lives throughout the Soviet Union.
26 Kollontai, A. 1920. Emphasis added showing the materialist value is all that counts in communism as well as capitalism! www.marxists.org/archive/kollonta/1920/communism-family.htm.
27 James Heckman. https://ifstudies.org/blog/nobel-laureate-james-heckman-the-family-is-the-whole-story-.
28 Cooper, D. 1971, p. 5.
29 Recall that Thatcher's poll tax was levied not on households or families, but on *individuals*.
30 Weatherill, R. 2017.
31 Someone who took part in, or otherwise supported, the civil unrest, characterised by student protests and widespread strikes, in France in May 1968. This also refers to a fierce social activist or protester.
32 Putnam, R. 2000.
33 Booth, M. 2015, p. 358.
34 Fraser, D. 2018.
35 Glynn, M. 2011.
36 Enright, S. 2007.

37   These include implicit racism, denigration of lone parents, misogyny, attacks on the poor.
38   Lammy, D. 3 August 2012.
39   Gallagher, C. 2017.
40   www.reuters.com/article/us-usa-fathers-idUSN0419185720070614.
41   Pownall, S. 2017.
42   Studnicki, J., Fisher, J., and Sherley, J. 2020.
43   https://twitter.com/RepBurgessOwens. 30.9.21.
44   www.esri.ie/system/files/publications/RS119.pdf; Smyth, E. and Darmody, M. 2021, p. 86.
45   Mayock, P. and Bretherton, J. 2016.
46   Bokoni, P. and Patrick, T. 2009.
47   Brussioni, M. 2020.
48   https://etcanada.com/news/298840/bill-maher-fumes-over-metoo-movement-warns-of-creating-police-state-on-sex-and-love/. And he continues, 'and they're – some millennials who grew up screaming at their parents – are so f★★king fragile!'
49   "Psy" stands for psychologist, psychotherapist, psychoanalyst, psychiatrist, etc.
50   Miller, J.-A. 2005, pp. 50–51.
51   Ibid., p. 51.
52   Wynarczyk, N. 2018 and McDonald, H. 2018.
53   www.tandfonline.com/doi/abs/10.1080/09546550490509775.
54   Owens, L. 2016.
55   Hamilton, H. 2018.
56   Hennessey, M. 2019.
57   John Simpson cited in Weatherill, R. 2004, p. 126.
58   https://obamawhitehouse.archives.gov/administration/eop/nsc/transnational-crime/threat.
59   https://pjmedia.com/news-and-politics/matt-margolis/2021/10/08/democrats-have-tried-to-distance-themselves-from-defund-the-police-but-the-rnc-has-the-receipts-n1522660.
60   www.thejournal.ie/ireland-response-to-human-trafficking-5133626-Jun2020/.
61   www.irishtimes.com/news/crime-and-law/more-than-3-000-domestic-violence-999-calls-marked-cancelled-by-garda-1.4601760.
62   www.bbc.com/news/uk-56384600.
63   *The Sunday Times*, (Irish edition). 3 October 2021.
64   Wojtyla, K. 2017, p. 174.
65   Davies, E. 2021. https://commentcentral.co.uk/sarah-everards-murder-must-kickstart-action-on-fatherhood/.
66   Eberstadt, M. 2020.
67   Eagleton, T. 2014, p. 186. Emphasis added.
68   Miller, J.-A. 1997.
69   Wolin, R. 2012, p. 304.
70   WAP (The World Association of Psychoanalysis) 2004. All quotes refer to this document unless otherwise stated.
71   Freud, S. 1923, p. 25.
72   Ibid., p. 45.
73   Freud, S. 1926, p. 196.
74   Lacan, J. 2005, pp. 78–79.
75   Dalrymple, T. 2017. *The Knife Went In. Real-Life Murders and our Culture*. London: Gibson Square.
76   Laplanche, J. and Pontalis, J.-PB. 1973, p. 103. See also Chapter nine in the present volume.
77   Lacan, J. 1969–1970, p. 35.
78   Cited in Heidegger, M. 1959, p. 163.
79   Žižek, S. 2003, p. 95.
80   Ibid., p. 98.

81 Sloterdijk, P. and Heinrichs, H.-J. 2001, p. 277.
82 Steiner, G. 1989, p. 127.
83 Weatherill, R. 2017, p. 182.
84 A reference to, Deleuze, G. and Guattari, F. 1980.
85 Richardson, W. 1998, p. 26.
86 Levinas, E. 1981, pp. 118, 122).
87 Levinas, E. 1993, p. 165.
88 Winnicott, D. 1971, pp. 89–93.
89 Weatherill, R. 2011, pp. 114–115.
90 Radical Orthodoxy is a Christian, mainly Catholic, theological and philosophical school of thought which seeks to combine radical postmodern philosophy in order to reject the paradigm of modernity.
91 Levinas, E. 1981, p. 18.
92 Weil, S. 1947, p. 18.

References

Alibhai-Brown, J. 2013. "My Week in the Man Desert: In Some Parts of Britain, 70% of Children Live without Fathers". *Mail Online*. https://www.dailymail.co.uk/femail/article-2359643/My-week-man-desert-In parts-Britain-70-children-live-fathers-YASMIN-ALIBHAI-BROWN-visited-discovered-devastating-consequences.html

Bion, W. 1962. "A Theory of Thinking. In *Second Thoughts*. London: Heinemann, 110–119.

Bokoni, P and Patrick, T. 2009. "Rough and Tumble Play." University of Arkansas for Medical Sciences. https://www.ucy.ac.cy/nursery/documents/Agrio_Pexnidi_sta_Nipia.pdf.

Booth, M. 2015. *The Almost Nearly Perfect People: Behind the Myth of the Scandinavian Utopia*. London. Vintage.

Brussioni, M. 2020. "Kids Benefit from Rough and Tumble Play with Dads". University of British Columbia's Dept. of Pediatrics. http://www.spph.ubc.ca/kids-benefit-from-rough-and-tumble-play-with-dads/

Cooper, D. 1971. *The Death of the Family*. London: Allen Lane the Penguin Press.

Dalrymple, T. 2017. *The Knife Went In Real-Life Murders and our Culture*. London: Gibson Square Books, Ltd.

Deleuze, G., and Guattari, F. 1980. *A Thousand Plateaus. Capitalism and Schizophrenia*. Trans. Massumi, B. London and New York: Continuum, 2004.

Dick, P. 1977. "If You Find This World Bad, You Should See Some of the Others". Essay in *The Shifting Realities of Philip K. Dick*. New York: Random House. (Page nos unavailable). http://empslocal.ex.ac.uk/people/staff/mrwatkin/PKDick.htm

Eagleton, T. 2014. *Culture and the Death of God*. New Haven and London: Yale University Press

Eberstadt, M. 2020. "The Fury of the Fatherless". *First Things*. https://www.firstthings.com/article/2020/12/the-fury-of-the-fatherless

Enright, S. 2007. "Are we failing our children?" *BBC. Newsnight*, Feb 13.

Etchegoyen, A. 2001. "Psychoanalytic Ideas about Fathers". In J. Trowell and A. Etchegoyan (Eds.) *The Importance of Fathers: A Psychoanalytic Re-evaluation*. New York: Brunner-Routledge, 20–41.

Frazer, D. 2018. *Licence to kill: Britain's surrender to violence*. London: Book Guild Publishing Ltd.

Freud, S. 1923. *The Ego and the Id*. SE 19, 3–66.

Freud, S. 1926. *The Question of Lay Analysis*. SE 20, 179–258.

Freud, S. 1930[1929]. *Civilisation and Its Discontents*. SE 21, 59–145.

Freud, S. 1939[1934–38]. *Moses and Monotheism, Three Essays*. SE 23, 3–140.

Gallagher, C. 2005. *My Teaching*. Trans. Macey, D. London and New York: Verso. 2008.

Gallagher, C. 2017. "You Can't Go around Shooting Your Mouth Off about Things When You're a Judge". *Irish Times* article, May 5.

Gane, M. (Ed.) 1993. *Baudrillard Live: Selected Interviews*. London and New York: Routledge.

Glynn, M. 2011. "Dad and Me. Research into the Problems Caused by Absent Fathers". *Addaction*. http://www.sakkyndig.com/psykologi/artvit/glynn2011.pdf

Hamilton, F. 2018. "Police Ignore Third of All Crimes after a Single Call." *The Times*. https://www.thetimes.co.uk/article/police-ignore-third-of-all-crimes-after-a-single -call-j79nlnjlr

Hennessey, M. 2019. "Thousands of Crimes, Including Rape, not Prosecuted Due to Serious Failings in Garda Youth Scheme". *The Journal.ie*. https://www.thejournal.ie/ garda-scandal-youth-referral-4445018-Jan2019/

Heidegger, M. 1959. *On the Way to Language*. Trans. Hertz, P. New York: Harper & Row Paperback, 1982.

Klein, M. 1928. "Early Stages of the Oedipus Conflict". In *Love, Guilt and Reparation and Other Works (1921–1945)*. London: Hogarth Press, 186–198.

Kollontai, A. 1920. "Communism and the Family". *Selected Writings of Alexandra Kollontai*. Trans: Holt, A. Allison & Busby, 1977.

Lacan, J. 1955–1956. *Seminar 3*. Miller, J.-A. (Ed.). Trans. Grigg, R. New York and London: W.W. Norton, 1993.

Lacan, J. 1958–1959. *Seminar 6. Desire and its Interpretation*. Trans. Gallagher, C. Dublin. Available at: www.lacaninireland.com/web/wp-content/uploads/2010/06/THE-SEMINAROF-JACQUES-LACAN-VI.pdf.

Lacan, J. 1963. *On the Names-of-the-Father*. Miller, J.-A. (Ed.). Trans. Fink, B. Cambridge: Polity Press.

Lacan, J. 1969–1970. *Book 17: The Other Side of Psychoanalysis: The Seminar of Jacques Lacan*. Trans. Grigg, R. New York: W. W. Norton.

Lacan, J. 1974–1975. *Book 22: R.S.I, The Seminar of Jacques Lacan*. Trans. Gallagher, C. http://www.lacaninireland.com/web/wp-content/uploads/2010/06/RSI-Complete -With-Diagrams.pdf

Lammy, D. 3 August 2012a. "David Lammy: My Fatherless Childhood Helps Me to Understand London's Rioters". *The Telegraph*. https://www.telegraph.co.uk/lifestyle /9449732/David-Lammy-My-fatherless-childhood-helps-me-to-understand-Londons -rioters.html

Lammy, D. 2012b. *Out of the Ashes. Britain after the Riots*. London: Cornerstone.

Laplanche, J., Pontalis, J.-B. 1973. *The Language of Psychoanalysis*. London: Hogarth.

Levinas, E. 1961. *Totality and Infinity*. Trans. Linguis, A. Pittsburgh: Duquesne University Press

Levinas, E. 1981. *Otherwise than Being or Beyond Essence*. Trans. Linguis, A. Pittsburgh: Duquesne University Press.

Levinas, E. 1993. *God, Death and Time*. Trans. Bergo, B. Stanford: Stanford University Press, 2000.

Mayock, P. & Bretherton, J. (Eds.) 2016. *Women's Homelessness in Europe*. London: Palgrave Macmillan.

McDonald, H. 12 March 2018. "Northern Ireland 'Punishment' Attacks Rise 60% in Four Years". *The Guardian*. https://www.theguardian.com/uk-news/2018/mar/12/northern -ireland-

Miller, J.-A. 1997. *Psychoanalysis in Close Touch with the Social*. Trans. Sowly, T. https://www.lacan.com/jamsocial.html

Miller, J.-A. 2005. *The Pathology of Democracy*. London: Karnac Books.

National Fatherhood Initiative. 2017. "Father Absence and Involvement: Statistics". https://www.fatherhood.org/fatherhood-data-statistics

Owens, L. 10 March 2016. "The UK's Response to Organised Crime and National Security". *Speech at RUSI*. http://www.nationalcrimeagency.gov.uk/publications/679-lynne-owens-speech-to-rusi-10-march-2016/file

Pownhall, S. 18 June 2017. "Dads Being Denied Equal Parenting Rights 'One of the Biggest Taboos We Face Today'". *The Irish Mirror*. https://www.irishmirror.ie/news/irish-news/dads-being-denied-equal-parenting-10641116

Putnam, R. 2000. *Bowling Alone: The Collapse and Revival of American Community*. London and New York: Simon and Schuster.

Richardson, W. 1998. "The Subject of Ethics". *The Letter* 14, 3–26.

Sachs, J., Sandel, M. 2018. "Morality in the 21st Century". BBC Radio 4. (3 September 2018). Podcast. https://www.bbc.co.uk/programmes/p06k4ztd

Sloterdijk, P., Heinrichs, H.-J. 2001. *Neither Sun nor Death*. Trans. Corcoran, S. Los Angeles: Semiotext(e).

Smyth, E., Darmody, M. 2021. *Risk and Protective Factors in Adolescent Behaviour. The Role of the Family, School and Neighbourhood Characteristics in (Mis)Behaviour among Young People*. Ireland: ESRI. Research Series 119.

Studnicki, J., Fisher, J. and Sherley, J. 2020. "Perceiving and Addressing the Pervasive Racial Disparity in Abortion". Sage Journals. August 18. https://doi.org/10.1177/2333392820949743

Steiner, G. 1989. *Real Presences*. London: Faber and Faber.

Trakl, G. see Heidegger 1959 above.

Vanheule, S. 2011. *The Subject of Psychosis*. London: Palgrave.

Verhaeghe, P, Declercq, F. 2002. "Lacan's Analytic Goal: the *Sinthome* or the Feminine Way". In Thurston, T (Ed.) *Re-inventing the Symptom*. New York: The Other Press.

Weatherill, R. 2004. *Our Last Great Illusion*. Exeter: Imprint Academica.

Weatherill, R. 2011. *Forgetting Freud. Is Psychoanalysis in Retreat?* Paulo Alto: Academica Press.

Weatherill, R. 2017. *The Anti-Oedipus complex: Lacan, Critical Theory and Postmodernism*. London and New York: Routledge.

Weil, S. 1947. *Gravity and Grace*. Trans. Crawford, E., von de Ruhr, M. London and New York: Routledge, 2002.

Winnicott, D. 1971. *Playing and Reality*. London: Hogarth.

Wojtyla, K. 2017. "Pope St. John Paul II, Karol Wojtyla". In Rzepa, J. (Trans.) *God's Hands. The Spiritual Diaries 1962–2003*. London: William Collins.

Wolin, R., 2012. *The Wind from the East. French Intellectuals, the Cultural Revolution, and the Legacy of the 1960s*. Princetown and Oxford: Princetown University Press

Wynarczyk, N. 12 September 2018. "Shot by My Neighbour: Young Belfast Boys are so Terrified of Vigilante Thugs that They Agree to Meet Them and be Shot in the Knees – or Worse, Receive a "Six-Pack'". *The Irish Sun*. https://www.thesun.ie/news/3109791/young-boys-agree-shot-knees-belfast/

Zizek, S. 2003. *The Puppet and the Dwarf. The Perverse Core of Christianity*. Cambridge, MA: MIT Press.

Flim

Doing Money. 2018. Dir. Miller, L.

3 Loving the Father into Life

This chapter takes a number of illustrations (from literature, case studies, and culture generally) to underline the importance of the father in all manner of ways. Charles Melman provides a moving account of the father created through love. Arthur Miller's plays stress the ethical failure of fathers. Hemmingway in the "Indian Camp", evokes the son's love of his father. Hugo Hamilton survives a brutal father who supports the Nazis. Marcel Czermak provides a case history of a man who tries to die like his father. Brian Friel's *Philadelphia, Here I Come!* reveals a missed meeting between a father and son. Stephen Poliakoff's *Joe's Palace* represents an atonement for a father. Steinbeck's *The Grapes of Wrath* shows fathers who were silent but strong. A clip from the Coen brothers' *No Country for Old Men*, shows the longing for a father. Lionel Shriver's killer son has an ineffectual father. Orhan Pamuk's character Cem Çelik searches the world for Oedipal stories out of love for a father who leaves him. Turgenev's *Fathers and Sons* introduces us to the fathers overthrown. Emmanuel Carrère: 'If I, who am not the best father in the world, can show my sons such tenderness, *how much more tenderness must the Father have for me?*'

- Oh yes, (the questioner has a look between irony and contempt, head on one side) remind me again why do you so nostalgically emphasise the father?
- Firstly, the assumption behind your question is wrong. It is not a question of MY emphasis on the father, nostalgic or not! The father simple IS, whether or not his place in the structure is filled. It is not nostalgia or reactionary politics. My thesis is to report on the absence and/or a forced retreat of the father.
- Clinically we note, the father is central for mental health. In fact, without him, mental health has no meaning.
- But there are many families are there not *without* fathers and they are doing well?

DOI: 10.4324/9781003225010-4

– There are a million families without fathers now in the UK and this is, let us say, a quiet catastrophe, a catastrophe in the making and one of unknown proportions.[1]

★★★

Chosen

Chosen, a Channel 4 film,[2] consists of the testimonies of three men recalling their days in the latter part of the last century at a prestigious boy's preparatory school in southern England, where they excelled at rugby, but were "chosen" by the charismatic rugby teacher/coach[3] for special secret treatment. Wright photographed them in their kit, kept notes on their sports performance, and provided special treats, like being driven in his open-topped sports car to matches. Thus chosen, this influential teacher was able to take them from their beds, separately in the evenings after lights-out. Each recalls the fatal "crossing the line of complicity" as they entered his room, where he was often naked and sexually aroused. They remembered exact details – the room, the bed, the smells, the sweat, the sexual acts performed.

In those days young boys who were sent to board in these schools were often from homes where normal affection was not expressed adequately. Referred to by one inmate as, 'Orphanages for people who have parents'.[4] Indeed, each spoke separately of their mothers and fathers being "remote", preoccupied with status, work, golf, etc., and in one case, extra-marital affairs. They recalled being sent from home to board at the age of 8 or 9 and the loneliness of it all. They needed love. They got perversion, shame, and isolation, the sense of *no* return to normality and finally the fatal self-disgust at going back to his room time and again. They were unable to tell anyone for fear of blame or disbelief.

These accounts told with honesty and sincerity after many intervening years of reflection and soul-searching bear witness to the need for the love of a father who chooses us and esteems us into being. This rugby teacher–paedophile acted originally in the place of the father only to cruelly mutate into a monster. Abuse occurs on multiple levels: 1) the blast of the Real otherness of the erotic; 2) soiling the mystery of future erotic love; 3) annulling the secret of trust that is naturally given to the adult figure; 4) knowing that there is no going back, no undoing of the shame – of having one's body aroused repeatedly and horribly pleasurably.

One may learn to live with this over a period of time, they concluded.

Loving the father into life

Speaking at the time of the death of George Best in November 2005, French psychoanalyst and cultural theorist, Charles Melman, speculated that, alcoholism is one of the ways of living the love of the father but the love for the father is unbearable ... and it is therefore an attempt to realise or produce the enjoyment that he as father has forbidden. Alcoholism is another way of loving the father, but an intolerable love. *Love is what makes the father exist.*[5]

Thus, 'In loving my father, I want him to exist'.[6]

The love for the father may *not* exist, but it may come into being over time. There is nothing simple or automatic about the father existing, except biologically somewhere, even as an anonymous sperm donor. Although we can describe in detail some aspects of the relationship between the father and child, ultimately all explanations fall short of the Real. *Love is what makes the father exist.* Love brings the father into being *ex nihilo*. Such love brings enjoyment, disappointment, misunderstanding, or hatred. Even appalling fathers will be loved into being. Fathers that do not exist will be loved into spectral being. And Melman goes all the way to assert, 'Life is simply a *semblance,* a preface, while we are waiting to finally rejoin the dwelling place of the Father'.[7]

★★★

Consider the Loman boys, Biff and Happy, and their love of their father, Willy, in Arthur Miller's *Death of a Salesman*.[8] Willy believes his own myth of being a great salesman adored by all his customers across the States. In reality, he lives up to his name (Loman) as he is failing and is about to be let go by his young boss, Howard, whom he knew as a child, a rather dull child he thought. By contrast, Willy loves his boys, whom he praises as young Adonises for their sporting prowess. As the play opens, the two sons, Biff and Happy, are together again in the house after more than ten years. Like their father, both have extravagant dreams and plans that never really come to fruition. There is underlying tension in the household, only just held together by the suffering mother, Linda. Neither of the boys is successful in any way. Since those early days of fun and of promise, the atmosphere between Biff and his father has turned sour. Something happened after the climax event of the Ebbet's Field football game. That summer Biff failed his maths examination, and he travelled to Boston on the spur of the moment to seek out his beloved dad to persuade him to talk to his maths teacher, so that the result might be changed. He is certain his powerful dad will be able to remedy the situation.

He is knocking at his father's hotel room in Boston. Willy's fancy woman, unseen by Biff, has been hurriedly dispatched to the bathroom. 'You gotta talk to him [the maths teacher] ... Because if he saw the kind of man you are, and you just talked to him in your way, I'm sure he'd come through for me'. But then Biff hears the woman laughing, and realises in a moment of traumatic disillusion, the *real* weakness of his father's position. His father is with this floozy every time he goes out West. He loves *her*. He gives *her* stockings that he denies his wife. His father has fallen. His father died at that moment. At that point the love of Biff for his father ended and Biff's life collapsed. But Willy never really gets it – why both boys are failures and now treat him derisively; why nothing works for him and Howard reluctantly sacks him after a moving scene in which Willy tries to interest him in the new tape recorder he has purchased.

In his autobiography,[9] Arthur Miller was amazed how so many men and women called him to say that Willy Loman *was their father*. At the end of the first performance of the play, there was no applause. People began to put on their coats. Others were bent forwards, hiding their faces. Some men, he notes, were openly weeping. And then, after a while, someone began to applaud, and then the applause was endless.

Writing in his Group Psychology paper, Freud asserts that,

> Identification is known to psychoanalysis as the earliest expression of an emotional tie with another person. It plays a part in the early history of the Oedipus Complex. A little boy will exhibit a special interest in his father; he would like to grow like him and be like him and take his place everywhere. We may say simply that he takes his father as his ideal. This behaviour has nothing to do with a passive or feminine attitude towards his father (and towards males in general); it is on the contrary typically masculine. It fits in very well with the Oedipus Complex, for which it helps to prepare the way.[10]

In another Miller play, *All My Sons*,[11] a denied truth haunts the Keller family. Joe Keller, the businessman father, has lied about selling a few defective plane engines during the war, thus escaping prison and responsibility for the subsequent plane crashes arising from these defects. He placed the blame on his inefficient partner and one time neighbour, Steve Deever, who goes to prison in his place. However, the suspicion in the neighbourhood remains that Keller is to blame. Keller's son Larry (an airman in the war) is to marry Deever's daughter Ann. As the play opens, Larry has been "missing" for over three years. In fact, he had written secretly to Ann, explaining that he had discovered his father's crime (from a US paper distributed among the troops) and that he intended to commit suicide on his next sortie. Meantime the family, chiefly the mother Kate, needed to continue to force themselves and others to believe the lie that Larry was still alive and about to arrive home, so that the father's crime could continue to be denied/erased and the blame continue to be carried by Deever. It falls to the idealistic Chris Keller, Keller's remaining son, to expose the truth about his father. The dramatic unfolding of this truth, the money and comfortable post-war lifestyle that has flowed from the crime and its cover-up, ends up destroying the family. Through Joe Keller's suicide comes the realisation that all those pilots who died in the planes with their defective engines: '*they are all my sons*'. Can a father really kill his son? Indeed, by reverse, can a son (Chris) really kill his father – with *truth*? Here, as in *Death of a Salesman*, the idealised and loved father, the very embodiment of the American Dream, crashes with the suicide of the father.

Willy Loman and Joe Keller are flawed, and love is withdrawn from them. *They cease to exist.* The loved father is a tragic figure because he fails in the idealisation. He is no longer master. The Miller fathers fail. Biff and Happy agree to mother Linda's suggestion that they should treat Willy to a meal in a restaurant and bring back the old times. But the boys get drunk with two women they have picked up and leave old Willy – 'some old man' – they call him, when one of the girls just asks as they are leaving the restaurant without him.

Spokesman

The father comes between us and our death. Psychoanalysis regards the father as the "spokesman", the person who tells us about life, the Symbolic, and the world. Exemplary in this respect is Hemingway's short story, "Indian Camp". Very young Nick and his doctor father visit an Indian woman in the northern woods of Michigan, late at night. She has been in labour for two days. In the shanty, she was in the lower bunk screaming in pain and her husband was in the upper bunk. He had injured his foot badly a few days earlier. The doctor explains to Nick that the woman is going to have a baby. Nick says he knows and understands, but the father tells him he does not. The baby wants to be born and she wants it to be born. All her muscles are trying to get the baby born. That is what is happening when she screams. He goes on to explain that babies are meant to be born headfirst; he might have to operate. Nick's Uncle George and three Indian men have to hold the woman while his father operated to deliver the baby boy. Nick held the boiling water. Nick turns away while his father does the stitching.

As they are leaving, the father checks the silent husband on the upper bunk, shining his lamp having pulled back the covers. The Indian lay with his face towards the wall, his throat cut, in a pool of blood where his body sagged down in the bunk. The razor was edge up on the blanket. The father tells George to take Nick outside, but Nick has already seen the dead man.

As they leave the father apologises to Nick for bringing him along. They are back in the boat and Nick asks his father, 'Do ladies always have such a hard time having babies?' 'No that was very very exceptional'. 'Why did he kill himself daddy?' 'I don't know Nick, he couldn't stand things, I guess'. 'Do many men kill themselves Daddy?' 'Not very many, Nick'. 'Do many women?' 'Hardly ever'. 'Is dying hard daddy?' 'No, I think it's pretty easy, Nick. It all depends'.[12]. In the early morning on the lake sitting in the stern of the boat with his father rowing, Nick felt quite sure he would never die.

Love makes the father exist

Consider Gar O'Donnell and his silent father in Brian Friel's *Philadelphia, Here I Come!* At the age of 25, Gar is about to depart from Ireland for Philadelphia – 'Leaving you forever', he tells his father. The play is set on the night before Gar leaves for America. Gar works for his uncommunicative father – Screwballs he calls him – yet there is a link between them. Gar is recalling a time 15 years earlier when he and his father sat in a blue boat on a lake on an afternoon in May. On that afternoon a great beauty happened, a beauty that has haunted the boy ever since, because he wonders did it really take place or did he imagine it.

> The paint was peeling, there was an empty cigarette packet floating in the water … and you had given me your hat and had put your jacket around my shoulders because there had been a shower of rain. You had the rod in your left hand – I can see the cork nibbled away from the butt of the rod – and maybe we had been chatting – I don't remember – it doesn't matter – but between us at that moment there was this great happiness, this great joy – you must have felt it too – it was so much richer than a content – it was great, great happiness, and active, bubbling joy – although nothing was being said – just the two of us on a lake on a showery day – and young as I was I felt, I knew this was precious, and your hat was soft on the top of my ears – I can feel it – and I shrank down into your coat – and then for no reason at all except that you were happy too, you began to sing.

> All around my hat I wear a green coloured ribbono,
> All around my hat for twelve month and a day
> And if anybody asks me the reason why I wear it,
> It's all because my true love is far, far away.[13]

Back in the present, on the eve of his departure, Gar complains to the silent man: there is only the two of us, he says. Each of us is all the other has; and *why can we not even look at each other*? Have pity on us, he says; have goddam pity of every goddam bloody man jake of us.[14]

The love for the father is unbearable

Hugo Hamilton, in *The Speckled People*,[15] attempts to come to terms with a father who loved Ireland so much that he wanted only Irish spoken in his house, flying into a rage if he heard English uttered. A father who was so close to his son that he might beat him senseless if his son went against him. The father used to say that *we* were the new *Irish* children and soon the whole country would be speaking Irish in the shops. Hugo's sanity was saved by his friend Packer down at the harbour. Hugo's mother was German and she had been deeply affected by the war. Hugo's German cousin Stefan went on the run from his father. Stefan had been told by his father that during the war he had seen people, including naked women, being massacred in a forest in the Ukraine. Stefan feared that his father was a murderer and he wanted to get as far away from him as possible, so he went "missing" in the West of Ireland.

At the height of his conflict with his father, Hugo wakes from a nightmare to find his father in a frenzy of violence, hitting him, punching him, even while he is still asleep: all the punishment in history being passed on blow by blow, here in my bedroom. He can see him remove his watch, roll up his sleeves, smell his sweat, and see the spittle on his mouth. Hugo runs from the house. He is full of murderous feelings for his father. But later returns, wanting to forgive him and remember the good things.

Stefan returns from the West and Hugo tells him of his father's beating. Stefan admits to hitting his father, knocking him to the ground in the garden, leaving him there while his mother had to help him to his feet. Stefan says he now wants to return to Germany, because that injustice that he had done to his father had begun to haunt him as much as the story [about the murders] that had been passed on to him from the war.

Hamilton's book, *The Sailor in the Wardrobe*[16] is really a tale of *three* fathers – Stefan's, Hugo's, and Hugo's father's father, whose picture is hidden in the wardrobe: John Hamilton, the sailor with the soft eyes who got locked in the wardrobe by Hugo's father. He lost his life when he fell on board a British navy ship during World War II. And after the Irish liberated their country from British rule, he disappeared, because my father wanted Ireland to be fully Irish and thinks his own father betrayed his country.

★★★

Melman continues, 'In loving my father, I want him to exist, to be one, and for that reason I accept that my life is a journey that will bring me to him'.[17]

Consider this case vignette reported by French analyst, Michel Czermac.[18] His patient had caused a fire; he admitted it in court, saying he started the fire, 'like a robot'. He had already made several suicide attempts. Once, he had tried to hang himself but the rope broke. On another occasion he had tried to gas himself, but his mother had stopped him in time. On this last occasion he set light to newspapers in a cupboard and had tried to kill himself through smoke inhalation. The analyst noted that in all his suicide attempts the respiratory channel is involved. At the time of these attempts, the patient was divorcing his wife and she was getting custody of the children. She used to provoke him saying: 'how are you a father, what sort of father are you?' The suicide attempts occurred when he was supposed to have the children and she had again prevented this on some pretext or other. Keeping the children, barring him, also kept him from realising his paternal function. His own father had been tubercular and died when his son was very young, from asphyxiation.

When his wife keeps the children, the patient reaches an impasse. He "answers" her question – *what sort of father are you?* – with a suicidal act in the Real, the message being: a father is someone who dies from asphyxiation; someone who dies from not being able to breathe; this was my father. I will *not* be a father, like a normal father, who breathes and brings words to life, but one who becomes a fatal absence, one who breathes in, inhales, smoke, death. In the desperation of his suicide attempts, there are fatal questions.

> Father do you not see that I am choking like you?
> Is a father just air?
> A father should be something, but what?

If this "something" is not given in the first instance, if there is *nothing* to draw on or to breathe in, the enigma of what is a father becomes brutal, becomes for this man quite literally a "burning question".

***

The guilt felt on behalf of a rich and powerful father is movingly illustrated in Stephen Poliakoff's television play, *Joe's Palace*. Here Joe (Danny Lee Wynter), the "weird kid" on his estate, acts as an unlikely concierge in the large, empty, Mayfair mansion of billionaire, Elliot Graham (Michael Gambon). Graham mysteriously wants to give away his money, to do something useful with his wealth. He forms friends with the lonely souls around him, especially Joe, whom he wines and dines, as well as Richard (Rupert Penry-Jones), a young cabinet minister, and Charlotte (Kelly Reilly) his secret lover. But Graham is troubled and depressed throughout, by how precisely his father came upon his excessive wealth. Here is the link. Graham discovers after extensive research, confiding in Joe, that his father forged business links with very successful Nazi firms in pre-war Germany. A letter reveals that back then, one sunny afternoon, while walking in a park in a German city, with his new-found business colleagues, Graham's father witnesses the truly shocking sight of German police rounding up a group of Jews at random, ordering the men and boys to strip naked and crawl like animals on all-fours along the path and ordering the women and girls to climb the nearby trees and utter sounds like birds.

Graham's father does nothing after witnessing such humiliation, only commenting later in a letter to a friend, with masterly ethical relativism: 'they certainly seem to do things differently here'. It is Graham himself who wants and feels compelled to atone on behalf of his deceased father. Joe intervenes to prevent him from shooting himself.

***

Contrary to current expectations, fathers must not reveal their hand. Psychoanalytically, the phallus must not be revealed. The postmodern view (he has no phallus!) is quite the reverse: talk and reveal your feelings. You've quite literally *nothing* to hide. In truth, in order to remain strong, men must remain hidden, just as God must remain utterly hidden and unfathomable.

As this extract from *The Grapes of Wrath* shows us, when men hide their emotions, everyone feels safe. The scene, from John Steinbeck's classic 1939 novel, set in dust-bowl Oklahoma during the Depression, is the aftermath of a disastrous dust storm which has destroyed farmers' crops.

> Men stood by their fences and looked at the ruined corn, drying fast now, only a little green showing through the film of dust. The men were silent, and they did not move often. And the women came out of the houses to stand beside their men – to feel whether this time the men would break. The women studied the men's faces secretly, for the corn could go, as long as something else remained. The children stood nearby, drawing figures

in the dust with bare toes, and the children sent exploring senses out to see whether men and women would break. After a while, the faces of the watching men lost their bemused perplexity and became hard and angry and resistant. Then the women knew that they were safe and there was no break. Then they asked, 'What'll we do?' And the men replied, 'I don't know'.

But it was all right. The women knew it was all right, and the watching children knew it was all right. Women and children knew deep in themselves that no misfortune was too great to bear *if their men were whole.*[19]

It is worth noting here that both men and women are separate, each in their own domain. Things were arranged so that men and women were not expected to integrate, not expected to communicate. Radical difference is allowed and indeed essential. Nevertheless, there is absolute human solidarity; without that they were doomed.

★★★

Without a father, or without an effective father, there is the real likelihood of a psychical disaster. Clinically this can be shown over and over. For what has happened to the Symbolic father is that he has been ejected from the Symbolic register.

Boy A., the boy who does not even bear his father's name, was a powerful Channel 4 drama, based on the novel by Jonathan Trigell,[20] brought to the screen by director John Crowley. Jack Burridge, formerly Eric Wilson, has a new identity, by which he must conceal, or cover over, his appalling past crime. When he was 10, he and his psychopathically tough friend Philip murdered a girl of about the same age beside a railway line. We get glimpses of their escalating crimes and Jack's very bleak early life. Bullied at school, then at home, his mother is dying of cancer and his father spends the day drinking and watching daytime television. Philip is raped by his older brother, who will later hang himself in prison. The parallels with Jon Venables and Robert Thompson and the murder of Jamie Bulger are immediately present.

More than ten years on and apparently rehabilitated, Jack has a fresh start, with a job in freight transport. He shows a simplicity and excitement at being out in the world together with a constant fear of his true identity being discovered. When he and work colleague Michelle fall in love, he desperately wants to tell her who he really is – but is advised urgently by his case worker that he must never tell anyone. In the meantime, the press is on his trail, with rewards being offered for anybody who can find him. Jack seems remarkably "soft" after spending 14 years in a secure unit. Coming upon a car accident, for instance, he saved a little girl's life – an illustration, maybe, of how much he'd changed for the better.

What makes this drama stand out is the commitment, solidarity, and love that develops between Jack and three key figures, Michelle, Terry, and his fellow truck driver, all of whom create a space for Jack to find real life worth living. Until, that is, the evil of the original crime and the evil of the tabloid press close the circle we know will shockingly reveal the true identity of Jack.

As his supports fall away in a catastrophic instant, when suddenly *no one answers his urgent calls*, Jack/Eric becomes zero – *Boy A*. Plunged into renewed isolation, all the more painful for the kindness and friendship he has been shown, he escapes from the house via a fanlight, to avoid the journalists outside, hurts his leg in the fall from the roof and hobbles off through the backstreets of Manchester and takes the train to Blackpool. Here a kind old lady tells him that this is the end of the line. At the end of the line, at the end of the pier, he briefly hallucinates his friends who might forgive him in due time, but not before he exits the scene.

★★★

In a similar vein, in a "community" without fathers, a BBC One documentary, *Stabbed: The Truth About Knife Crime* (Marc Sigsworth).[21] 'Mothers, sisters and survivors reveal why they are releasing CCTV footage of fatal stabbings and opening coffins to shock the nation into action'. A Glasgow sink estate is divided into gangland areas. Stray into the "wrong" area and you risk being knifed in an unprovoked attack. Youths bare their scars and joke about the dangers they face. Academics are interviewed giving their analyses of the rise in knife crime. A hospital consultant who stitches up the wounds of the victims is overwhelmed by what is happening and his work overload. He shows graphic pictures of the victims. One has a kitchen knife sticking out of his back. Another shows deep, long machete wounds. Another shows an exposed open lung.

The police are marginalised, and most knifings go unreported. One youth did report the crime against him and was subsequently knifed to death in a revenge attack. In his memory, his mates daubed his name on a derelict wall. Mothers and sisters grieve. But where are the fathers? There is no mention of the fathers. Without fathers and surrogate fathers (youth and community workers and volunteers), barbarism returns potentially without limit, except the fierce brutal authority wielded by the gangs in place of the father. There are no limits in the Real. Here we should recall Lacan's formulation: what is withdrawn or expelled from the Symbolic (the father, order, castration, etc.), reappears in the Real, 'erratically, like a punctuation without a text'.[22] Erratically, without control, and punctuation with a knife, and mothers grieving with no speech, no text. We are speech-less.

★★★

At the end of the neo-Western crime thriller, *No Country for Old Men*, a 2007 film based on a novel by Cormac McCarthy and directed by Joel Coen and Ethan Coen, Sheriff Bell (Tommy Lee Jones) recounts a dream to his wife. He and his father were riding horses through a snowy mountain pass. Bell says his father, who was carrying fire in a horn, quietly passed by Bell with his head down. Bell then relates that his father was 'going on ahead, and fixin' to make a fire', in the surrounding dark and cold, and that when Bell got there, his father would be waiting. We know this is no more than a momentary wish fulfilment in the bleak darkening landscape of criminal immigration, drug gangs, drug deals gone wrong, random killings, firefights in the street, and 'young boys going grey'. This is a world destroyed where killing is normal. Sheriff Bell, who has retired feeling "overmatched", is told by his Uncle Ellis that this region has always been violent. This is *no country* for old men; no country for young men, anyone. Period.

★★★

At around the time of the Columbine High School massacre (April 1999), which resulted in the deaths of 13 students and the wounding of 25 others, news footage showed in its extended coverage a youth with an assault rifle on a mountainside taking potshots at a television which he had positioned at some distance on the other side of a small valley. When asked what he was doing shooting at a television monitor, he said in a deadpan voice that 'he was shooting the babysitter'.

★★★

Lionel Shriver's *We Need to Talk about Kevin*, recounts the fictional story of Eva Khatchadourian's retrospective account of her son's life up to and beyond the day he went to his high school and began shooting his classmates. The BBC book club discussion about the Shriver book focussed on Shriver's sneaking liking for Kevin but failed to discuss Eva's obvious narcissistic coldness and her possible unsuitability for having children. It also omits any mention of the father, Franklin, and his lack of authority – he always gives his son the benefit of the doubt and avoids any conflict situation. Not that either of these factors should excuse the (fictional) crime committed by Kevin and those like him.

However, there is a type of father who is indistinguishable from his son. He regards his son as his mate. They are both cool, wear the same gear, listen to the same music, own the same gadgets, follow the same teams, and use the same drugs. Such fathers admire their children's anti-establishment attitudes wishing that they had had the same kind of spunky attitude. Novelist and journalist Tim Lott, wrote: 'At the heart, our children are as much a riotous, disrespectful, anti-establishment bunch of awkward cusses as the rest of us have always been. And I wouldn't have it any other way'.[23] Another way to neutralise the father–son tension.

★★★

The father should disappear. About 15 years ago, an early morning show on RTÉ Radio interviewed two young male workers involved with children and child protection in Ireland. All talk is of caution around children, to the extent that specifically male adults must *never be alone* with a child or a group of children. This is normal now, so much so that as a man you would never go swimming with your children alone, you would never help out with super-vision if you were left on your own, never comfort a child (except verbally) when the child is hurt, except maybe in the presence of other adults, in an office or suitable place. Acknowledging that 'things had probably gone too far down the road of risk aversion', they reported that a priest who took his nephew to the cinema was spat at and had to leave the cinema. The father-hating ethos means now that everyone is suspect. Recently, applications for the urgently needed vaccinator role had to show proof of Garda vetting.[24] No one will be trusted until they can prove their innocence.

As trust has disappeared from the Symbolic it returns as universal suspicion in the Real. *There is no speech. Just download and fill out the vetting form.*

There is a sign in a Dublin park that says, *Adults must be accompanied by a child.* Adults on their own can no longer be trusted to be safe around children. This is a complete Oedipal reversal where the children are in charge!

As with Greta Thunberg, the leader of "Extinction Rebellion", who award-winning *Irish Times* journalist Fintan O'Toole believes is a modern-day prophet.[25] Indeed, when the diminutive 16 year old greeted the Climate Change Conference in Madrid in December 2019, she said 'Hello Madrid!', sounding for all the world like a Pope. And she declared: 'People are under-estimating the force of angry kids'.[26] Greta's father declared that her nervous symptoms were decreasing the more she campaigned on the world stage. As the BBC's Justin Rowlatt says, 'A key reason her "How dare you!" message hit home so hard in the UN this week was because she seemed so jarringly out of place in the air-conditioned formality of the UN's New York HQ'.[27] *HOW DARE YOU* is jarringly out-of-place for another reason: another role reversal, unimaginable until very recently, outside that is of totalitarian systems that always *used children.*

The nihilist

> We base our conduct on what we find useful. In these days the most useful thing we can do is to repudiate – and so we repudiate.

> Everything?
> Everything.
> What? Not only art, poetry … but also … I am afraid to say it …
> Everything, Bazarov repeated with indescribable composure.[28]

Turgenev popularised the term "nihilism" through the radical figure of Yevgeny Bazarov. Turgenev wrote *Fathers and Sons* to explore the growing cultural conflict between the liberals of the early 19th century and the growing nihilist movement in Russia. Both the nihilist sons and the liberal men like Nikoláy Petróvich Kirsánov, the modest father of Arkády and follower of Bazarov, want change, but the latter wants *total* change. Back then it was science that was to be the vehicle of total change – a chemist is 20 times more useful than a poet.[29] Whereas today we might speak of secular reason. Back then, Turgenev had discovered, 'the young iconoclasts bent on total annihilation of his world in the certainty that a new and more just world would emerge'.

Turgenev 'trembled before' these new Jacobins and their 'hunger for blood'.[30] And Berlin, introducing this novel, could have been referring precisely to today's anxieties when he speaks of being, 'morally repelled by both the hard faces to their right and the hysteria and mindless violence and demagoguery on their left'.[31] In the introduction, Rosemary Edmunds suggests the book is 'perfectly constructed as a drama of Sophocles ... the universal clash between generations'.[32] Take, for instance, Arkády's father Nikoláy with his modest estate, Marino and Bazarov are somewhat contemptuous in their attitude to him and Nikoláy's brother Pavel, in spite of their hearts being in the right place. Bazarov's attitude to his own parents reveals his contempt for their traditional values and virtues, not to mention their simple and generous hospitality. And as for the peasants generally, well Bazarov reveals unconscious contempt for the very people he claims to want to save. 'Only when the poorest peasant has a house like that [the clean, tidy cottage of the bailiff] will Russia achieve perfection, and we must all of us work to this end'. However, in the next breath Bazarov says, 'But I have developed a hatred for that "poorest peasant" of yours ... for whose sake I am ready to sacrifice my skin and who won't even thank me for it'.[33] And as for Arkády's Uncle Pavel – 'What did you call Uncle Pavel? I merely called him what he is – an idiot'.[34] Apparently, Bazarov liked to stroll into the village to engage some peasants in banter:

> Well brother, pray expound to me your views on life. For I am told the whole future of Russia lies in your hands, that with you a new epoch in history is about to begin – you are to give us a real language, and legislation.

After getting no credible reply, Bazarov shrugged his shoulders contemptuously, and walked off. And the peasants stood around asking what he was talking about! 'Bazarov the self-confident did not for a moment suspect that in their eyes he was after all nothing but a buffoon'.[35] But almost by poetic justice, Bazarov catches typhus from a dying peasant, and it is too late to save him from succumbing to the disease, leaving his stricken parents, generous to the last, in 'unutterable bewilderment'.

> Who is it crying there? Mother. Poor mother. Who will she feed now with her wonderful beetroot and cabbage soup?
> My son, my dear beloved son!
> What is it father?[36]

> There is a small village graveyard in one of the remote corners of Russia ... it has a melancholy look ... sheep wander over the graves ... But there is one among the graves which no man molests and no animal tramples upon

... two young fir trees have been planted there ... Yevgeny Bazarov lies buried in this grave ... two frail old people ... supporting each other ... fall on their knees and weep long and bitterly ... exchanging a brief word, they brush the dust from the stone ... then resume their prayers unable to tear themselves away.[37]

★★★

The father is probably the only person in the world who really wants the best for us, while at the same time leaving us free. As Emmanuel Carrère says in his search for Christianity, 'The Father isn't some kind of slave master', as he is supervising his young boys playing in the park. He continues, 'I'd be worried ... if they spent the whole time with me, watching me, wondering what I'm thinking and if I'm happy with them'. Carrère wants to be a benign presence in their lives. 'If I, who am not the best father in the world, can show my sons such tenderness, *how much more tenderness must the Father have for me*?'[38]

★★★

One day, when I was 7, my parents took me to a beach on Heybeli Island. They wanted to teach me how to swim: my mother would lower me belly-first into the water, and I would flail and splash trying to reach my father standing three steps away. Every time I came close he would take another step back. 'Daddy don't go!' I'd scream so much. 'There's nothing to be afraid of, son. I'm here, all right'. 'All right', I'd gasp, basking in the joy and comfort of his arms.[39]

This is Cem Çelik in Orhan Pamuk's *The Red-haired Woman*, present with his father's body on the day of his death.

Cem is the son of a pharmacist whose left-wing politics take him away from home and from these comforting arms. To help his mother, Cem goes to guard his aunt's cherry and peach orchard. In the garden next door to the orchard, a well was being dug. Against his mother's wishes, Cem goes to work as an apprentice well digger with Mahmut, who gradually becomes a "father", who tells Cem stories about life and danger while they work on the well near an imaginary Turkish town called Öngören.

From time to time, they go into town and sit at the cafe. Cem catches a glimpse of the mysterious and beautiful red-haired woman. Among other stories, as they dig deeper and deeper,

> Master Mahmut warned me always to be careful: unless he has his wits about him, a well digger's apprentice can risk maiming his master, and if he is careless, he could even end up killing him. Now remember, your eyes and ears must always be alert to what is going on down in the well.[40]

Mahmut also warned that the deeper they dug the closer they got to the after-life. The well digging became a metaphor for a life and death struggle. Already the Oedipal outline is unmistakably forming with Mahmut and the red-haired woman as protagonists. 'If you want to be a good apprentice, you will have to be like a son to me'.[41] Then there is the incident.

> A father is a doting, charismatic figure who will until his dying day accept and watch over the child he sires. He is the origin and the centre of the universe. When you believe you have a father you are at peace even when you can't see him, because you know he is always there, ready to love and protect you.[42]

However, this story, like Oedipus, is a tragic story. The adult Cem becomes obsessed with investigating Oedipal stories. Stories, for instance, of a father bedding his beautiful daughter-in-law while his son is away from home on military service. Discovering the truth on his return, the son would murder the father. Or, a son might force himself on his mother in a fit of insanity. The father would try to stop him and the son would end up killing the father. *These* sons were hated, not because they had killed their fathers, but because they had violated their mothers.

There is a scene from Ferdowsi's epic *Shahnameh* in which Rostam weeps over his son Sohrab, whom he has killed without recognising him after many days of fighting. This is Iran's national epic. Cem says, 'Whenever I read about Rostam and Sohrab, I felt as if I were reliving my own memories'.[43] There is Abraham preparing to cut his son's throat. Ilya Repin's oil painting *Ivan the Terrible and His Son* (Moscow: Tretyakov Gallery) shows a father cradling his bleeding son whom he has just killed. Also, at the time of the new Ottoman sultan, their first act upon ascending the throne was to execute all other princes, whose deaths he would subsequently mourn.

And what should we make of Cem whose leftish father did not watch over him and Cem's son Enver, in his turn similarly neglected, who emerges late in the book to complete the Oedipal scandal?

★★★

The postmodern father leaves the mother of his child, maybe not even know-ing, being told, or caring that he *is* the father. He avoids responsibility; he avoids commitment. But the culture no longer seems to care whether or not he is there. He too is speechless. He has *been* disappeared. As poverty increases in cities across the world with income inequality, news stories abound of struggling young *mothers* unable to put food on the table, find affordable childcare, educate their children, and *so on*. Never! Never, is there a question about the absent father. *The father does not exist.* This is called freedom. Quite the reverse.

Researching her book, Hanna Rosin[44] meets Bethany and her daughter and enquires about Bethany's partner. 'Well, there's Calvin', she said, meaning her daughter's father. She looked over at her daughter and tossed her a granola bar and they both laughed. 'But Calvin would just mean one less granola bar for the two of us'. Without saying as much, she communicated what her daughter seemed already to understand and accept: by keeping Calvin at arm's length, Bethany could remain queen of her castle, and with one less mouth to feed, they might both be better off!

Rousseau left his five children so that they could make it up on their own and be free of constraint! And with the father out of the way, *the culture* can do what it likes!

The leader of the men's group continues, reading from a worksheet:

> Let's see. What are the four kinds of paternal authority? Moral, emotional, social, and physical. But you ain't none of those in that house. All you are is a paycheck, and now you ain't even that. And if you try to exercise your authority, she'll call 911. How does that make you feel? You're supposed to be the authority, and she says, 'Get out of the house, bitch'. She's calling you 'bitch'![45]

A "paycheck", or merely, as the later Lacan put it, a "spermatozoon".[46] Lacan was never one to be found behind the curve.

The father has been hated out of being. The father has been ejected from the Symbolic.

Melman distinguishes between conduct (*conduit*) and behaviour (*comportment*); the former is linked to moral agency, in other words, the father, and the latter can be evaluated or measured in its success or failure on a pragmatic behavioural compliance scale, *without* the father being necessary. The analogue romance of the Oedipal and the paternal has been overtaken by the cold calculation of cybernetic policing and social credit systems *without appeal*. It operates in the absence of humanity. It is becoming truly *trans*-human and poses itself as real freedom!

> [t]oday we no longer want to understand or hear the unconscious, but we want to *directly enjoy it* ... everything that was hidden or repressed [by the father], everything that was associated with modesty, shame, or decency, today all of that, which is what makes up the unconscious, in other words everything we have put aside ... and belongs to what we would call obscene – off the stage – today we all think we have a *right to a full enjoyment ... all of that*.[47]

In the old symbolic order, every presence invokes a possible absence, culminating the phallic signifier, which through the psychoanalytic notion of castration evokes its own absence. Soon, there will be *no* absence as *everything will transpire*, even thoughts before we think them, with neural implants. Enjoyment without limit. Knowledge, information, connection.

Own nothing and be happy, be nomad. Don't get married or have children. No one is coming.

Castration

Finally, what does the old term "castration" refer to? This effect which appears to be so lacking today? In *Seminar 15*, Lacan makes the point that Freud's theory of subjectivity's contribution to a psychoanalytic theory of subjectivity can *be summed up* by the term "castration", being in some way always cut off from enjoyment, *jouissance*.

> Let us not forget that up to then the religious signs, incarnations, for exam-
> ple in which we recognise this castration complex, circumcision for exam-
> ple, to give it its name, are again one or other form of inscription, of mark
> in the rites of puberty, of tattooing, of everything which produces marks,
> impresses on the subject, in connection with a certain phase which in an
> unambiguous fashion is presented as a phase of accession to a certain level,
> to a certain stage of desire. All these things make their appearance always
> as a mark and an impression.[48]

In the same seminar Lacan notes that James Joyce as a child was cruelly tied to a barbed wire fence by another child and beaten. Yet, Joyce bore the perpetrator no malice. This "castration", this mark on the body is seemingly just let go; it does not register at the level of the body, at the level of the Real – castration *not* acknowledged, which Lacan links with psychosis. 'He expresses this by saying that [his body] is like a fruit skin'.[49]

Add to this that Joyce was not functioning as a father. Neither was his grand-father. Both were alcoholics. Joyce's brother Stanislaus accused Joyce of creating a 'rootless life' for his family, with 'the constant shift from country to country, from language to language, and the continual rupture of ties with friends and relatives'.[50] Lucia became psychotic. Joyce's wife Nora blamed him 'for giving her and Lucia an unbearable life … drunkenness every night'.[51] There were rumours of incest. And Joyce was accused of "malignant self-absorption".[52]

Without the father, there is loss, radical loss, rootlessness, rupture, unbear-able life. In major cities, such as London, Liverpool, Manchester, Birmingham, and Leeds, over 50 per cent of children live in fatherless families.[53] With the radical loss of security this inevitably brings for so many women and children it still remains largely unremarked in the media for fear of stigmatising single par-ents, overwhelmingly female. The State is expected to be "father". According to James Heckman, 'What we really have come to understand is that some of the major growth of inequality has … to do with the change in family struc-ture … as single-parent families grow, inequality itself grows'.[54] Every year in the UK an additional 20,000 people, mainly women, join the throngs of those raising children more or less singlehandedly.[55]

***

Protect. Procreate. Provide.[56] These three values, not exclusively male, are remarkably constant across cultures. The protector role is the least shared between the genders, being most firmly rooted in the physiology of the stronger male body. A world without fathers, even at the reductive level of biology and cyber-operationalism, is a world without real protection, given initially by the father and later by the Symbolic structures supported by the father. A world without procreation, with less children being born and the increasingly free availability of abortion. A world without provision, where men are increasingly free *not* to be providers of sustenance and resources, but to go off on their own alone.

Notes

1 Richardson, H. 2013.
2 Woods, B. 2008.
3 Peter Wright, recently convicted aged 83 and serving time. www.youtube.com/watch?v =tOQ5glZfi6w.
4 De Bernieres, L. 2021.
5 Melman, C. 2006, p. 64.
6 Ibid., p. 65.
7 Ibid., p. 62.
8 Miller, A. 1949.
9 Miller, A. 1987.
10 Freud, S. 1922, p. 105.
11 Miller, A. 1947.
12 Hemmingway, E. 1944, pp. 86–87.
13 Friel, B. 1965, p. 74.
14 Ibid., p. 85.
15 Hamilton, H. 2001.
16 Hamilton, H. 2006.
17 Melman, C. op. cit., p. 65.
18 From an unpublished lecture given in Ireland in 1984.
19 Steinbeck, J. 1939, p. 4.
20 Trigell, J. 2004.
21 *Stabbed: The Truth about Knife Crime*. BBC One. 20 January 2009. www.bbc.co.uk/pro-grammes/b00h45s1.
22 Lacan, J. 1970, pp. 324/388.
23 Cited by Tony Sewell. 18 Feburary 2007. *Independent*. www.independent.co.uk/voices /commentators/tony-sewell-the-grown-ups-need-to-grow-up-who-must-grow-up -children-need-grown-up-adults-436779.html.
24 "Vaccinator, COVID-19 Vaccination Programme Recruitment FAQs". https://hbsrecruitmentservices.ie/vaccinator-covid-19-vaccination-programme -recruitment-faqs/.
25 O'Toole, F. 2019.
26 www.cbc.ca/news/world/greta-thunberg-climate-summit-madrid-1.5382070.
27 Rowlatt, J. 2019.
28 Turgenev, I. 1862, p. 123.
29 Ibid., p. 97.
30 Berlin, I. 1970.
31 Turgenev, I. 1862, p. 55.
32 Ibid., p. 70.
33 Ibid., p. 211.
34 Ibid., p. 212.
35 Ibid., pp. 275–276.

36 Ibid., pp. 283–285.
37 Ibid., pp. 294–295.
38 Carrère, E. 2014, p. 79. Emphasis added.
39 Pamuk, O. 2017, p. 174.
40 Ibid., p. 31.
41 Ibid., p. 38.
42 Ibid., p. 219.
43 Ibid., p. 140.
44 Rosin, H. 2012.
45 Grose, J. 2010.
46 Lacan, J. 1969–1970, p. 127.
47 Melman, C. op. cit., p. 67. Emphasis added.
48 Lacan, J. 1957–1958, Session 26 March1958.
49 Lacan, J. 1975–1976, Session 11 May1976.
50 Maddox, B. 1988, p. 292.
51 Ibid., p. 283.
52 Ibid., p. 292.
53 Office for National Statistics, www.fathers-4-justice.org/about-f4j/fact-sheet/.
54 Mrozek, A. 2021.
55 Guy, C. 2013, p. 3.
56 Gilmore, D. 1990.

References

Berlin, I. 1970. "Fathers and Children". *The Romanes Lecture*, in Turgenev, I. 1862, 57.

De Bernieres, L. 2021. "Reader Boarding School Stories". *The Sunday Times*, April 23. https://www.thetimes.co.uk/article/readers-boarding-school-stories-the-cruelty-scarred-me-for-life-at-75-i-am-still-hurting-2jgbw69zx

Carrère, E. 2014. *The Kingdom*. Trans. Lambert, J. London and New York: Penguin Books.

Freud, S. 1922. *Group Psychology and the Analysis of the Ego*. SE. 18, 67–144.

Friel, B. 1965. *Philadelphia, Here I Come!* London: Faber and Faber.

Gilmore, D. 1990. *Manhood in the Making: Cultural Concepts of Masculinity*. Yale University Press.

Grose, J. 2010. "The End of Men". http://www.theatlantic.com/magazine/archive/2010/07/the-end-of-men/308135/

Guy, C. 2013. *Fractured Families. Why Stability Matters*. Centre for Social Justice. June.

Hamilton, H. 2001. *The Speckled People. A Memoir of a Half-Irish Childhood*. London and New York: Fourth Estate.

Hamilton, H. 2006. *The Sailor in the Wardrobe*. London: Fourth Estate.

Hemmingway, E. 1944. *The First Forty-Nine Stories*. London: Arrow Books.

Lacan, J. 1957–1958. *Seminar V. The Formations of the Unconscious*. Trans. Gallagher, C. Dublin: St Vincent's University Hospital.

Lacan, J. 1969–1970. *Seminar 17. The Other Side of Psychoanalysis*. Trans. Grigg, R. New York: W.W. Norton, 2005.

Lacan, J. 1970. *Ecrits. The First Complete Edition in English*. Trans. Fink, B. London and New York: W.W. Norton, 2002.

Lacan, J. 1975–1976. *Le séminaire de Jacques Lacan: Livre 23, Le sinthome*. Paris: Seuil. Seminar XXIII, 11.05.1976.

Maddox, B. 1988. *Nora: The Real Life of Molly Bloom*. Boston, New York: Houghton Mifflin Company. Mariner Books Edition.

Melman, C. 2006. "George Best and the Name-Of-The-Father". *The Letter, Journal of Lacanian Psychoanalysis* no. 36, 62–68.

Miller, A. 1949. *Death of a Salesman*. London and New York: Penguin Modern Classics, 2001.

Miller, A. 1987. *Timebends. A Life*. London: Bloomsbury.

Miller, A. 1947. *All My Sons*. London: Penguin Classics, 2000.

Mrozek, A. 2021. *Citing James Heckman (Nobel Laureate) in "The Family Is the Whole Story"*. Institute for Family Studies. https://ifstudies.org/blog/nobel-laureate-james-heckman-the-family-is-the-whole-story-

O'Toole, F. 2019. "Greta Thunberg is a Prophet, Preacher, Rulebreaker, Avenging Angel" 28.9.19. https://www.irishtimes.com/opinion/fintan-o-toole-greta-thunberg-is-a-prophet-preacher-rulebreaker-avenging-angel-1.4030064?mode=sample&auth-failed=1&pw-origin=https%3A%2F%2Fwww.irishtimes.com%2Fopinion%2Ffintan-o-toole-greta-thunberg-is-a-prophet-preacher-rulebreaker-avenging-angel-1.4030064

Pamuk, O. 2017. *The Red-haired Woman*. Trans. Oklap, E. London: Faber & Faber.

Richardson, H. 2013. "A Million Children Growing up without Fathers". *BBC News*, June 10. https://www.bbc.com/news/education-22820829

Rosin, H. 2012. *The End of Men: And the Rise of Women*. New York: Riverhouse.

Rowlatt, J. 2019. "Climate Change: Greta Thunberg Calls out the 'Haters'." *BBC*, Sept 28. https://www.bbc.com/news/science-environment-49855980

Steinbeck, J. 1939. *The Grapes of Wrath*. Penguin Modern Classics, 2005.

Trigell, J. 2004. *Boy A*. London: Serpent's Tail.

Turgenev, I. 1862. *Fathers and Sons*. London and New York. Penguin Modern Classics, 1965.

Woods, B. (Dir.). 2008. *Channel 4 True Stories*. 15 December 2008. https://www.youtube.com/watch?v=WoOzqebOU1k

4 Being (not) in the World without a Father

The violence of civilisation falls on the poorest children. The father begets the soul of the child (Lacan); without him there is a loss of "affective density". Much of the misery seen in the courts is caused by the lack of a father figure in offenders' lives. Badiou asserts that we live in an *atonal* world without ordering. The notion "child" is part of outdated mommy–daddy (Oedipal) language. The child no longer exists except as simulation and bureaucratic notion – "Children First". Twenty children die "in care" each year in Ireland. How should we understand extreme states, such as autism, Tourette's, hyperactivity, "asocial" *jouissance*, cutting, etc.? Maybe as 'the revenge of the Real' (Baudrillard), the return of "child" in virulent brutal forms having been exposed to "not-me" impingements? Children who murder their parents. Levinas is cited as he describes the bare horror of the "there is" – *existence without existents*. Finally, how should we medically treat extreme states? Adaptation (CBT, etc.) or the Lacanian ethic that each child is a singularity?

- Yeah, I have a 2 year old.
- Do you see him much?
- Nah. I did for a while, but there were problems. So, I left it all up to her. It's better that way. She's better with 'em. She prefers it. It's not fair to keep coming and going.
- Yeah, you're right. Leave 'em at it. That's what I say. Leave 'em at it.[1]

We have noted that fathers are in a *weak position* vis-à-vis the loosening family structure against the hidden power of the mother's *jouissance*. How much more perilous is the child's position in a time of autonomy for all? The ease of divorce and separation – "you will have several partners in your lifetime" – is freedom for the adults in liberal society, and, "won't the children be happier too?"

To *have a world*, as such, is thus not a simple description of reality out there – it is the fruit of a sustained act of faith – to have a world requires a coherent belief which Lacanian and Freudian psychoanalysis in the past linked strongly

DOI: 10.4324/9781003225010-5

to the father. Without a father, there is the risk of atonality and psychosis, the kind of permanent state of agitated infantilisation, which, as says Žižek, with the absence of the father, 'far from bringing about the non-pathological state of full desiring capacity, leads, rather to total psychotic catastrophe, to the dissolution of the subject's entire universe'.[2] There is no big Other to guarantee the consistency of the Symbolic space within which we can dwell and *have a world*. Instead, there are only contingent, local and fragile points of stability which may come and go, grow and dissolve, but do not constitute a world.

There was a Bernardos' report some years back alleging "hatred" of children in the UK. Bernardos produced a video based on the language used online: three men are talking about "vermin" and "animals" that are "feral" before grabbing shotguns and taking to the streets. They are chasing gangs of children that they want to shoot. These are words used daily in reference to children. Barnardos' chief executive and former director general of the Prison Service, Martin Narey, said,

> these are not references to a small minority of children but represent the public view of *all* children. Despite the fact that most children are not troublesome there is still a perception that today's young people are a more unruly, criminal lot than ever before.[3]

The video shows white males in the manners of racists, but their targets are children. Children are seen running in fear of their lives as shots ring out. The video is intended to shock, and places the blame squarely on violent adult men attacking youths.[4]

This evidence of underground (Oedipally derived) hatred of children is part of the systemic violence involved in "civilisation" *per se*, which bears most heavily on children, no longer shielded as they once were by the father's protection. Now in the virtual world he has absolutely no function. With the so-called "Igeneration",[5] childishness is now prolonged into adulthood. They are less confident, less optimistic than millennials. They think it's cool *not* to need anybody, to be very individualistic. To be "thirsty" (to want to form loving relationships) is considered pathetic – they may be "catching feelings". They are the most physically safe on the one hand, yet the most mentally fragile generation on the other. Suicide, self-harming and depression continues to rise.

Thus, there is a crisis of social solidarity, lack of trust in institutions, crisis of purpose/meaning. Paralysed by choice, they believe that freedom is absence of restraint.

Recently, in the new non-world, British children are being warned to be careful about what they say online as it could ruin their future careers. Police have already recorded thousands of "non-crime hate incidents" involving children. These non-crime hate incidents could show up if an employer conducted a deep background check.[6]

There are some young adults now that live their lives online – out of contact with real people. Change is coming so fast that parents and other adults are always behind the curve. Some 45 per cent of teens say they use the internet 'almost constantly', a figure that has nearly doubled from the 24 per cent just three years earlier.[7] Children and teenagers are watching or maybe stumbling across pornography from an earlier age – in some cases as young as 7 or 8.[8]

Here is pathetically inadequate advice for parents: 'having an understanding of what's out there – and what your child might see at some point – can be an important part of helping your child have a healthy and safe relationship with real sex at the appropriate time'.[9] Is this advice in any way a match for the Real of obscenity out there, increasing in accordance with the inexorability and exponentiality of Moore's Law. Similarly with drugs: 'give them the information on risks', and *so on*. But how can mere education *qua* information compete with the Real *jouissance*?

I recently participated in a one-day conference, the first in Ireland, for professionals working with children psychoanalytically. With nearly 100 participants, *all* women save for three male participants (no one questioned the gender imbalance). I was one of 16 contributors. All day the focus was the psychoanalytic preference for enabling the young person *to speak*. The "autonomous child" is front and centre – parents are way back, in a "supportive" role. But when I remonstrate, 'Where are the fathers?', there is brief acknowledgement, with smiles or even assent, before it dies down. And then someone murmurs, do we really need them?

Tom Madders of the charity, YoungMinds, said:

> We are facing a mental health crisis for children and young people. We know that teenagers are facing a wide range of pressures, including stress at school, bullying, body issues and the added pressure of the 24/7 online world. Girls may also be affected by early sexualisation, and the feeling that their lives need to be as perfect as pictures in newsfeeds.[10]

Family structure, school, neighbourhood emerged as having a significant and consistent relationship with adolescent behaviour, with poorer behaviour across *all* domains for those in lone-parent families or families that experienced separation during adolescence. This pattern held even taking account of the socio-economic characteristics of these households and was not fully explained by other factors[11]

The child does not exist

Fourteen years ago I wrote about the "simulation" of childhood, citing the widespread belief that education, skills training for parents, lessons in "emotional intelligence", teaching children about rights, democratic families, and all manner of educational domestication, will bring progress and individual freedom. 'All these rational solutions, coming from the final phases of the enlightenment tradition in the West, fail to take account of the *unchanging real* of human relationships. These have always been based on power, force and hierarchy, and yet in the special case of children we have pretended to relinquish these'.[12]

The phantasy is that the real issues of power, hierarchy, and *so on* have been reset. Post-psychoanalysis, we no longer believe in 1) the Real of the drive and 2) the inevitable assertion of *some* "authority". But if not from the family from where?

Indeed, *real children no longer exist.* Caught in an autonomous zone, like a demilitarised zone: **the drives** on the one side and **criminal exploiting Other** on the other – drug dealers, internet trolls, online and offline paedophiles, lone wolves, bullies, the mentally ill, etc. Where is the child? We naively believe that reason alone will dispel the powerful forces.

The child as simulacrum occupies a thematic zone – to do with "care". New medical categories pathologising behaviour*s* (plural), special needs, and many new professionals requiring training to deliver these goods that stand in place of protective authority.

Meanwhile, the governmental strategy contains pieties, such as "harm reduction", "monitoring evolving trends", "controlling, regulation and supply of drugs", provision of "performance indicators", "maintenance treatments", and "needle exchange".[13] Real increasing devastation becomes the simulacrum of harm reduction. Devasted victims become "service users" who should be encouraged into more "healthy lifestyles".

The new business model "County Lines" is the practice of trafficking drugs into leafy rural areas and sleepy small towns, away from police presence in major cities. Traffickers recruit feral children, excluded from home and school and now in the greatest danger of their lives. These children are referred to as "vulnerable" in need of "care". Katie Razzall (BBC *Newsnight*) spent months in 2019 reporting on the plight of teenagers in the UK, placed by their councils in unregulated, unsupported accommodation. Those children, it was alleged, were 'treated like dogs'.[14]

Children these days exist in departmental bureaucratic models, the documentary outpourings from which are to be studied by the professionals. Thus, with a clear conscience they can say "Children First!"[15] All the politicians can say "Children First". And all can shout – *there will be no more child abuse.* Yet, an average of 20 children die in the "care" of the Irish State each year, which goes largely unremarked. In 2014, Tusla (The Child and Family Agency in Ireland) reported 26 deaths.[16] Yet there is no real outcry, no national programmes devoted to the issue, no resignations.

Thus, "Children First" might also signify, the *first* to suffer, the *first* to die. Before being born, there is a largely unavoidable 60 per cent risk of dying by natural miscarriage. Survive that, and you may be at risk of being "terminated", more so if you are a girl. Back in the sixties there were three abortions for every live birth in Russia, now down to two.[17] In France you have an even chance of dying from abortion or continuing to live.[18] And if you are unfortunate enough to be a late termination, you are going to suffer a very painful death: 'A group of nurses and doctors have said the use of potassium chloride [to cause foetal heart attack] in late-term abortions is causing excruciating pain to babies before they die'.[19]

Once born, infanticide, according to the Society for the Prevention of Infanticide, was a crime committed by some mothers in medieval times, but such a fate still remains occasionally true today. As many as 43 per million under 1-year-olds represent the group at *greatest risk* of homicide in the UK.[20]

Get beyond that age, then comes the question of gender. When it comes to a child who wants to transition, the medical team will need "to work with you" as parent/guardian, to bring you onboard with a process that ultimately might *not* require your consent. Recall Victoria Gillick in 1983, a Roman Catholic mother of ten, who challenged the right of doctors to prescribe contraception to girls under the age of 16 without their parents' permission or even knowledge. How did that go? Only two years later the British House of Lords affirmed the doctors' right, ruling that 'the parental right to determine whether or not their minor child below the age of 16 will have medical treatment terminates if and when the child achieves sufficient understanding and intelligence to fully understand what is proposed'.[21]

Children first. Believe the child

Children First is a sentimental notion, a virtual signalling that hides a serious failure in adult confidence around children. Adult authority has ceded itself to children. There is an erosion of solidarity. Adults are likely to spy on each other and are increasingly afraid to ask other adults to mind their children. Adults are no longer allies to each other or to children. One statistic was cited where a majority (75 per cent) of men surveyed said that they would not intervene to help a distressed child that wasn't their own. Children are taught to be suspicious about adults, who, in turn, are frightened that children will be believed and that they will be found guilty. Children make the rules; adults must obey. Adults now defer to children.[22]

Children First is the lie that means children *last*, with adult freedoms trumping the child's, as family structure becomes "less rigid". Of course, in the so-called democratic family all members are equal! To get round the embarrassing thought that adults do in fact exert more power, with less responsibility, make the children autonomous and fool them into thinking that they *are* adults by giving them similar rights as adults at earlier and earlier ages. We are so reasonable! Give them the information – on drugs, trans issues, porn, sex, divorce – let *them* decide. Give them an iPhone! Let *them* decide. Education! Education! Provision without protection. Freedom without protection. Obscenity without protection. There is no father. It cannot end well.

There are some children who do not know they exist. In seriously non-functioning families, without the foundational provision of "primary illusion-ment", they merely survive as entities. Because no one helps them feed, clothe, clean themselves, they have no self-care. Maybe, later in childhood if they are fortunate, someone – a teacher, another adult, adoptive parents – might call them forth so that they can begin to know that they exist, *for the first time*, only to be beset by all the horrors of symbolisation and a feeling of terrible loss. They are faced with whether to live or to go back to being dead? In order to live for the first time, they feel the urgent need to check everything obsessively and frantically on Google because they cannot trust anything in the absence of primary illusionment. Uncertain and paranoid in the extreme, they are easy prey for every conspiracy. Suicide always beckons.

Nostalgia lingers

Even the natural world does not exist. The *Oxford Junior Dictionary* has cut out around 50 words connected with nature and the countryside.[23] "A" was for acorn, "B" for buttercup, and "C" for conker, not Attachment, Blog, and Chatroom. Almond, Blackberry, and Crocus made way for Analogue, Broadband, and Celebrity.

Recall Winnicott's understanding of psychosomatic unity and felt aliveness,[24] brought about by children's agile play in what used to be called the natural world. Now, more often, plugged into the matrix, the body and mind can wither away together or become over-extended and obese as a counter-reaction.

Twenty-eight authors refer to what they euphemistically call 'a decline in natural play and the decline in children's wellbeing'.[25] These authors include Margaret Atwood, Andrew Motion, Michael Morpurgo, and Robert Macfarlane. They cite research a generation ago when children still existed and 40 per cent of them regularly played in natural areas, compared to 10 per cent today, with a further 40 per cent never playing outdoors. Obesity, anti-social behaviour, friendlessness, and fear are the known consequences. Walk through any suburban estate a generation ago and there were children tearing around on bikes, kicking a ball, and *so on*. Now those roads are more or less deserted.

> 'Wassat then?' a man at the bar says to the barman, early on a quiet week-day evening, as my child jumps up to peer through the bevelled glass of the pub's front door. He had been sitting at the picnic bench outside with his grandmother.
>
> 'Is that a little kiddy?' he asks no one in particular. This was clearly a rare sighting.

Nostalgia lingers. The chief inspector of schools in the UK complains that nursery rhymes are no longer taught in nurseries or schools.[26] Also fairy tales, folk tales, Greek and Roman myths, and religious parables. In his groundbreaking book, *The Uses of Enchantment*, Bettelheim[27] described how myths offered a framework within which to help children work through their unconscious Oedipal wishes, that is, the darker feelings that terrified them, that found a perfect outlet in fairy tales, myths, and Bible stories. Everyone understood what the big bad wolf represented, or the wicked stepmother, or little Red Riding Hood who strayed from the path, or Icarus, or Prometheus, and *so on*. They understood that these stories were valuable lessons in living with danger, with kindness and warmth possibly winning out in the end. These rhymes and stories at one time were known by heart, were part of what Winnicott called the "transitional space", a protected zone in early childhood against impingement.

These myths and fables have for millennia helped children understand the world and created a moral framework. Now as the State has taken over education, there are new parables. Old stories and rhymes are replaced by ideological "stories" not unlike the old Soviet propaganda, with directives on speech and language compliance, warnings about "hate speech" enforced by the State, as well as White Privilege, Climate Change, LGBTQ issues, and *so on*.

The new language, the nobodaddy language, is the universal anti-hierachical language of rights and equality. Officially, the "child" changed from being an *object* with rights that need protection, to becoming a *subject* with rights to be demanded. The shift was from the child's *charitable* status (that is, worthy of love and protection) to a *political* one. The old notion of child was always a Western pedagogical one that prevailed in Europe and the rich North in the recent past and does not stand comparison with young persons from poorer parts of the world, or even young people from just a few centuries ago in Europe who had/have no childhood. Thus, 'the way children are conceptualised in society creates … the Image [simulacrum] of Childhood of that particular society … thus ideas concerning the rights of children are strictly dependent on the prevailing "Image of Childhood"'.[28]

Once we ask, 'Is a child a micro-adult or a *species sui generis?*'[29] then, as we have emphasised, there is no such thing as a child anymore.[30] The child has become an abstraction, a performance, a virtual entity, a dissected object. Thus, the modern child stages himself in various ways, acts out his childhood ironically, albeit very enthusiastically. Children are pliable and biddable. That has always been the case but now even more so as their lives become more precarious – both parents working, moving, splitting up, moving on, realising themselves anew, fulfilling themselves, and *so on*.

The usual story when the parents are separating: oh, the children will adapt, of course they will; they might even benefit from having new brothers and sisters.

- No! Believe me, the children will be very happy.
- We will still love you. In our separate ways, of course we love you.
- Yes, of course. And I love you.
- And, I love you too.
- No more worrying. Okay? No more. You know you can always tell us if there is anything bothering you, don't you?
- Yes, I know. Thanks. That's good to know.
- Just so long as you know that. We'll be here for you.

We might still slip into the old language by dint of habit! - "adult", "child", "mother", and *so on*. Postmodern anti-foundationalism strongly insists that there is no father as there is no authority (except one's own). Nothing exists in terms of the old Oedipal differentiations: no child, no father, no mother, no sexual difference, and no generational difference.

Equality is the master signifier in the (non)world. And nobody notices the staggering losses, or if they do they have no place to say so. Postmodernism recognises *no* losses, only gains. And as in Soviet times, if you fail to understand, there is always the threat of the psychiatric hospital.[31] We are learning what happens when you allow the "children" to run the playground and there are no adults around – they have all become children. *In*-tolerance is rife. Adult children have stopped *having* children[32] maybe because they have *become* children and they do not want responsibility. The child no longer exists because we have become children!

Think of "The Teddy Bears' Picnic", but *without* the mummies and daddies coming to pick them up to take them home to bed because they're tired little teddy bears. But there will be **no one** at six o'clock to take them home to bed. **No one is coming** because there are no more mummies and daddies.

Revenge of the Real

One should wonder if the "child" – the young subject – whom we allege is always "free to speak", as "subject with their own rights", the "Children-First" child, the child from whom we should learn, who deserves education and information, who is a "stakeholder" – with all these false privileges, and *so on*: does he/she ever get caught up *in the revenge at its own disappearance* in hyper-reality. A revenge that it can know nothing about; a revenge that *it is subject to*. Not chosen, it is a revenge of the ravaged Real against the ubiquitous hyper-real, a revenge of brutal intensity, an archaic roar into the void.

Recall the autistic boy who had several so-called meltdowns that greatly upset the guests in a Spanish resort hotel.[33] Recall also the fictional Kevin of Lionel Shriver's *We Need to Talk about Kevin*[34] fame. The story was rejected by Shriver's literary agent: 'I just don't think anyone is going to want to publish a book about a kid doing such maxed-out, over-the-top, evil things, especially when it's written from such an unsympathetic point of view'. The agent suggested a rewrite: 'Don't make him a mass-murderer … have him actually have a soft spot for his sister because she is easily humiliated and poses no threat'.[35] But it was mass readership that made this book a success.

The fascination with the evil child is already spoken for.[36] This is the trouble with what Baudrillard calls the "Integral Real"; no stone will be left unturned by the "maxed-out, over-the-top" postmodern global media. There is nowhere to hide. Are autism, Asperger's, and *so on*, the medical names we give to mediate, rationalise, tame, and control a massive global resistance – an autistic resistance on the level of the Real psyche–soma – to the impingement of this unreal or hyperreal noise-world, against which some are bound to erect massive defences, to create a minute mental safe space where nothing is allowed. Such is the tsunami of the artificial world at max volume. Is it any wonder that one may want to cover one's ears and curl up in a corner and rock? Or scream back, scream to let you know how absolutely alien the world has become. I can match alien for alien. I can match rage for rage. I can wake the hotel guests. I can destroy the high-school kids. But there is no "I", that is, there is no choice, there is no decision, as Baudrillard says, 'the subject has the passion to be object, to become object … taking revenge, becoming refractory, impenetrable, "crystalline" object'.[37]

The animal–object–machine of the pre-subject reacts to the inhumanity of the post-human that advances towards us on an invisible and unstoppable wave, by becoming robotic in advance of robotics, by becoming artificial in advance of artificial intelligence (AI). A switch flips and the lights go out. A fuse is blown; all goes black. How else to cope with the white heat of technology bearing directly on the neurones?

This is total exposure. I cannot speak. I have "locked-in syndrome". This must be how you kill a child without him dying, without him knowing. He "functions" (note the already common usage of this machine word) normally even if he is consumed, enveloped by (virtual) reality, no longer a child but an embedded terminal in a neural-electronic network. He is a cyborg. There is no opting-out. Everything and everyone are wired. And because we are in postmodern times, we feel we must try to keep up with the latest …

These are extreme states in extreme times. The last vestiges of the human recede and a whole new generation with a zero attention span screams "this is 2021" as if NOW is what is important and the past is past – what we know now is all that counts. This is the refusal point, blanking out critical thinking, demanding safe spaces, trigger warnings, whole swathes of people not allowed to speak. As Eagleton says about the postmodern, 'If God is dead, then man himself, who once dreamed of filling his shoes, is also nearing his term. There is not much left to disappear'.[38] It is in this general catastrophic context that the child no longer exists.

The child is just a casualty of a much bigger white-out. The blizzard of information and stimulation pre-empts the discovery of the world, and comes between us and the world out there, thus creating an ever-new virtual world of more febrile intensity, confusion, and chaos where there can be no lack. No lack of anything, especially porn and crime, which are unstoppable. Paul Virilio called this the "Information Bomb", detonated by the energy of mass information.[39]

Let us step back from the all-out blizzard, its impersonality and its "transhuman" effects, and return to what little remains of the personal. No wonder that Peter Sloterdijk concluded that 'the world-soul project' failed and, as a consequence, he recommends 'death by exposure', a long, hard, cold look at the dissolution of meanings and what he calls, 'the riven bonds of life'.[40] Death by exposure is what I attempt by writing. But the "riven bonds", the riven *social* bond? Starting with the father. "Get rid of the father" was the message of at least the last half-century, now more or less shamelessly avowed. And getting rid of the father – the Symbolic father – means the whole (Oedipal) structure collapses. Parricide, according to psychoanalysis, was one of the crimes secretly wished for, making way for incestuous relations to become normalised and unanalysed. In the absence of the father, the phallic mother enters onto the scene, with a complex mixture *of seduction and archaic dominance without limit.* There will be no longer any repression of the child's polymorphous perversity, but rather its hyperrealisation in the wild excesses of late capitalism and the global market.

For some, the blizzard of *jouissance* is all too much. Christopher Boone in *The Curious Incident of the Dog in the Night-Time* has a favourite dream, that we can summarize as follows: nearly everyone on the earth is dead, because they have caught a virus. It's like a computer virus ... and he can go anywhere in the world and know that no one is going to talk to him or touch him or ask a question.[41] Christopher prefers white noise to block out the blizzard outside. He has been impinged upon by what Frances Tustin refers to as the "not-self" at a time in early life when he is totally unable to contain it. For Tustin, the autistic child is not "object-related". She is asymbolic, lacks phantasies and imagination, cannot "not-me" play, has little inner life, and lacks a 'psychic floor'.[42] Thus, 'pathological autism is seen as a system of protective manoeuvres by which "not-me" reality is avoided'.[43] The child with autism gets others to do things for them to maintain the delusion-of-fusion with the object. The aim of psychotherapy here is 'to re-establish the primary situation of *flowing-over-at-oneness*, which has been agonisingly disturbed by experiences of sensuous disconnection from a sensation-giving mother'.[44]

The issue here is that "not-me" impingements have greatly increased since Tustin's pioneering work in the last century when autism was considered a rare disorder. Since then, there has been at least a twenty-fold increase in cases diagnosed. However, Linda Blair warns, 'It's unclear, therefore, whether the higher rates reflect a real increase in ASD (autism spectrum disorder), or whether the increase is down to a relaxation of the diagnostic criteria coupled with an increased awareness of the condition'.[45] This new diagnostic awareness coincides with a number of major trends in the new century. These include what Žižek refers to as the retreat or regression in the West 'to an autistic-masturbatory, "asocial" *jouissance* whose supreme case is drug addiction'.[46] Retreat from the (non)world, beyond envy and ressentiment into a deafening autistic roar, as we discover that anyway, the "self is an illusion",[47] an illusion of the user, and *so on.*

Irrefutably, the *inhuman* space of the "not-me" is expanding. Autism has coincided with automation. Protective measures – Tustin suggests they are extreme defences – are required to shut out the horrors of the (non)world. Levinas referred to the uncanny "noise" of the *il y a*, the impersonal "there is", existence (Being) without existents (beings), the pure anonymous glacial materiality of Being itself. He asks,

> How are we going to approach this existing without existents? Let us imagine all things, beings and persons, returning to nothingness. What

remains after this imaginary destruction of everything is not something, but the fact that there is [*il y a*]. The absence of everything returns as a presence, as the place where the bottom has dropped out of everything, an atmospheric density, a plenitude of the void, or the murmur of silence … And it is anonymous: there is neither anyone nor anything that takes this existence upon itself.[48]

Perhaps Levinas was referring to the inhuman, where the final (human) absence is decipherable today as a massive electronic presence, the "there is" of automated voices, automated empathy, and AI, all bleeps and beeps and robotic totality? Was this one meaning of "death by exposure"? For there is now less and less possibility of hiding from this radical exposure trans-human penetration. Privacy is becoming impossible. The autist is the canary in the coal mine.

Singularity or integration

Among the treatment approaches to autism, the behavioural approach encourages certain behaviours and discourages others through a subtle reward and punishment (called a "correction") system to bring about 'meaningful and positive changes in behaviour'.[49] These techniques focus on breaking complex tasks into smaller, more achievable steps. As children learn each step, they get praise and rewards. Difficult behaviour is ignored. In the developmental approach, the teacher or therapist sets up a situation that encourages the child to initiate a desired behaviour and then to build on this, hoping to improve communication and learning.

Developmental approaches aim to help children form positive, meaningful relationships with other people. They focus on teaching children social and communication skills in everyday structured settings. They also aim to help children develop skills for daily living. Trial and assessment are key – what works when teaching children new behaviours and skills by using a variety of specialised, structured techniques. These interventions have a normative aim, governed in part by the assumption that autism has a genetic cause.

From a psychoanalytic perspective, an object relational approach attempts to understand the psychotic terror that leads to autism. Following Freud, Klein, and Bion in particular, Anne Alvarez emphasises the "here and now" affective processes in the analytic session, especially 'sensitivity to and familiarity with primitive, nearly unbearable states of mind',[50] that are repeated with the therapist. Her approach is 'more relational, less reductionistic and mechanistic, and more able to accommodate novelty, growth, change and the mentalness of mind'.[51] She points to the simple but profound notion that we need to understand that people talk with the idea of a listener in mind. She says, 'their words are aimed and if there is felt to be nowhere to aim them, why talk? Autistic children occasionally talk *at* someone, but almost never *to* someone'.[52] And the comparison she is making here is with earlier theories of Freud (before object relations) and arguably with behavioural methods described above. That is, by ignoring the child's relation to the external mother and the internal object, there is no way of understanding autism. As the title of her book suggests, Alvarez is trying to breathe life back into the rigid, dead, autistic manoeuvres against terror, the sorts of "unthinkable anxieties" or "primitive agonies" that Winnicott[53] outlines: falling forever; going to pieces; having no relation to the body; having no orientation; complete isolation because of there being no means of communication – which all relate to autism and childhood psychosis.

In Kanner's early account of autism do we not see precisely the postmodern atomised world being anticipated in the autistic child? The autist is a bellwether:

> There was, on his side, no affective tie to people. He behaved as if people as such did not matter or even exist. It made no difference whether one spoke to him in a friendly or harsh way. He never looked at people's faces. Whether he had any dealings with persons at all, he treated them or rather parts of them, as if they were objects.[54]

Kanner was the first to introduce the very controversial notion of the "Refrigerator Mother", who by her alleged coldness brings about the lack of 'affective tie'.[55]

Learning from the autist, on the other hand, characterises the Lacanian orientation. The autist is regarded first and foremost as a singularity, a one-off. There is no attempt made to change behaviours or indeed to encourage relating *per se*, but rather to facilitate the development of this unique subject against any "normatising discourse". To quote Neus Carbonell, 'For [Lacanian] psychoanalysis, considering autism as being in relation to an *unfathomable decision of the being* entails also thinking about a treatment for the subject. All that remains of the other treatments is the correction or re-education of alleged anomaly'.[56]

With other treatments, there is no consent asked for or given. Dawson points to science's, 'history of conjuring experiments, evidence, and data to prove that prevailing prejudices are justified. We did not find out a lot about women until women became human beings with human rights'. If science was serious about human rights and ethics, [a]utistic behaviours would be found to be compatible with learning, intelligence, and achievement; and these behaviours, however different, would be valued. Society would receive the message that it is alright to be autistic, and that it is alright for an autistic person to be different from a typical person.

Commenting on the so-called "splintered" intelligence of autists, '[t]his *is* the place to state that it is unethical, and unscientific, a *priori* to deem untreated autistics unintelligent and unable to learn because our intelligence and our learning fail to be typical'. She concludes, 'The poverty of autistic social outcomes, regardless of our abilities, is consistent with persons who have no rights and merit no ethical consideration'.[57]

The trenchant critique offered here by Dawson, is focussed on the "ABA industry".[58] Significantly, there is no mention by Dawson of other psychoanalytic approaches mentioned above, *only* the Lacanian critique which stands alone in its emphasis on the singularity of the subject with its ineffable *unfathomable decision of the being.* Period.

In the Lacanian view, the subject should not be coerced into relating, adapting, and *so on*, rather celebrated as exemplifying "neurodiversity", indeed forging new pathways in being. However, is this not just another example of the denial and prolongation of the Real of pain and suffering with many an autistic subject trapped forever in the hellhole of the Real?

Sophie Robert's documentary *Le Mur* (or *The Wall*) includes interviews with a number of prominent Lacanian analysts in which they discuss their perspectives on autism. A court in Lille upheld complaints taken by several key analysts who saw themselves on tape and did not like how they were portrayed, claiming that they had been selectively edited.[59] The video is no longer available with English subtitles, although the French version is available.[60]

When years back I asked Lacanian analysts if there had ever been any studies to verify the efficacy of Lacanian analysis, they looked at each other and could not conceal their amusement at my question! How can you measure ethics?

Recall the good news/bad news joke: the bad news is you've been diagnosed with autism, but the good news is your (neuro)difference will come to be differently valued in time as culture evolves.[61] Or, the good news is that we understand autism and have a very moving psychoanalytic account of its psychogenic etiology, but the bad news is, no one now with their scientific worldview will ever believe us and will continue to treat autistic subjects as objects.

A BBC programme on France's treatment of autism[62] highlighted the bad news. As the psychiatric world in France is dominated by Lacanian psychoanalysis, only 20 per cent of autistic children in France are in school, and often only part-time. The rest are either in psychiatric hospitals, or in medico-social centres, or living at home. The real tragedy is with France's autistic adults, many of whom languish in a state of total incomprehension or even self-mutilation. Seventy-five per cent of families with autistic children end in divorce, and normally it is with the mother that the autistic person stays. Today these elderly women are looking after their adult children with no knowing what will happen when they die.

Notes

1 Author's observation overheard on a suburban train.
2 Žižek, S. 2000, pp. 116–117.
3 Samuel, M. 2008.
4 The original video does not seem to be available.
5 Twenge, J. 2017.
6 Squires, B. 2021.
7 Anderson, M. and Jiang, J. 2018.
8 "Children see pornography as young as seven, new report finds". 2019. BBFC. www.bbfc.co.uk/about-us/news/children-see-pornography-as-young-as-seven-new-report-finds.

9 www.children1st.org.uk/help-for-families/parentline-scotland/guidance-advice/por-
   nography/.
10 cited in Smyth, C. 2017.
11 Smyth, E. and Darmody, M. 2021, p86.
12 Weatherill, R. 2004, p. 69.
13 "Reducing Harm, Supporting Recovery. A Health-Led Response to Drug and Alcohol
   Use in Ireland 2017–2025". Dept. of Health.
14 "Teen in care treated 'like stray dog'." BBC *Newsnight*. 9 October 2019.
15 "Children First" or "Child First" is a generic term used to refer to the protection and
   welfare of children in Ireland. It is linked to the Children First Welfare Act 2015.
16 Buckley, H. 2015.
17 Ponars   Eurasia.   www.ponarseurasia.org/abortion-in-russia-how-has-the-situation
   -changed-since-the-soviet-era/.
18 www.cairn-int.info/article-E_POPU_1904_0409--recent-demographic-trends-in
   -france.htm.
19 "Potassium chloride use in late term abortion causes excruciating pain". https://gript.ie
   /medics-say-potassium-chloride-used-in-late-term-abortion-causes-excruciating-pain
   -for-foetus/.
20 Motz, A. 2008, p. 274.
21 Doward, J. 2020.
22 See discussion on *The Moral Maze*. BBC Radio 4. 23 January 2008.
23 Flood, A. 2015.
24 Winnicott, D. 1949, p. 244.
25 Flood, A. 2015.
26 Wilby, P. 2018.
27 Bettelheim, B. 1975.
28 Veerman, 1991, p. 398.
29 Ibid., p. 397.
30 Postman, N. 1982.
31 Now there are reports that the old Soviet misuse of psychiatry is returning. See Roache,
   M. 2017.
32 "The End of Babies". www.nytimes.com/interactive/2019/11/16/opinion/sunday/
   capitalism-children.html.
33 White, V. 2011.
34 Shriver, L. 2010.
35 Shriver, L. 2011.
36 Renner, K. (ed) 2013.
37 Smith, R. 2010 (ed), p. 143.
38 Eagleton, T. 2014, p. 192.
39 Cited in Armitage, J. (ed) 2001, p. 168.
40 cited in Weatherill, 2017, p. 47.
41 Haddon, M. 2004.
42 Tustin, F. 1981, p. 18.
43 Ibid., p. 17.
44 Ibid., p. 22.
45 Blair, L. 2014.
46 Žižek, S. 2006, p. 311.
47 Nørretranders, T. 1991.
48 Levinas, E. 1947, pp. 46–47.
49 *Challenging Autistic Behaviour*. BBC, 25 February 2017.
50 Alvarez, A. 1992, p. 7.
51 Ibid., p. 11.
52 Ibid., p. 191.
53 Winnicott, D. 1962.

54 Kanner, L. 1943, p. 217.
55 See for instance, Cohmer, S. 2014.
56 Cited by Goldenburg, M. 2012. Emphasis added.
57 Dawson, M. 2004.
58 ABA is Applied Behavioural Analysis and it is a pragmatic approach to helping people with autism. It focusses on improving specific behaviours such as social skills, communication, reading, as well as adaptive learning skills, such as fine motor dexterity, hygiene, grooming, domestic capabilities, punctuality, and job competence. Whatever works.
59 Autism   scandal.   www.lacanonline.com/2012/01/news-january-2012/?fbclid=IwA R0k2HdnPzW46QIlm09Bh-JWvdI4bORoU9VVl4qQkMGF6wwRt2kD9qUP-DWE.
60 *Le mur, la psychanalyse à l'épreuve de l'autisme.* www.youtube.com/watch?v=PS2dlJh5U60.
61 See for instance, Lyons, V. and Fitzgerald, M. 2013.
62 Schofield, H. 2012.

References

Alvarez, A. 1992. *Live Company. Psychoanalytic Psychotherapy with Autistic, Borderline, Deprived and Abused Children.* New York and London: Routledge.

Anderson, M., Jiang, J. 2018. "Teens and Social Media & Technology". *Pew Research Centre,* May 31. www.pewresearch.org/internet/2018/05/31/teens-social-media-technology -2018/.

Armitage, J. (Ed.) 2001. *Virilio Live. Selected Interviews.* London: Sage Publications.

Bettelheim, B.1975. *The Uses of Enchantment: The Meaning and Importance of Fairy Tales.* New York: Vintage.

Blair, L. 2014. *The Key to Calm.* London: Hodder & Stoughton.

Buckley, H. 2015. *National Review Panel. Annual Report 2014.* https://www.tusla.ie/uploads /content/NRP_Annual_Report_2014.pdf

Cohmer, S. 2014. "Early Infantile Autism and the Refrigerator Mother Theory (1943– 1970)". *Embryo Project Encyclopedia* (2014-08-19). ISSN: 1940-5030 http://embryo.asu .edu/handle/10776/8149

Dawson, M. 2004. *The Misbehaviour of Behaviourists: Ethical Challenges to the Autism-ABA Industry.* http://www.sentex.net/~nexus23/naa_aba.html

Doward, J. 2020. "High Court to Decide If Children Can Consent to Gender Reassignment". *The Guardian.* Jan 5. https://www.theguardian.com/society/2020/jan/05/high-court -to-decide-if-children-can-consent-to-gender-reassignment

Eagleton, T. 2014. *Culture and the Death of God.* New Haven: Yale University Press.

Flood, A. 2015. "Oxford Junior Dictionary's Replacement of 'Natural' Words with 21st-Century Terms Sparks Outcry. *The Guardian,* Jan 13. https://www.theguardian .com/books/2015/jan/13/oxford-junior-dictionary-replacement-natural-words

Goldenburg, M. 2012. "Autism: An Ethical Stake for Our Time". *The Symptom* 13. http:// www.lacan.com/symptom13/autism-an.html.

Haddon, M. 2004. *The Curious Incident of the Dog in the Night-time.* London: Vintage.

Kanner, L. 1943. "Autistic disturbances of affective contact." *Nervous Child,* 2, 212–250.

Levinas, E. 1947. *Time and the Other.* Trans. Cohen, R.. Pittsburgh: Duquesne University Press, 1987.

Lyons, V., Fitzgerald, M. 2013. "Critical Evaluation of the Concept of Autistic Creativity". *Recent Advances in Autism Spectrum Disorders - Volume I, Michael Fitzgerald.* IntechOpen, DOI: 10.5772/54465. Available from: https://www.intechopen.com/books/recent

-advances-in-autism-spectrum-disorders-volume-i/critical-evaluation-of-the-concept
-of-autistic-creativity

Motz, A. 2008. *The Psychology of Female Violence. Crimes against the Body*. London and New York: Routledge.

Norretranders, T. 1991. *The User Illusion: Cutting Consciousness Down to Size*. New York and London: Penguin, 1998.

Postman, N. 1982. *The Disappearance of Childhood*. London: Vintage Books.

Renner, K. (Ed.) 2013. *The 'Evil Child' in Literature, Film and Popular Culture*. London and New York: Routledge.

Roache, M. 2017. Is Soviet-era Punitive Psychiatry Making a Return? In *Al Jazeera*. https://www.aljazeera.com/indepth/features/2017/05/soviet-era-punitive-psychiatry-making-return-170530141852510.html

Samuel, M 2008. "Bernardo's Survey Reveals Disturbing Intolerance of Children". *Community Care*, Nov 17. https://www.communitycare.co.uk/2008/11/17/barnardos-survey-reveals-disturbing-intolerance-of-children/

Schofield, H. 2012. France's Autism Treatment "Shame". *BBC News Magazine*, April 2. http://www.bbc.com/news/magazine-1758312

Shriver, L. 2010. *We Need to Talk about Kevin*. New York: Serpent's Tale Classics.

Shriver, L. 2011. "Lionel Schriver's Talk about Kevin". *The Guardian*. https://www.theguardian.com/film/2011/may/17/lionel-shriver-we-need-talk-kevin

Smith, R. (Ed.). 2010. *The Baudrillard dictionary*. Edinburgh: Edinburgh University Press.

Smyth, C. 2017. "Women More Unhappy than Men Until They Reach Mid-80s." *The Times*. December 14. https://www.thetimes.co.uk/article/women-more-unhappy-than-men-until-they-reach-mid-80s-j868mxzkv

Smyth, E., Darmody, M 2021. "Risk and Protective Factors in Adolescent Behaviour. The Role of the Family, School and Neighbourhood Characteristics in (Mis)Behaviour among Young People". Ireland: ESRI. Research Series 119. https://www.esri.ie/system/files/publications/RS119.pdf

Squires, B. 2021. "The UK's Shocking Secret Police "non-crime" Speech Lists Put Kids' Future Careers at Risk". https://reclaimthenet.org/non-crime-speech-lists-kids/

Tustin, F. 1981. *Autistic States in Children*. London and Boston: Routledge.

Twenge, J. 2017. *Igen. Why Today's Super-Connected Kids Are Growing Up Less Rebellious, More Tolerant, Less Happy--and Completely Unprepared for Adulthood--and What That Means for the Rest of Us*. New York: Simon & Schuster.

Veerman, E. 1991. *The Rights of the Child and the Changing Image of Childhood*. Boston and London: Martinus Nijhoff Publishers.

Weatherill, R. 2004. *Our Last Great Illusion*. Exeter: Academic Imprint.

Weatherill, R. 2017. *The Anti-Oedipus Complex: Lacan, Critical Theory and Postmodernism*. London: Routledge.

White, V. 2011. Victoria White: Our Family Holiday was Ruined by the Treatment of Our Autistic Son. *The Herald*. May 5. https://www.herald.ie/opinion/victoria-white-our-family-holiday-was-ruined-by-the-treatment-of-our-autistic-son-27979250.html

Wilby, P. 2018. "Offsted Head: 'The Last Thing a Chief Should be is a Crusader.' Oh Really? *The Guardian*. Feb 6. www.theguardian.com/education/2018/feb/06/ofsted-chief-inspector-amanda-spielman-hijab

Winnicott, D. 1949/1975. "Mind and its Relation to Psyche-soma". In *Through Paediatrics to Psycho-analysis*. London: Hogarth, 243–254.

Winnicott, D. 1962/1972. "Ego Integration in Child Development". In *The Maturational Processes and the Facilitating Environment*. London: Hogarth, 56–63.

80   *Part I*

Žižek, S. 2000. *The Fragile Absolute*. London and New York: Verso.
Žižek, S. 2006. *The Parallax View*. Massachusetts: The MIT Press.

Television Programmes

Challenging Autism Behaviour. 25 February, 2017. London: BBC Television Programme. https://www.youtube.com/watch?v=O8j3LsHcnNc
Newsnight. 13 February, 2007. *BBC news and Current Affairs Television Programme.*
Newsnight. 17 May, 2017. *BBC News and Current Affairs Television Programme.*

Part II

5 The Mystical Origin of Psychoanalysis in Ireland[1]

This chapter describes the unique form that psychoanalysis initially took in Ireland during the last century. The founder was Jonathan Hanaghan, regarded by some of his followers as a mystic or an Old Testament prophet, with his original fusion of Freud and Jesus. From Luke 12: *I have come to bring division* (the Oedipus complex). In analysis you become "undefended as little children". The "forth-giveness" of the libido – key to mental health versus spiritual retreat. The primacy of the spirit (evolution) versus phantasy ("devolution"). The superego terrifies (make cowards) whereas the ego ideal "invites". Let go hate. Undo fixations. Marriage as foundation of society. Men and women must encounter each other in an experiment in living. Against hypocrisy and the Pharisees as life-haters. He was criticised for lofty idealism and for isolationism

- Hanaghan.
- Who?
- *Hanaghan*!
- Who's he?
- Not sure.
- Did somebody say he started psychoanalysis in Ireland back in the day?
- Dunno …
- Hey! Does anyone know? It's so long ago.

★★★

In the middle of World War II, Jonathan Hanaghan founded The Irish Psycho-Analytical Association in Southern Ireland. He brought psychoanalysis to Ireland in 1917, encouraged by Ernest Jones who identified with him as "another Gael". Hanaghan had been analysed by Douglas Bryan[2] during World War I, who in turn had been analysed by Freud.

Hanaghan was a Freudian, but he brought a teaching which was a *revelation*. Into the quiet fading gentility of leafy Victorian Monkstown in South Dublin came a radical preacher, a larger-than-life, self-taught charismatic figure, with a shock of white hair and a great presence. He demonstrated a provocative

DOI: 10.4324/9781003225010-7

interpretation of classical psychoanalysis, correct and to the point, but with a dynamic twist. He linked Freud with the New Testament. No one before or since has combined Freud *and* Jesus[3] in such a dramatic and apocalyptic way as Hanaghan.[4]

The "Monkstown Group"

He did not preach in churches, instead he set up his psychoanalytic practice in No. 2 Belgrave Square in Monkstown where he began to see people for what he called "psychoanalytic healing". There he trained a small number of other analysts in Freudian theory to carry on the work, which he regarded as nothing less than lifesaving.

To his small band of followers from all walks of life, some of whom became his disciples no less, he was known simply as "Jonty", because of the very personal nature of his mission. To some he became known as "Jonty of Monkstown" such was his stature. Indeed, there was even talk of the *three* key figures who mattered more than anyone else in the world: "Jonty of Monkstown", "Jesus of Nazareth", and "Freud of Vienna". To all, he was a father figure at a time when fathers still mattered, but upon whom the sun was already setting.

He respected Freud's atheism, but Hanaghan's claim was that Freud revealed the unconscious as essentially man's sinful nature. To Hanaghan, Freud had revealed the repressed truth about human nature. A further claim: European civilisation was defended, walled-off against its own erotic and murderous impulses, criminally acted out in the two world wars. Thus, for Hanaghan, mental illness on a personal level is ultimately a *spiritual* malaise, a *dis*-ease, a type of dereliction of the soul. Only the psychoanalytic situation, with its space to speak and particularly *to feel*, with its regularity of sessions, allows individuals to become painfully aware of their suffering and thus be helped.

However, he believed that psychoanalytic treatment *per se* was insufficient to sustain the healing. What was needed, according to Hanaghan, was a healing fellowship, a beloved community: an informal group of like-minded analysed individuals willing to reach out and support the other in crisis.

Long before "Group Therapy" became fashionable as such, Hanaghan formed what came to be known as "The Monkstown Group". It had no fixed membership, no structure, no office, no organisation, and no hierarchy. Anyone could join the group for as short or as long a time as they needed. Analysts, patients, friends, as well as psychiatrists, philosophers, poets, and theologians, on most Saturday evenings in winter, would crowd into the large double reception rooms in Jonty's Victorian house in Belgrave Square to hear talks given by him standing in front of an open fire.

In these group meetings there was no therapy as such, Hanaghan would talk on philosophical, theological, and Freudian themes in some detail – the Oedipus complex, the castration dread, the anal personality, greed, envy, existential crises, marriage, fellowship, family life, and *so on*. He linked biblical themes with psychoanalytic. He also illustrated his talks with folklore, poetry

– Blake, Tennyson, Longfellow, Wordsworth, Shakespeare's sonnets – and *so on*. He referenced Greek myth as well as religious thinkers – Augustine, Thomas à Kempis, Nonconformists like minister Isaac Watts.

This was a communal experience, of thought, conflict, and creativity, of great importance to participants, a few of whom came from far and wide in some instances, to listen and imbibe Jonty's wisdom. Some would eventually seek analysis. Hanaghan's influence was wide and profound for "those who had ears to hear", spread mainly by word-of-mouth. However, many ordinary folk living close by were indifferent or even hostile.

After the talk and discussion, there was a cup of tea, sandwiches and cakes would be passed around, made by the women in the group who took it in turns to help out. There was no charge, no publicity, nothing asked in return for the evening except fellowship.

And some of the people of the Group formed the approximate and loose-knit healing fellowship that comprised nothing more than the human souls that made it up. People were energised by what they felt were the revolutionary insights offered by Hanaghan in those rather dark days in Ireland. Later, after his death at 81 years in 1967, the Saturday night group was led in turn by the five other analyst-healers whom he had trained. And it still meets I believe in much reduced numbers today.

The clear detail of the unscripted presentations on Saturday nights, which had a very strong redemptive message, meant that some followers never missed a group. In-between, there would be analytic insights aplenty, with people interpreting each other's dreams and symptoms. Sometimes, there were wild interpretations and ad hominem put-downs. There was talk of people "not being analysed enough" and analysts even intervening in marital disputes that sometimes did not end well. People fell in love and others listened and healed each other.

Hanaghan risked conflict, bringing truth into the open, while preaching community and fellowship: let go hate; let go resentment; analyse the Oedipal rivalries and transferences; make fellowship with your brothers and sisters in the new community; leave the neurotic past behind. There was a book of his sayings,[5] beginning with Hanaghan's formula, 'I utter what men mutter', followed by impish sayings, mystical sayings, on the themes of love, hate, envy, imagination, death, marriage, Adam and Eve, and *so on*.

What was original and riveting for people at that time was the demonstration of the ordinary psychopathology of everyday life, precise psychoanalytic links made with everyday examples of how lives could be psychologically damaged, of how *unfree* every "free-thinking" person was. With Platonic illumination – the light of understanding, people said – Hanaghan spoke to them directly. He could explain the precise nature of the Falling. Hanaghan referred to his followers as "seekers after truth". And people reported that their lives had been changed forever.

In his presence, people could just break down sobbing as they 'received themselves unto themselves' as he would say, or as they *became as little children*

(Matthew 18:3). People became undefended and thus moved to painful sobbing and abjection in the aura of his presence. He was a strong, steady, and
steadfast presence while he retraced the unconscious patterns of painful childhood events. What was required was the long process of "working through"
as Freud had recommended in the normal psychoanalytic process, sometimes
taking years.

Although acclaimed, Hanaghan claimed nothing for himself. He believed
that his teaching might spread organically. He wrote little and refused contact
with the International Psychoanalytic Association (IPA), what Masud Khan
later in a private communication called the 'Jewish castrating machine'.

Hanaghan knew that his view of Freud was a step too far for the atheisti-
cally minded IPA in London and New York. Although he spoke with great
erudition, he claimed that the academic focus of psychoanalysis as a defence
against simplicity. Simplicity was key. For Hanaghan, psychoanalysis was truly
a folk psychology, explicable to all although resisted by most. Explicable yes,
but heard by only a few. Anna Freud was full of praise for Hanaghan saying
that, 'the mantle of her father's work had fallen on his shoulders', as was British
journalist and broadcaster Ludovic Kennedy, who named Hanaghan 'as the
most interesting person he had ever met'. Arland Ussher, past President of the
Irish Academy of Letters, named Hanaghan as 'one of the greatest figures of
the century'.[6]

Libido

Hanaghan differentiates two registers: actuality and reality. Actuality is the
practical, pragmatic realm of truth and untruth, of masks and semblances of
everyday hypocrisies, compromises, and *so on*. As against reality which is the
higher realm of values, the *meta*-physical, moral imperatives and the Aristotelian
virtues. The corresponding psychical agencies are the actuality-ego and the ego
ideal.

Central for Hanaghan's theorising, as for Freud, was the Oedipus complex
and its legacy of neurosis or psychosis. Hanaghan cites that well-known passage
in Luke 12: 49–53,

> *I have come to set fire to the earth, and how I wish it were already kindled! Do
> you suppose I came to establish peace on earth? No indeed, I have come to bring
> division. For from now on, five members of a family will be divided, three against
> two and two against three; father against son and son against father, mother against
> daughter and daughter against mother, mother against son's wife and son's wife
> against her mother-in-law.*

'In my judgement', Hanaghan says, 'Jesus is right and Freud, a non-Christian,
has amazingly come to the same conclusion searching only along psychological
lines in trying to understand the sane and insane'. He goes on to explain the
Oedipus complex in the simplest terms:

The son falls in love with his mother and the little daughter falls in love with her father and tries to become like her mother and the little son is jealous because he can't get all that daddy is getting and the little daughter is similarly jealous of the mother and this causes a terrific battle of jealousy of envy of hate and distress.[7]

Thus, the child's ego becomes embattled in what Hanaghan describes as an "ego fortress" arising from *secondary* narcissism. Primary narcissism was thwarted within the family and so the libido is not able to flow out to others and to the world. Thus, we are not able to love our neighbours as ourselves, because we no longer love ourselves. 'At first the baby falls in love with itself, and only when its love has been drawn out by its parents can it go forward to object-love'. This is the key to the Hanaghan paradigm, namely, the ability, or the ease, with which the libido is able to flow forth to the world of others and enrich itself by contact with the world. He was guided by Freud and his famous formula:

A strong egotism is a protection against falling ill, but in the last resort we must begin to love in order not to feel ill, and we are bound to fall ill if, in consequence of frustration we are unable to love.[8]

Here Freud had in mind Heine who had imagined God saying, 'Illness was no doubt the final cause of the whole urge to create. By creating, I could recover; by creating I could become healthy'.[9]

'We must begin to love in order not to fall ill', underpinned Hanaghan's key notion of what he called "forthgiveness", an active process of libidinal investment of the outside world, particularly the world of others. Beyond forgiveness for specific wrongs, and *so on*, forthgiveness implies a generosity of spirit, a love of life itself, participation in the gratuity of being beyond narcissism. This is the key to mental health and the aim of analysis itself. Forthgiveness is the key to community, fellowship, healing, and *so on*.[10]

Freud makes clear that the early ego was first of a *body* ego.[11] The libido, in Freud's mythology, is a reservoir within the id. This narcissistic libido flows out to objects (in love). Hanaghan makes use of Freud's *Amoeba* analogy,[12] likening the outflow of libido to the protrusions called pseudopodia that the single-celled creature extends and retracts. We can go out to the world or withdraw from it. We withdraw in sleep, in autoerotism, and especially in organic illness, where 'the libido which is withdrawn is found in the ego once more, as an increased cathexis of the diseased part of the body',[13] leading to hypochondria, narcissistic states, or indeed the psychotic over-valuation of the self as in megalomania.[14] Conversely Freud states, 'for complete health it is essential that the libido should not lose this full mobility'.[15] Mobility is key, as is *free* association, its linguistic counterpart. In depression or melancholia (as well as all neurotic illness) this mobility is lost. Freud's well-known passage on the "shadow of the object" is critical for Hanaghan's theorising. Here an object-attachment, the attachment of the libido to a loved object, is broken and withdrawn because of some slight or hurt. And, instead of being able to flow out to a new object,

> [T]he free libido was not displaced onto another object; it was withdrawn into the ego ... not employed in any unspecified way, but served to establish an *identification* of the ego with the abandoned object. Thus the shadow of the object fell upon the ego, and the latter could henceforth be judged by a special agency, as though it were an object, the forsaken object. In this way an object-loss was transformed into an ego-loss and the conflict between the ego and the loved person into a cleavage between the critical activity of the ego and the ego as altered by identification.[16]

Hanaghan praises what he calls Freud's 'spiritual discerning' in detecting 'an insincerity *of voice* in the ruthless self-accusations' of the melancholic. This "voice" was really the voice of the abandoned *other*, with which the ego has identified.

Hanaghan explains how the pseudopodia of the libidinal cathexes flow out to the other in love, 'the richer our love outflowing, the more differentiated our object-libido'. When we lose that object by death or betrayal, the pseudopodia retract into the ego, but the now differentiated libido cannot easily be reabsorbed, 'it becomes a free-floating foreign libido causing anxiety and depression'. In taking it back the person becomes changed, 'becoming in character like the person lost'.

In mourning, the object-libido is gradually reabsorbed and as Hanaghan puts it, 'After a season joy comes, because the retreated libido, now sublimated, flows forth in faith once again to love others'. In melancholia however, 'when the object-libido flows back into the self it is rejected utterly [still hated]. Because of its non–absorption, it remains unaltered in character'. It becomes a foreign hated object now "inside" the ego. What follows then, is 'bitter unconscious warfare in which the invaded ego seeks to cast out the invader [now inside] even at the cost of his own life'.[17] Where Hanaghan refers (at least in part) to bitterness, hatred, betrayal, love – part of his folk psychology – Freud prefers cathexis, libido, object, etc., and bitter self-hatred is for Freud the full sadism of the death drive – the 'pure culture of the death drive' to describe the superego of the melancholic.[18] Hanaghan makes use of Freud's "scientific" signifiers, but also mixes in a much closer language of human drama, tragedy, life and death, with ethical overtones of love and betrayal.

Self-preservation

When it comes to the self-preservation instinct, Hanaghan's revision of Freud is again original. For Freud, self-preservation is primary and essentially Darwinian. As Freud says: 'To begin with, sexual activity attaches itself to functions serving the purpose of self-preservation'.[19] Initially, the attachment is to the oral drive securing the basic self-preservative function of nutrition. Thus, initially the sexual drive is described by Freud as autoerotic. Later, Freud's conflict model of the drives will pit the sexual drive against the self-preservative instinct or the ego instincts. He refers to, 'the undeniable opposition between the instincts which subserve sexuality, the attainment of sexual pleasure, and those other instincts, which have as their aim the self-preservation of the individual – the ego instincts'.[20]

However, Hanaghan notes that the human infant is born more helpless and more vulnerable than any other animal. The higher mammals have the longer and the most dependent infancies. Instead of the atomistic, survivalist notion implied by Freud's theory, Hanaghan notes very paradoxically: 'it is the utterly undefended human baby [that] is more adequately self-preserved than all non-human babies'. He continues, the infant 'has achieved self-preservation by *self-abandonment* to the answering beloved parents'.[21] He asserts that the radically helpless baby's cry evokes optimally the attuned love response of the parents which thus, 'call[s] forth from frail parent hearts God-like qualities and libidinal out-pourings *until then in slumber* ... courage, patience, foresight, endurance, affection'. The archaic cry embeds the baby in the wider family that he himself evokes and calls forth into being.[22] The infant causes love to happen for its own protection. Thus, as Hanaghan believes, 'his self-preservation cry has created the beloved human community on earth'.[23]

However, the trusting infant's cry of the pre-ego often goes unmet and thus the infant must reverse his primary self-abandonment lest he be overwhelmed by the oral drive. He turns away from openness to the mother into secondary defensive autoerotism and starts sucking his thumb. Thus, 'the rejected infant constructs his ego out of his *reversed* self-preservation instinct. He seeks to preserve himself by turning against all'.[24] This mechanism recalls our discussion in Chapter 4 of this volume on contemporary atomism and the (non)world.

The spirit

Thus, beyond the reductive drive mechanics of the id, ego, and superego, and thus at this point beyond Freud also, Hanaghan preferred to think in terms of the primacy of the human spirit, at least part of which, he believed, remained uncontaminated, untainted by the corrupt world. Thus, he developed the notion of the ego ideal, in a very different direction to Freud, as a 'still small voice' leading us *outwards*, away from ourselves, towards our own unique (ethical) ideal, a Platonic Idea(l) lying dormant in the unrepressed unconscious.

Contrast this ideal, as Hanaghan does, with the primitive superego, which for Hanaghan is the collective harsh voice of the ancestors, of the gang or the herd *within* so-called civilisation, part of everyone's personal and archetypal history post-Oedipus. Hanaghan maintains that it is the might of the superego that strikes fear, dread, and terror into the child – castration dread – under the guise of moral training, a ubiquitous pathological outcome of the Oedipus complex. Castration is an archetypal 'engram' in the psyche.

The people of the Group thus espoused this anti-Oedipal message, locating the "true" enemy in the established churches, the vicars, the priests, the Holy Family, the schools, doctors, psychiatrists, philosophical intellectuals, politicians, the rich, and *so on*.

The Group saw itself as embattled against its own host culture, allegedly inhabiting a "spiritual wasteland" ruled over by tyrants and priests. As Hanaghan railed against these authorities every Saturday night, the disciples listened and noted the good news of liberation via psychoanalysis. The host population's reaction in South Dublin and further afield varied between not knowing, indifference to occasional outright hostility. Hanaghan's provocative preaching received several credible death threats. Many outsiders referred to "strange-goings-on" in Monkstown: was it free love, devil worship, a religious cult, and *so on*? All this hostility was proof to the Group adherents of what Hanaghan indeed had told them – these (unenlightened) people are locked inside life-hating egos. They need *our* message to save their souls, people said, not so much for God *per se* but for exuberant *life itself and free-living*. And the word of Hanaghan of Monkstown did spread, and a steady stream of people found their way to him to listen to the teachings of Freud and Jesus and thence possibly to be analysed. Hanaghan believed in the inevitable upward movement of the human spirit towards truth.

Imagination

The ego ideal according to Hanaghan, set against this reactionary superego, is the agency of spiritual vision that perceives beauty, goodness, and truth – radically at odds with tradition, orthodoxy, and civilisation itself. Hanaghan encouraged the people to believe that the ego ideal will emerge from even the worst detritus of personal experience during the psychoanalytic process. Man is spirit essentially (as well as mind and body). According to analyst Dick Cameron, 'An analyst invites a man to be what he – the man – wants to be, according to his own ego ideal'.[25] Imagination is central and primary, as are the Platonic notions of illumination by the *light* of Goodness and insight, emanating from the One. The good things that we achieve, coming from the abundant goodness of the universe, are obscured by the evil of the world, in particular the ego-defendedness of the individual living in fearful neurotic seclusion.

Identification proceeds via imagination, particularly identification with the parents. However, Hanaghan explains that children identify with a great many elements in their environment, via dramatic imitation. Thus, one child who later becomes an elite runner imitated the running style of his cat. Hanaghan recalls seeing his grandson running and darting to and fro like the swallows overhead.

> By identity-play a child becomes a creature, a plant or a thing … as he earlier incorporated his mother's milk he now incorporates existent being … The strength, courage and swiftness of creatures … By becoming the river, the clouds, the sea, he enters into their being.[26]

Mother's milk extends symbolically to mother nature.

The imagination is key to self-formation. Hanaghan says, 'Man's primal presentations, therefore, are in the imagination. Before thought, before act, man is presented within his imagination with evolutional and devolutional purposes'.[27] The primordial choice: vision versus phantasy. Vision (the ego ideal) leads to evolution (the life drive or Eros). Phantasy (id and superego presentations) leads to *de*volution (the death drive). The subject is key: *we* are the site of *choice* between phantasy and vision, between, for Hanaghan, ultimately barbarism and creative living and loving.

Thus, for Hanaghan, like people today who worry about their carbon footprint, *our* choices have cosmic reverberations. The superego coerces us through fear and threat (potentially contributing to evil) leading us into slavery. The ego ideal *invites us*, i.e. without threat, to act freely in accordance with our vision which participates in the Platonic Good beyond Being. And so, to follow the ego ideal (sublimation) requires courage and a capacity to stand alone. Thus, Hanaghan, the pagan, believed in a universe governed by a dualism of forces, implicit in Freud's final instinctual dualism.[28]

Imagination makes possible the resolution of the Oedipus complex. Classically the complex is "cut" via castration, but Hanaghan believes that it might be "untied" rather than cut. The frustrating Oedipal deadlock might be relieved by another myth – the compensatory story described by Otto Rank,[29] the myth of the royal birth of the hero. The child imagines himself to really be of noble birth rather than the child of his humble parents. His true father is a king and his mother a queen. By this noble vision of himself he lifts himself out of the family. The desire to be loved by his "Frustrating" parents is transferred to his royal dream parents, "solving" the problem of unsatisfying object-love. His loss of self-esteem is healed by the discovery of his royal lineage. In his daydreaming his royal parents come and claim him from his now despised "foster parents".[30] Hanaghan links this myth with the New Testament.

> As Jesus revealed, we are born into biological, sociological family, but we must be born again into the family of the Kingdom of Heaven. When Jesus asked, *Who is my father and my mother*, he asked a question whose profound meaning is only now becoming scientifically understandable.[31]

Creative imagination is key. Although strongly Freudian, particularly the later Freud, Hanaghan as we have indicated was against what he called the "sterile intellectualism" of the universities, saying 'you cannot seek God through logical argument … There is only one way … through the awareness of your own overwhelming in loneliness and the cry of your own heart … God is discovered in relationship, not in detachment: the relation of father and son'.[32] The analytic recall of childhood events became, in Hanaghan's thinking, linked to Christ's injunction, *Unless you turn around and become like little children, you will never enter the kingdom of heaven. Let a man humble himself until he is like this child* (Matthew 18:3). Not so much recall of memories but cathartic regression to the 'desolate overwhelming', preferably in analysis, of childhood memories.[33]

His message, and it was a *message*, couldn't be clearer: *let go hate!* 'In repentance, sadism and masochism are sublimated'.[34] Acknowledge destructiveness:

> When we greet the madness in us we are safe enough. I am a most venomous person. It lies in us all: in the Nazi and the Jew. It is what we do with the venom that is important. All that lies in evolution lies in us.[35]

Love, on the other hand, the love of the analyst could withstand the anger, coldness, desertion, etc. of the other (negative transference).

> Love is sustained volition willing the Good: *Thy will be done on earth as it is in heaven.* It is the undefended self forth-flowing despite coldness, contempt, disdain and hate.[36]

Phantasy

All mental illness, according to Hanaghan, is down to this wholesale spiritual retreat from life and unwillingness to love: 'the rivers of love are frozen within us'.[37] Thus neurosis and psychosis are caused and maintained by blocked passion (affects) leading to psychological, even physical, illness. But Hanaghan warns analysts, 'In concentrating on the psychoses and neuroses they are concentrating on the *repressed* unconscious and therefore on phantasies. Unless they correct this bias by a study of the *unrepressed* unconscious [the river] they can well become disoriented'.[38] Here, he invokes sublimation and vision leading to integration. He praises psychoanalysis for 'its rediscovery and scientific explanation of repressed phantasy', but its weakness is, for Hanaghan, its ignorance of 'the divine civilisation' in the unrepressed unconscious.[39] Ultimately, *The Kingdom of God is within you* (Luke 17:21).

Phantasies risk the disintegration of the psyche and the problem here is fixation. Fixations exist at various levels of libidinal development. Fixations affect what we might call the psychopathology of everyday life. He was thinking in particular about the disruption of the "beloved community" by these devolutionary forces seeking expression in life, weakening or destroying relationships and community. For instance, the oral leads to destructive gossip, bad-mouthing the other, addictions, alcohol abuse, and *so on*. This is the first level of fixation and the most disturbed and narcissistic, classically understood to be determinant of the worst mental illnesses – schizophrenia, paranoia, and deep depressive psychosis. The anal leads to obsessionality, meanness, hoarding of money and possessions, smearing of others, sadism and controlling behaviours, and intellectual defensiveness, taking up rigid positions in thinking, and *so on* – *My will* be done, Hanaghan was fond of typifying the anal character. The phallic can lead to aggressive intrusion, rapaciousness, and *so on*.

The European medieval castle was, for Hanaghan, a metaphor for the regressive psychological defensiveness of modern men and women en masse. We are locked into ourselves with ego defence. Hanaghan declared the truth to be that the modern city was dereliction and spiritual decay. It begins not so much in the conflict between the id and the superego, but 'in the depth of man's spirit as a personal volitional act whereby phantasy wish-fulfilment is chosen rather than vision-fulfilment ... [this] begins his devolutionary in-turning ... Europeans, in their personal retreat, have withdrawn their love and their interest from their civilisation'.[40]

Phantasies are temptation situations: 'The seductive wish-phantasy is presented to you with its opposing painful feelings of revulsion, shame, self-reproach and guilt'.[41] The link for Hanaghan is with Jesus alone in the wilderness with the wild beasts (the libidinal drives). For Hanaghan, *the whole of creation groaneth and travaileth in pain together until now* (Romans 8:22). However, the analyst can only bring the patient to that critical point, 'for in temptation you are brought face to face with the mystery of fallen nature ... in a momentary flash you come face to face, not only with your repressed outcast self, but with repressed, regressed, outcast creation'.[42]

At this point, you are most alone. As a loving father helping his child to walk, allowing him to stumble again and again, the analyst, 'as a loving father holds out his hands to his baby learning to walk, so does a spiritual healer aid a seeker. But he can no more meet his crisis than a father can do the walking for the child'.[43] At the point when you are most alone and in abjection, the atheistic analyst has nothing to say, but Hanaghan believes the psalmist should come to mind: *be still and know that I am God* (Psalm 46:10). And, *The peace of God that passeth all understanding* (Philippians 4:7).

Marriage

Marriage was key for Hanaghan, 'the foundation-stone of our society', but *not* what he regarded and condemned as the type of "loveless", so-called "Christian" relationship with the two people allegedly walled off from each other in 'suits of armour'.[44] He claimed that less than 5 per cent of couples in Europe have real marriages of sexual-spiritual fulfilment. He deplored the dirty (anal) repressed-inhibited attitude to sexuality. Hanaghan sought to rejoin sexuality and spirituality – 'the disrobing of the spirit before the disrobing of the body'[45] – against the sexologists and Freud who merely reduced the erotic to an instinct, or a need in a materialistic world.

He thought that it took ten years to make a marriage, 'where you are learning patience with each other ... learning understanding ... [of] the profound mystery of sexual difference ... until they reach the point where, like the Greeks, they are filled with wonder [of] the real beauty of a fulfilled sexual relationship'.[46] Hanaghan's approach advocated building a relationship through the barely tolerated vicissitudes of love and hate, withdrawal 'into the wilderness' and coming together again in renewed openness, undefendedness, holding nothing back, hiding nothing, involving the totality of the person, conscious and unconscious, thus enabling both, with the help of God ('waiting prayerfully without recrimination'), to create what he termed with no trace of sentimentality, a 'holy marriage'.[47] This necessarily involves striking at the 'fundamental selfishness' of the other, fighting the fight 'to cleave all the pretence, and let the hate and anger expose itself'. With this acceptance of the dangers of marriage,

> your wife or your husband lays bare everything that is in him ... you are naked opposite each other, two wild things [not just with the personal unconscious, but also] of the primeval forest, with all the Palaeolithic and Neolithic elements that belonged to primitive man out-pouring in this home of yours.[48]

Hanaghan's psychoanalysis stretches from the very highest reaches of the human soul to the abysmal that predates personal birth. He refers to the Book of Common Prayer: 'for richer, for poorer, in sickness or in health, to love and to cherish, 'til death do us part, according to God's holy ordinance; thereto I plight thee my troth'. In his folk and ironically contemporary way, he also refers to, 'unmasking the brute and the bitch that are in every man and woman'.[49]

For Hanaghan, men and women are utterly different, necessarily so. Nothing sentimental here about marriage, but quite the opposite: only radical difference, risking everything in the struggle can make a real bond where each has freedom, and each can love. Similarly, for the children to 'learn control [of the drives] by conscious suffering', if the parents are prepared to go, 'step by step and day by day with its [the child's] inner life'.[50]

Hanaghan was a modernist insofar as he idealised youth – including youth teaching adults; adults learning from children. He envisaged some adults whom he deemed too alienated in their defensive anti-life attitudes, their Oedipal envies, to be open to the idealism of youth. For Hanaghan, 'The child and Plato are one ... Child and philosopher are measuring the temporal against the eternal and finding the temporal wanting'. However, with(out) sentimental idealisation, he acknowledges that, 'what confuses us is that he [the adolescent] is also a child of nature [i.e. subject to drives], revealing to us his animality whilst concealing from us his dawning awareness of his divinity'.[51] Children join gangs fulfilling an apparent "deep hunger to belong", but could Hanaghan have imagined today's gangs, when his 1950s' version were only stealing sweets?

As if anticipating the breakdown of the nuclear family, he claims on a note of Freudian pessimism, 'I have also tried to show that the family is quite unfitted to deal with its problems ... the jealousies and envies ... of little children'. And he jumps assertion to, 'the whole of the devastation that has smashed our civilisations, including bloody war, is nothing but the break-out of these envies, maladies and hatreds in great social, volcanic upheavals because they were never controlled within the family'.[52] Was he giving assent to alternative forms of family life? For a while he formed and lived in a commune.

With Wordsworth, too much getting and spending, we are out of tune, laying waste our powers, and *so on*. Thus, for Hanaghan, 'the family today may be judged as guilty ... we present no creative vision to our children'.[53]

Sublimation was key to forging passion into power, transforming the death drive:

> We must give up our masochisms and endless self-pity ... that makes us weary and so sad and sorry for ourselves. We are in such great need and somebody must take care of us – poor, poor me! So we endlessly nurse ourselves while there are people crying out in ultimate, real need ... in the grip of real mental illness ... real physical illness ... of poverty and want ... loneliness; and we have nothing to give ... So I want to say again ... you and I [must] repent of our unknown hates, or our implacable hates ... *Repent for the kingdom of heaven is at hand.*
>
> (Matthew 4:17)[54]

Critique

Hanaghan's theory is largely affect based. Libido, the drives, forces, and counterforces dominate his thinking and practice. In some respects, Hanaghan is closest to maybe Michel Henry and François Roustang, who rejected the Lacanian emphasis on the signifier.

At work here is a pagan, Dionysian celebration of life over and against the stultifying effects of 20th century materialism and its corresponding ego-resistance – resistance to the free flow of life itself. For Hanaghan, language and free association is only en route to the greatest freedom, via the Holy Spirit: *Come to me all you who are burdened and heavy-laden, and I will give you rest* (Matthew 11:28).

Hanaghan spoke strongly to the disaffected, lonely, alienated youth of the late fifties and early sixties,[55] prior to the great Cultural Revolution of the late sixties. The generosity of spirit which was the Group was welcomed by many as a real Christian community of sharing and equality.

Hanaghan died in 1967 aged 80, which was also the year of the "Summer of Love", of which he would have approved. The small group of analysts and their patients very slowly became somewhat interned, *without links* to other analytical, radical political, or religious groups.[56] In the years after his death, the temperature was cooling and people were looking outwards to myriad psycho-therapies and "growth groups" in Britain and Europe. Study groups and reading groups were set up in Dublin during the seventies by the many younger followers interested in Freud and Klein. Speakers, such as R.D. Laing and Masud Khan were invited from abroad. Aspiring analysts underwent apprenticeship-type trainings with the older analysts, gradually taking on patients themselves under supervision.

Visiting analysts today sometimes ask: 'Why did psychoanalysis start so late in Ireland?' The dominance of the Catholic Church, biological psychiatry, the innate conservatism of the people, and *so on*, left no space for psychoanalysis. Hanaghan was regarded as perhaps an outlier, an anomaly, or even an aberration, as psycho-therapy became more formalised and institutionalised during the eighties.

Hanaghan's faith, his vocation, his rhetoric that was more mystical than theoretical, more intensity than reason, more Platonic-Christian than Freudian, and his deep commitment to the work of analysis was largely sidelined after some four decades. For Hanaghan, professionalisation with its insurances and protocols, which later developed, in short, the formalisation of psychoanalysis in the university, would have been seen as a defence against life, encounter, and engagement. The installation of agreed standards and codes of ethics, and *so on*, would have doubtless been seen by Hanaghan acolytes as part of a broader resistance to/repression of the Real of the erotic.[57] Freud himself had much earlier repressed the Seduction Theory and all that went with it and Baudrillard joked that even at that point he had destroyed psychoanalysis.[58]

In his cultural polemics, Hanaghan was anticipating the future state of things. His passionate diagnosis of a deeply repressive reality describes fifties Ireland. Had he lived, Hanaghan would have been surprised and maybe delighted at how easily the theocratic moral edifice tottered then collapsed under the wave of social reform and scandal for the half century after his death.

Soon after the sixties, concerns for the public good were quietly forgotten and traditional notions in every sphere tumbled. *Anti-Oedipus* was a best seller.[59] Soon there was no public good to defend. The new public good was that there was no *public* good. We had been freed from any transcendental notion of the Aristotelian common good and this was the absolute good in itself! Now, there are as many goods (ego ideals) as there are people. That is now claimed as the real freedom. No one can tell us what *our* good is.

His rage against the institutions – the Holy Family, the Church, the schools, the universities, the army, and *so on*, might have seemed all well and good to a new generation growing up after the Cultural Revolution. His message was the clearest exposition of this type of writing-speaking which was popular around that time, made so by writers as different as Paul Tillich, Ivan Illich, Erich Fromm, and Harry Williams all of whom combined some variant of analytic thinking with its open permissiveness and attention, with the agape quality of early Pauline Christianity. Hanaghan, like Jesus in the temple (Matthew 21:12–13), spoke in messianic tones with the rage that belongs to authority with compassion.

The story was told of how he once gave a talk in a school, to the teachers and parents, on masturbation! Who was this Jonty of Monkstown talking about sex and the castration threat and the terror it posed for little boys? By what authority? And yet there were the few who listened and understood, believing they were hearing the most unusual understanding and compassion.

In the consulting room, it was generally observed that his psychoanalytic practice and that of his colleagues was a model of patient listening and understanding. They charged variable fees (as low as 1d per session!) so that no one was turned away.

Hanaghan's attacks on *all* institutions would come to be named, in time. as Cultural Marxism. Hanaghan was well ahead of the posse. He had already, 'marched through the institutions'.[60] However, Hanaghan was beyond politics and was without the sophistication of Marcuse,[61] for instance, who had already noted *de*-sublimation in the name of an illusory "freedom" under capitalism. He called it "*repressive* desublimation".[62] Materialist conformity *demands* that you *should* 'give into temptation';[63] you have no choice!

Hanaghan seemed to think that freedom from the castrating, fear-inducing superego would lead via faith to emergence of the Holy Spirit. Clearly, one does not readily follow from the other in a *post*-Christian world. The adolescent who throws off the repressive authority of the parents may not find God or freedom, after a period "in the wilderness". Against Hanaghan, the wilderness may just expand; the wilderness may just beckon; the wilderness may seem to be all there is – with no realisation of the Platonic Ideal of the Good beyond being.

Perhaps Hanaghan should have been careful what he had wished and preached for. The throwing off of the old patriarchal superego can lead to far worse – the archaic persecutory superego predicted later by Freud and Klein.[64] Also, there is no simple route to the beloved ego ideal – a vision of truth and justice to replace the ancient superego. Insofar as the ego ideal could possibly be realised in some form, it requires at the very least faith, great educators, and maybe many gifts besides.[65] Also, what is there to stop the ego ideal of the "still small voice" from morphing into some terrifying opposite, demanding an endless upping of your game to an extreme of perfection and self-denial as in the anorexic, or the extreme drive of the obsessive?

The retreat of the spirit

However, there was at least one occasion where Hanaghan came close to defending the superego, like Freud, who at one point refers to the superego as a 'precious cultural asset',[66] reducing the civilisational requirement for *external* coercion. Speaking of European man's 'inner retreat' in times of conflict, Hanaghan blames the State, 'for the purposes of total war, siding with the repressed impulses against the superego'. He continues, 'the State's desertion of the internalised superego whose projection it is, and its reinforcement of the inner repressed impulses, altered the character of many men and women'. Hanaghan recounts meeting with battle-hardened soldiers with devastating psychological changes. He continues, 'The State-supported repressed impulses were able to break-through the ego's repression barriers, entering consciousness as primitive wish-phantasies pressing towards action'.[67] This inner primitive breakthrough against ego and superego had three consequences identified by Hanaghan: 1) perverse acting out, 2) renewed attempts at repression leading to psychoneurosis and shell shock, and 3) rebellious conscientious objectors.

The devastation of the two world wars on European soil altered the 'mental stasis balance' of European men: 'Through a magnitude-increase in the repressed impulses, many men and women would be compelled into an inner retreat'.[68] Thus by re-energising id violence, the spirit is pushed further into the background.

Hanaghan has a triptych of his own: beyond Freud's id, ego, superego, Hanaghan posits biology, psyche, spirit – the highest of these being spirit. It is only in the realm of spirit that the human being is free. But when the spirit is in deep retreat, or is negated or disbelieved, human beings are really animals – the spirit becomes nothing more than a wish-fulfilling illusion.

Even Hanaghan did not anticipate the full retreat of the spirit under capitalism *and* socialism.[69] Hanaghan was a Teilhardian, believing in the telos of evolution and the eventual triumph of the spirit. However, he *also* anticipated things going into reverse gear with his concept of *d*evolution (unlike de Chardin), the death drive which he took from Freud without question. This gave Hanaghan his defiant prophetic edge and his outrage. It gave him authority. Nevertheless, even Hanaghan seems naively hopeful in his simple trust in the Holy Spirit and the 'still small voice' and with 'Jesus as the pinnacle of evolution'.[70] Hanaghan underestimated the collapse of Christian faith, and widespread anti-Christian hatred, that would be created by the combined effort of atheistic enlightenment thinking, Cultural Marxism, and Islamism in the new century.[71]

His message was always one of hope for all those who were suffering, but he was keenly aware of the pincer movement of hatreds, coming from the id on the one hand and the superego on the other. Thus, psychoanalysis was ultimately a question, as it used to be, of "facing one's demons". *You* are responsible for your demons.

However, with the shift towards seeing the sufferer as a victim and the abandonment of the aforementioned original sin, the demons are now firmly located in the Other *qua* Capitalist institutions and the like.[72] This is *not* a return to Freud, but a return to Rousseau. There are of course *real* victims. Nevertheless, the analytic process should bring about an increase in response-*ability* – the capacity to be open to the world of difference and the free flow of life itself, as well as the needs of the other closest to us.[73] The process of what we might now term deconstruction brought on by free association should loosen the knots of neurosis to facilitate responsibility.

Thus, Hanaghan was Old Testament *and* New Testament. Actively attentive to the suffering of the patient, as this term "patient" (never client) itself implies. But also clear about the masochistic or hysterical elaboration of symptoms which is part of every mental illness – our universal tendency to libidinise suffering for secondary gain, or in some cases the negative therapeutic reaction.

Clearly Hanaghan was an "object-relations" theorist before Fairbairn *et al.* became well known. For Hanaghan, 'To live alone is utterly alien to the self as spirit'.[74] His God was above all a *personal* God, a loving father who seeks us out. Hanaghan evoked the desolation of the cities, anonymous and lonely, and today half of all Americans live alone.[75] For Hanaghan nevertheless, there is a continuum from the love called forth by the child (his self-preservation instinct) to the mother, to the parents, the family, and the wider community, and finally to God. This is the child's "spiritual pilgrimage". Torn always between vision and phantasy, '*His most ardent desire is the desire to be loved. It is also his utmost need*'.[76] This assertion chimes with Freud's notion that psychoanalysis is a cure through love, although Freud stopped short of God's providential love as our final destination. And Lacan had insisted that we give up the desire of the Other and take on subjective-destitution. The desired approval or love of the Other is a universal neurotic trap.[77] Hanaghan would agree where the "other" is another human (small "o"), but when the other is the Other *qua* unknowable God it is quite the reverse: to believe in God's providence is *freedom* from neurotic suffering and an opening to *real* suffering.

Hanaghan invited an *experiment in living* via radical self-surrender, akin to subjective-destitution, which requires, 'a stripping of all dishonesties, of all leanings on external persons or things'.[78] And arguably, Hanaghan rushes all too quickly through the valley of the shadow of death, as it were, to the love allegedly on the other side. While we are told that God is closer to us than we are to ourselves (see Matthew 10:30), a lifetime of training and especially faith in this experiment, in the Pascalian wager in living, is required for this to become a saving possibility. And in a world of the wholesale "retreat of the spirit" – maybe Hanaghan's key insight – we prefer life-hating, hating our neighbour as ourselves, retrenchment, and *so on*.

Freud was clear that our *first* relation to the world is one of hate. To reprise Winnicott, hate is where we start from.[79] 'Hate, as a relation to objects, is older than love. It derives from the narcissistic ego's primordial repudiation of the external world with its outpouring of stimuli'.[80] Omnipotent hatred is our first response to life – absolute rejection of the world with all its otherness and difference. This is why analysts like Winnicott and Kohut have emphasised the mediating role of the mother and father in protecting the infant (via primary illusion) from the total shock of the external world.

Hatred maybe our first response to life, but also it might be our ongoing response unless we take seriously the forthgiveness advocated by Hanaghan. Melanie Klein would be in agreement in her (theological) analysis of envy.[81] And as C.S. Lewis says: 'Look for yourself, and you will find in the long run only hatred, loneliness, despair, rage, ruin, and decay. But look for Christ and you will find Him, and with Him everything else thrown in'.[82]

Freud indeed made clear that the so-called cure through love is accompanied by an ever-present adamant refusal, which he termed resistance: 'resistance accompanies the treatment at every step of the way, every single association, every act'.[83] And the journalist Janet Malcolm, surveying and writing sympathetically about American psychoanalysis, made resistance, let us repeat hatred of life, seem something of an absolute.[84]

Hanaghan underestimated the fundamentally *divided* nature of human subjectivity; original sin remains original, part of our DNA. Once we have discovered the unconscious, there is no going back. All human representation is false; all is a mask-like semblance. This is what is toxic about psychoanalysis, leading to the inevitability of the death drive.[85]

Thus, Hanaghan's ideal of the "lover of humanity", or in more mundane terms, the "fully analysed person" (a term that he did not use), or "the healer" should strictly be considered a myth, implicit in much of what Hanaghan and his followers proclaimed. The fallen nature of man is structural, not something that can be "healed". On the contrary, analysis exposes precisely this fallen condition, leading optimally to the "depressive position".

In his lengthy introduction to the 1992 edition of *Society, Evolution and Revelation*, Micheal O'Regan rightly cautions against "lofty idealism" and Hanaghan's "saying too much at one time". O'Regan's introduction offers a valuable comparison[86] for Hanaghan scholars seeking to link his writing with a wider circle of broadly existential psychotherapeutic writers, such as Fromm, Buber (Hasidism), May, Binswanger, Caruso, Frankl, Yalom, Bollas, and others, including first and foremost Meister Eckhart.[87]

There is however an urgency in Hanaghan's writing and speaking which sweeps all before it in a somewhat manic way. Hanaghan was promoted to guru-like status by some followers via their positive transference to him. The failure to properly analyse and loosen this transference became finally an incestuous failure for the Monkstown Group.

Inevitably, a new more conventionally trained younger generation of practitioners, who cared little for and knew nothing of Hanaghan and his religious teachings, took over in the nineties and reinvented psychoanalysis in Ireland along international and socially progressive lines, eschewing all that had gone before. And Hanaghan and the Monkstown Group became like that tree in the distant forest that falls (in every sense) and there is no one to bear witness to the "Event".[88]

Did it happen at all? Hanaghan! Who's he?

★★★

Finally, what Hanaghan was really clear about is that in relationships close up, spirit to spirit, infantile longings and hatreds are repeatedly re-enacted against the other. Each "other" is misunderstood in terms of the past. Each refuses to acknowledge the other *qua* other, by insisting that their demand is justified *in the present*. And there is in addition some secret pleasure in this demanding re-enactment of the past. Sadism and masochism are involved, i.e. perverse elements, which can be repeated over and over as part of the repetition compulsion. Lacan agrees: 'I have always reminded you that we must begin with the fact that transference, in the final analysis, is repetition compulsion'.[89]

Hanaghan clarifies these mechanisms and interpreted them in a way that would be rare today, as analysts eschew mastery in all forms. Each analysis comes upon the painful disappointments of failed love – *why wasn't I loved enough*? This has to be confronted, interpreted, worked through in the re-enacted endless disappointments of the transference.

The gulf of failure remains always. Maybe after analysis there are better solutions to the felt lack of love. Lacan reprises this gulf as lack on *both* sides: 'love is giving what you do not have to someone who doesn't want it'.[90]

C.S. Lewis too is circumspect:

> To love at all is to be vulnerable. Love anything and your heart will be wrung and possibly broken. If you want to make sure of keeping it intact you must give it to no one, not even an animal. Wrap it carefully round with hobbies and little luxuries; avoid all entanglements. Lock it up safe in the casket or coffin of your selfishness. But in that casket, safe, dark, motionless, airless, it will change. It will not be broken; it will become unbreakable, impenetrable, irredeemable. To love is to be vulnerable.[91]

Lewis and Lacan from different orientations regard love, beyond idealisation, as fragile, almost unlikely, and certainly ambivalent. And to cap it all the "loved" person may seem not to want love from you at all. For Hanaghan however, such hesitations are mere defences against the primordial sexual drive to unity, as recounted in *The Symposium*. Failure in this regard might be due to our hatred of life in its fullness, part of our being too "civilised", too educated, tamed, alienated, afraid of life flowing full, and *so on*.

Skelton appraises[92] Hanaghan's work, placing him in the context of other analysts who have attempted to embed psychoanalysis within religion or philosophy – a tendency Freud strongly resisted. Starting with Jung, who gave psychoanalysis a Pantheistic dimension, there was Binswanger and Medard Boss who developed existential-phenomenological analysis, also Igor Caruso and later R.D. Laing. But Hanaghan was the most avowedly Christian of them all, possibly closest to the Quaker tradition.

★★★

John Malkovich mentions a film director in Kazakhstan who tells him that after the fall of Communism he realised that they had all being living as orphans, they had all been in a giant orphanage. They had no father.

Notes

1 This is a personal account.
2 Douglas Bryan was the first secretary of the British Psycho-Analytic Society and translator of Karl Abraham.
3 The title of one of his books. Hanaghan, J. 1966.
4 Neville Symington, a member of the Middle Group of British Psychoanalysts, on the publication of *Cultural Collapse* (Weatherill, R. 1994) commented wryly on how psychoanalysis in Ireland always had a religious twist (personal communication).

5 Hanaghan J. 1960.
6 These quotes are taken from a leaflet about psychoanalysis in Ireland, assembled by Hartmann, M. 1985.
7 Hanaghan, J. 1979, p. 59.
8 Freud, S. 1914, p. 85.
9 Ibid., p. 85, n3.
10 See Weatherill, R. (ed) 1999, p. 219.
11 Freud, S. 1923, p. 26.
12 Freud, S. 1917a, p. 139.
13 Freud, S. 1917b, p. 419.
14 Ibid., p. 415.
15 Freud, S. 1917a, p. 139.
16 Freud, S. 1917c, p. 249.
17 Hanaghan, J. 1966, pp. 76–77.
18 Freud, S. 1923, p. 53.
19 Freud, S. 1905, p. 182.
20 Freud, S. 1910, p. 214.
21 Hanaghan, J. 1957, p. 21.
22 This theme recalls Charles Melman in Chapter 3 of this volume.
23 Hanaghan, J. 1957, pp. 20–21.
24 Ibid., p. 35.
25 Cameron, R. (ed) 1970, p. 34.
26 Hanaghan, J. 1957, p. 183.
27 Ibid., p. 60.
28 Freud, S. 1920; Weatherill, R. 1998; Weatherill, R. (ed) 1999.
29 Rank, O. 1909.
30 Hanaghan, J. 1966, chapter 7, p. 80ff.
31 Ibid., p. 85.
32 Hanaghan, J. 1957, p. 168. Here, echoing the theme of this book and the Lacanian notion of "lack" – 'your own overwhelming in loneliness'.
33 Ibid., p. 167.
34 Cameron, R. (ed)1970, p. 7.
35 Ibid., p. 33.
36 Hanaghan, J. 1957, p. 161.
37 Ibid., p. 160.
38 Ibid., p. 62.
39 Ibid., p. 69.
40 Ibid., p. 86.
41 Ibid., p. 73.
42 Ibid., p. 82.
43 Ibid., p. 82.
44 The title of the first chapter of Hanaghan, J. 1973, pp. 13–21.
45 Ibid., p. 113.
46 Ibid., p. 13.
47 Ibid., p. 33.
48 Ibid., p. 41.
49 Ibid., p. 47.
50 Ibid., p. 72.
51 Ibid., pp. 89–90.
52 Hanaghan, J. 1979, p. 88. Hanaghan was a conscientious objector and a pacifist. He claimed he had seen war at first hand through the terrible regression it causes to man's spirit. The ego's sublimations and achievements are forced to regress to primitive violence. In war, the old men *qua* fathers send the young men *qua* sons to fight and be killed

while the old men themselves survive. For Hanaghan this was the out-working of the old enmity between father and son from the Oedipus complex.

53 Ibid., p. 83.
54 Ibid., p. 77.
55 In some respects, Jordan Peterson comes to mind.
56 The group became rather like those families that are content within themselves, saying, 'Why would we need outside friends?'
57 Some Lacanians took this view also, refusing insurance and state registration.
58 For a development of this theme see, for instance, "The Seduction of Therapy" in Weatherill, R. 2011, pp. 75–92.
59 Deleuze, G. and Guattari, F. 1972.
60 Slogan coined by Marxist activist Rudi Dutschke around 1967, who was inspired by the work of Italian communist Antonio Gramsci.
61 Marcuse corresponded with Dutschke in 1971, approving his revolutionary approach to culture, the advance guard of today's social justice warriors.
62 Marcuse, H. 1964.
63 A slogan on supermarket trolleys at the time.
64 See Weatherill, R. 1994, p. 140ff.
65 Here mention must be made of Jordan Peterson whose YouTube presentations have attracted many followers because he speaks of responsibility, akin to Hanaghan's notion of the ego ideal.
66 Freud, S. 1927, p. 11.
67 Hanaghan, J. 1957, p. 72.
68 Ibid., p. 73.
69 It would take someone of the stature of Malcolm Muggeridge to record the spiritual sterility of *both* world systems which he realised as early as 1919 after a trip to Moscow to behold the new utopia. See Muggeridge, M. 1934.
70 Introduction to Hanaghan, J. 1957.
71 See for instance Weatherill, R. 2017, chapter 9 and Conclusion. The BBC, no less, refers to Christian persecution 'at near genocide levels'. www.bbc.com/news/uk-48146305.
72 For Lacan, the other is also the unconscious.
73 Maybe Hanaghan would have cited Levinas who takes our debt to the other to a sacrificial extreme.
74 Hanaghan, J. 1957, p. 163.
75 https://ourworldindata.org/living-alone.
76 Ibid., p213. A need unlike the Lacanian need he disavows vehemently.
77 Although in the later Lacan this extreme asceticism was modified by the sinthome, the saintly man – maybe a version of the Hanaghanian ego ideal.
78 Hanaghan, J. 1957, p. 168.
79 The title referred to: Winnicott, D. 1986.
80 Freud, S. 1915, p. 139.
81 Klein, M. 1957, pp. 176–235.
82 Lewis, C.S. 1952, p. 227.
83 Freud, S. 1912, p. 103.
84 Malcolm, J. 1977.
85 Hanaghan lacked a concept of the Real. The dereliction he describes with such force is 'the desert of the Real', a phrase that has entered the postmodern lexicon via a quote delivered by the character Morpheus in the 1999 film *The Matrix*.
86 O'Regan, M. 1992. Introduction to Hanaghan, J. 1957, pp. xi–xxxix.
87 Micheal O'Regan was the director of Eckhart House, Institute of Psychosynthesis and Transpersonal Theory until his death in 1997.

88 "Event" in the Badiouian sense, Badiou, A. 1988. The Event being sustained only by the faith of the followers so long as they remain faithful.
89 Lacan, J. 1960–1961, p. 172.
90 Lacan, J. 1960–1961, p. 147.
91 Lewis, C.S. 1981, p. 121.
92 Skelton, R. 1994.

References

Badiou, A. 1988. *Being and Event*. Trans. Feltham, O. London and New York: Continuum, 2005.

Cameron, R. (Ed.) 1970. *The Wisdom of Jonty*. Dublin: The Runa Press, 34.

Deleuze, G., Guattari, F., 1972. *Anti-Oedipus. Capitalism and Schizophrenia*. Trans. Hurley, R., Seem, M., Lane, H. London and New York: Continuum, 2004.

Freud, S. 1905. "Three Essays on Sexuality". SE 7, 125–249.

Freud, S. 1910. "The Psycho-analytic View of the Psychogenic Disturbance of Vision". SE 11, 209–218.

Freud, S. 1912. *The Dynamics of Transference*. SE. 12, 97–108.

Freud, S. 1914. "On narcissism. An introduction". SE14, 67–102.

Freud, S. 1915. "Instincts and their Vicissitudes". SE 14, 117–140.

Freud, S. 1917a. "A Difficulty in the Path of Psycho-analysis". SE 17, 135–144.

Freud, S. 1917b. *Lecture XXVI: "The Libido Theory and Narcissism."* SE 16, 412–430.

Freud, S. 1917c. "Mourning and Melancholia." SE. 14, 237–260.

Freud, S. 1920. *Beyond the Pleasure Principle*, SE 18, 3–64.

Freud, S. 1923. *The Ego and the Id*. S.E. 19, 3–66.

Freud, S. 1927. *The Future of an Illusion*. SE 21, 3–58.

Hanaghan, J. 1957. *Society, Evolution and Revelation. An Original Insight into Man's Place in Creation*. Dublin: The Runa Press.

Hanaghan J. 1960. *The Sayings of Jonathan Hanaghan*. Dublin: The Runa Press.

Hanaghan, J. 1966. *Freud and Jesus*. Dublin: The Runa Press.

Hanaghan, J 1973. *The Courage to be Married*. Cork and Dublin: The Mercier Press.

Hanaghan, J. 1979. *The Beast Factor*. Ireland, Enniskerry: Tansy Books, The Egotist Press, 59.

Hartmann, M. 1985. *Jonathan Hanaghan 1886–1967*. Dublin: The Runa Press.

Klein, M. 1957. "Envy and Gratitude". In *Envy and Gratitude & Other Works 1946–1953*. New York: Delta 1975, 176–235.

Lacan, J. 1957–1958. *Seminar IV, The Formations of the Unconscious*. Trans. Gallagher, C. Dublin: St. Vincent's University Hospital.

Lacan, J. 1960–1961. *Seminar 8. The Transference*. Ed J-A. Miller, Paris: Seuil 1991.

Lewis, C.S. 1952. *Mere Christianity*. London: C.S. Lewis Signature Classics Edition, 2012.

Lewis, C.S. 1981. *The Four Loves: Affection, Friendship, Eros and Charity*. London: Fontana.

Malcolm, J. 1977. *Psychoanalysis: The Impossible Profession*. New York: Jason Aronson.

Marcuse, H. 1964. *One-Dimensional Man. Studies in the Ideology of Advanced Industrial Society*. London and New York: Routledge Classics, 2002.

Muggerage, M 1934. *Winter in Moscow*. London: Eerdmans, 1987.

O'Regan, M. 1992. "Introduction to Hanaghan". In *Society, Evolution and Revelation*. Dublin: The Runa Press, pxi–xli.

Rank, O. 1909. *The Myth of the Birth of the Hero: A Psychological Exploration of Myth*. Trans. Richter, G., Lieberman, R.. Baltimore and London: The John Hopkins University Press, 2004.

Skelton, R. 1994. "Jonathan Hanaghan. The Founder of Psychoanalysis in Ireland". *The Journal of the Irish Forum for Psychoanalytic Psychotherapy* 4, no. 1, 60–78.

Weatherill, R. 1994. *Cultural Collapse*. London: Free Association Books, 1994.

Weatherill, R. 1998. *The Sovereignty of Death*. London: The Rebus Press.

Weatherill R. (Ed). 1999. *The Death Drive. New Life for a Dead Subject*. London: Rebus Press.

Weatherill, R. 2011. *Forgetting Freud. Is Psychoanalysis in Retreat*. California: Academic Press.

Weatherill, R. 2017. *The Anti-Oedipus Complex. Lacan, Critical Theory and Postmodernism*. London and New York: Routledge.

Winnicott, D. 1986. *Home Is Where We Start from: Essays by a Psychoanalyst*. London: Penguin Books, 1990.

6   Hanaghan Returns

This chapter imagines Hanaghan's return more than half a century after his death. He is continuing his psychoanalytic work in secret. A young student of psychoanalysis has found his writings inspiring and meets up with him to question him further. In his warm response to her, he acknowledges how much the world has changed and modernised towards the freedom that he himself espoused back then. But he points also to the dark side and the "inflection point", the rise of new totalitarianisms and his intense concern for the future with the outpourings of hate and *ressentiment*. He admits his past error in over-estimating youthful idealism.

Hanaghan is back in Monkstown and it is the 2020s. A young investigative journalist is lucky to catch an interview with him as he has been incognito since his return.[1] It is more than half a century since his death. The young journalist has studied psychoanalysis but has only heard the name of Hanaghan and "The Monkstown Group" quite recently. But in preparation for the interview, she has been trying to get up to speed. Below, is her account of their unusual meeting.

I meet him in a modest apartment in town and we are both masked-up as it is only a little over three years since the pandemic and people are still restricted in some situations. He suggested dispensing with the masks, and I agree.

The room in which we meet is big and airy. The first thing I am struck by is his presence. I'd heard of this thing called an aura, but I have never experienced it first-hand. With his longish white hair, he struck an imposing figure, immediately putting me at ease, before we had spoken. I had my list of questions carefully prepared, but I was put off following them by what I can only say was his overwhelming simplicity and peacefulness. It was the simplicity that I believed came from wisdom and experience combined. I am amazed to see myself writing this – wisdom and experience – these are not words I would normally use. Even authority, yes, that's the right word. Wow! Was that transference already, I wondered. Was he my father?

I leave aside my questions to live in the moment and go with the flow. Apparently, he has been seeing some people in secret for "healing" as he

DOI: 10.4324/9781003225010-8

prefers to call analysis. Some people have heard he is back. He asked me briefly about myself and my circumstances. I feel at ease to say as much or as little as I want. There was no need to put on the usual act. I talked spontaneously, with a delightful freedom I should say, about how I loved my father (now deceased) because he loved me. Already, I could feel my eyes welling up. But he let me change the subject.

So, almost reluctantly, I found myself asking what he thought of the world, the West now, and how it had changed in the last half century? I could immediately see his face darken and his body visibly shrink. But then he brightened and looked up at me:

> You know, what struck me first was the newness of everything! The bright sharpness of the modern buildings, the clarity of the yellow road markings, more traffic lights and *so on*. Such huge new cars with women driving! And colour, all the new colours. Instead of just dingy greens and blacks that I remember; colour everywhere. So, what I notice is a great flowering of new material goods and the range of exotic foods on offer, topped by the magical functioning of the internet and the mobile phone. The mobile phone must be a miracle. And the people, if one can generalise, so effervescent, so lively, so confident, so free. It was a wonderful surprise. It could not have been predicted!

And then his face darkened again, and he put his head in his hands …

> But all this material wealth and excitement covers dark forces, which are by definition hidden from view, as Freud said of the death drive. The death drive is mute. And these dark forces are increasing as material wealth is increasing alongside a kind of hyperactive happiness. And we seem to have lost the ability to properly locate or detect the dark forces and this is frightening. When I was here before, we still had some inkling, but now, none. And the reason we have lost this is because we have rejected Christianity – the science of theology – which sets this out clearly.
>
> We must recall that the psyche has a *theological* structure – 'a concave without a convex'.[2] I wanted to emphasis this in my writing;[3] that the Other *qua* God is closer to us than we are to ourselves. But we have rejected any of this thought and revelation. We have rejected the soul as intermediary between us as creatures and God, if I may put it like that.
>
> We wanted to go it alone, and that was all well and good, and I used to speak about "the holy atheistic" church to honour my sincere atheistic friends. We abandoned the transcendent, partly because of course some terrible things were done in its name in Ireland. I opposed the established Church, the Holy Family and all the rest of it back then.

It sounds like you're regretting that now, I asked. Surely nothing but good has come from our rejection of Catholic dominance, a new respect for minorities, and *so on*.

Oh yes. All that is good. No doubt about it. The Church was corrupt in its power structure. But at the same time we set *ourselves* up as gods. There was no God and we set *ourselves* up as gods. That was some risk, wasn't it?

Sounds like courage to me. Where is the problem? Didn't you yourself advocate the courage to face-down the horror of the superego that makes fearful conformists of us all? I thought that was one of your main challenges, to regain our lost freedom against terror?

Yes! Yes! A thousand times Yes! But I didn't stop there. The castrating superego has to be replaced by the light of vision, what I called the ego ideal, lest we fall into a new kind of slavery. You can end up with nothing, believing that you are free.

Let me explain more carefully. What I had noticed back then was that we lived in a kind of terrified normality typical of an outwardly imposed Catholic morality which, for instance, barred so-called "fallen" women from life in the community. The Holy Church and the Holy Family were at one on this. Young girls went in terror of bringing dishonour on the family. (Today, we still see this in Islam with honour killings and *so on*.) Destroy triumphantly this terrifying norm, give people the courage to rise up against it, which was actually happening around the world at the time of my death, and you can end up with chaos, not freedom.

Why so? Why chaos?

Let me put it like this. Power abhors a vacuum. Destroy the Church's authority and a new (worse) authority will take its place. There are so many examples to choose from. Robespierre and the Reign of Terror, Stalinism, Mao, and *so on* – so many springs followed by horrendous winters. We could call it the iron-law of the superego: defeat it in one place and it reappears in a worse form. Removal of the superego does not equal freedom.

Okay, that was then, but now we really are free! That hasn't happened with us. I was getting into my stride!

Has it not? If I was giving one of my Saturday night groups in Monkstown today, I'd be talking about the out-of-control gangs of youths in Dublin's north inner city terrifying young immigrant delivery drivers.[4] I'd be talking about an epidemic of drug addiction which is out of control.[5] More people dying each year in America from drug overdoses than died during the whole of the terrible Vietnam War.[6] I'd be talking about feral children at terrible risk in our cities – drugs, sexual exploitation, county lines, petty crime, anti-social behaviour, and *so on*. This is not down to the harsh superego, it is due to the NO superego, what even one of your mentors at college called the manifestation of "Id-Evil".[7]

No, but wait. That is all down to poverty and underprivilege.

Partly true, no doubt. Families struggling from pay cheque to pay cheque. That's true. But, more importantly, it's down to *spiritual* poverty – a much greater poverty underlying all forms of poverty. I used to talk about the European ego being like a medieval fortress. I think this is still true today and the fortress has become the gated community where the very rich live in their anal-retentive way, hoarding up their possessions. The elites are protected, with minders and security, and they communicate through PR people. They link globally not locally. Christopher Lasch pointed that out some time ago.[8] The elites have abandoned the masses to the gig economy.

Okay. Maybe you have a point. But you're losing me, I still think *we are free*. After all, this is the 21st century.

Yes. I know what you mean. But I think there are good grounds for think-ing this freedom is an illusion. In the fifties and sixties, when I was talking on the Saturday nights, people knew all too well that they weren't free. Curiously, that gave them a small margin of real freedom. For instance, in those days you could say you were going to Mass and, in reality, bunk off to play with your friends. This was the small freedom of Modernity. Now, during the Postmodern when, by definition, all of those old pro-hibitions have been abolished or resolved. We have developed rational ethical norms, there is no longer freedom, because now you should *want to do the right thing*. Before, as a child you were forbidden to smoke for example, but you could rebel with a quick smoke and hide your cigs. Now, you should not even want to smoke because it is known to be bad for your health. If you smoke now, you are not really asserting freedom from a ridiculous prohibition, you're just plain stupid. Likewise, a mobile phone gives me unlimited freedom, but in reality, one cannot live today without one.

And think of children in the twenty-first century! In the previous century, Irish short-story writer, Mary Lavin, said that as a child she could roam all day in Dublin! She had no fear for her safety in the capital city. That was freedom. Now, do I need to spell it out? Children have so many unanswerable worries. I have white skin, am I a bad person? Have we destroyed the planet? And, how can parents reassure a child when they are confused themselves and want to do the right thing?

Yeah! But this confusion as you call it is a good thing. The family has to figure these things out for themselves. Nothing is imposed. This is what freedom means. It means anxiety. (God! He's been away too long. This is hitting him hard – all these changes.)

> Did you ever think that *you* are very probably part of the elite! No joking. As a progressive and having been to university, and working in journalism, studying psychoanalysis, and *so on*, you almost certainly *feel* part of the elite even though you might be still quite poor in economic terms! Your (politicised) education separates you from the vast mass of humanity, for whom you often say and believe you care deeply. That mass of humanity, the rubes, are in effect despised by the elites. This is not admitted openly of course. This is the contemporary class divide. And you with your education passport (at third level) can leave the masses behind.

Is that a criticism? I personally feel in solidarity with the mass of humanity, *The Wretched of the Earth!*[9]

> No. Not necessarily. And, of course, I do not know how you think. But you'd have to wonder how youthful radicalism can join forces with the tech oligarchs, the main media organisations, and large corporations who all claim to be for social justice! How can this be youthful or radical? And where is the freedom when there is only one correct way to think! As the joke goes: a person claims he no longer can form opinions of his own, as he always waits to see what major corporate brands have to say on any given issue before he decides what he believes.[10]
>
> These days, censorship of certain political viewpoints can be automated via "machine learning". Twitter's Pranay Singh claims machine learning algorithms can select as many as, 'five thousand keywords to describe a redneck' and, he shamelessly continues, 'the majority are for Republicans'.[11] They seem to be totally unaware of how intolerant *they* are. It's the old question of the mote in the eye (Matthew 7:3). They even joked (Ha! Ha!) that the rednecks and their children should be put in re-education camps.[12]

Okay, that was a joke and the guy, Michael Beller, was sacked immediately. But, is the point you are making that we think we are free but we are still intolerant, is that it? There are swathes of people (we believe) who do not think and speak in the right way. As you claimed earlier, the superego is worse now than it was before. That's very counter-intuitive isn't it.

> True, as old father Karamazov said, 'If God is dead then everything is permitted', but Lacan rejoins, 'God is dead means *nothing is permitted anymore*'.[13]

Yeah. I see. I think? NOTHING is permitted! We are not at that point?
I feel free. I really do, I feel free. But you are insisting that that is an illusion born of hyper-materialism. Maybe a necessary illusion.

Yes, it is the traditionalists that are not allowed to exist. These are red-necks, the bigots, the 5,000 names.

And, personally, I wanted psychoanalysis for the masses, for the 5,000 names. I didn't want it to be only for the wealthy, the intelligent, the sophisticated, as it was at that time in the major centres despite the aspiration for free clinics.[14] Now that has changed and there is much more availability. I know that our little group was criticised at the time for being an Anglo-American outfit, we were colonial elitists, but we never turned anyone away in Monkstown.

And I wanted the language of psychoanalysis to be simple without being simplified. I disliked the use of Latin in the Strachey translation of Freud, rightly criticised by Bettelheim as concealing Freud's profound humanism.[15] And Freud's aim in his writing was to be absolutely clear; it was some of his French followers who have gone in for deconstruction. And Lacan's favourite signifier is "impossibility". So while patients are no longer drawn exclusively from the wealthy, the language of psychoanalysis has gone to those esoteric heights of *intellectual* wealth, at least in one of its incarnations, requiring years of dedicated study to what real end one wonders.

Well, I can confirm that!

In the old days, I believed in youthful idealism and I still do. I have seen it with my own eyes. Take the young analysts for instance. I have seen how they can sit with and listen openly to very unwell people who may have suffered multiple abuses. This is very moving to witness. It is at the heart of the psychoanalytic enterprise. It is life-giving and healing. And it is part of the training to remain 100 per cent patient. And these young analysts, mostly women it has to be said, are prepared to do that, day after day. Here is the new ego ideal fostered by the discipline of psychoanalytic trainings.

Yeah. Why do you think it is mostly women?

Well, maybe that is not strictly true. There are quite a few Lacanian men. They must like the castrating edginess of Lacan! But let's generalise, practitioners are mostly women in the caring professions. Women are closer, by virtue of fertility, to the beating heart of life, what Lacan called the *other jouissance*. Recall too that Lacan declared that 'the Woman ... is one of the names of God'.[16]

Psychoanalysis has inevitably drifted towards the feminine and the mother. There are problems with this which we might get to, not least the eclipse of the erotic and seduction in psychoanalysis, as Jean Laplanche has pointed out.[17] As Badiou and others have also noticed, the disappearance of the traditional figures of the feminine in modernity: fatal seduction, amorous gift, and the mystical sublime.[18] I used to be particularly interested in

these tropes. Now all that is regarded very cynically as mystical otherness, a kind of compensatory male imaginary. No more of what I wrote back then:
    'Beauty through woman has wounded man's soul'.[19]
    Maybe, these were just male phantasies to support the One. And now women are becoming the One – taking charge of the world. And, people say, now there will be no war with women in charge!

Yeah, it really seems like that. At last, women are being recognised. It feels so good!

    Yeah. Recognised in *one* register, but maybe lost to an all-important other dimension.
    But just as that has happened, I think something much more serious is afoot and it is around the signifier "trans". Identity politics is the warm-up gig. Here, I am coming back to the darkness that I mentioned earlier. When Lacan famously said, 'The Woman does not exist',[20] was he really anticipating the radical dissipation of a species, *qua* biological woman, for instance? Just as the woman comes into her own, she *qua* wom*x*n becomes non-binary, then finally non-existent. People now talk of birthing people, people who menstruate, and *so on*. Trans is the transition to the trans-human, the beyond-human, the creation of "mind files" – digital clones, with our consciousness (uploaded) on-line.

All this is, is a challenge to biological essentialism surely.

    Well, there is a passage in *Brave New World*: 'To say one was a mother – that was past a joke: it was an obscenity'.[21] And as for the father, 'The word for "father" was not so much obscene as … at one remove from the loathsomeness and moral obliquity of child-bearing – mere gross, a scatological; rather than pornographic impropriety, the comically smutty word'.[22] Remember, these beings have long since given up on viviparity.
    Well, when I was railing against the holy hypocritical Catholic family and demanding freedom, I never anticipated anything approaching 'Civilisation is sterilisation'.[23] And, 'Mother, monogamy, romance. High spurts the foun-tain; fierce and foamy the wild jet. The urge has but a single outlet. My love, my baby. No wonder those poor pre-moderns were mad and wicked and miserable'.[24] Does this not fit the view in the most radical circles today?
    I am ashamed to say that I never really anticipated the spiritual degra-dation that comes with trafficking, with sex slavery, international crime, and *so on*. And the worst thing is that people no longer demand an end to these things. We are caught in the headlamps of horror; we are stupefied into indifference …

Sorry to interrupt. Is this why you came back under cover? Did you come back to warn us about something? Did you feel it was unsafe to be seen in Dublin? I mean who would recognise you?

You're right! Who would recognise me? That is not important. Once you die you are forgotten. And that is the order of things. But when I start to talk, I start to make enemies. And remember American satirist H.L. Mencken: 'for every nugget of truth, some wretch lies dead on the scrapheap'.

Ah! But what about *The wind bloweth where it listeth, and thou hearest the sound thereof, but canst not tell whence it cometh, and whither it goeth: so is every one that is born of the Spirit* (John 3:8).

Absolutely yes. This, *The wind bloweth where it listeth*, was one of my favour-ite quotes in my Saturday night talks to the Monkstown Group. This is where we come back to analysis and the subject as primarily a *spiritual* sub-ject, who maybe has yet to find out that the she is a spiritual subject. What is ultimately the role of free association? Surely to free the spirit to partake of the Good beyond being. Desire is one thing, but we must go beyond desire to the spirit – to give one's life to the spirit, although no analyst can say or know where it comes from and where it is going.

But if you remain incognito how will anyone know about the spirit? Before you had the Group every Saturday night to publicise psychoanalysis: Freud and Jesus? Yes?

Well, each person I see will know. But like the wind, the spirit cannot be contained in words and words today are already part of the degradation – a fading simulation of the Real. The spirit is in the register of the Real and there is no knowing where it will go. Everything else by definition is *unreal*, or as Lacan insisted, lacks. The lack is the lack of the Real. If we go back to my favourites Augustine and Aquinas, the lack is the lack, or privation,[25] of the Good.

We do not see the Good. But the world is held together by the Good of ordinary people, which was remarked upon so well by Chesterton. When asked about poetry, he mentioned as an example the railway timetable as pure poetry![26] What he meant was that the fact the trains run on time was in effect the poetry of the goodness of ordinary people giving their lives for others. This is the Platonic Good beyond being and unseen within being. It is nobody's good, it is invisible, incognito, and *so on*. But many participate in the Good without making a big thing of it.

What is hyper-visible on the other hand, *forced* to appear, is evil. There was Baudrillard's famous work: *The Transpiration of Evil*.[27] What we notice in hyper-visibility is the lack. So many are getting caught up in the hyper-visible and becoming suicidal, particularly children, as I said earlier. They cannot bear the lack – any imperfection that they see in their image, and they become terribly anxious to correct it. They have not learnt the Lacanian lesson that all beings lack – they are *not* God.

We lack and we are wholly responsible for what we do with our lack. Do we act through vision or through phantasy? Do we follow desire or spirit, or can the two coincide?

Do we not need a notion, a hierarchical notion of right and wrong, for your vision/phantasy dichotomy to work, for people to be able to choose? And this agreement about what is right and wrong has long since gone. I think you have made that the central point to your vision.

I agree. And when I was talking earlier about the idealism of the young analysts and how impressive that was, how they were able to listen patiently and without judgement – all good. But they *cannot* judge. They are unable to judge. No! That is not quite true because sometimes they are *very* judgemental over certain things to do with the so-called new normal – climate change, racism, patriarchy, meat eating, smoking, and *so on* – the list is getting longer and longer.

But the Ten Commandments! Yes, they MUST be broken! That is the new commandment. The Jewish law is to be hated. This is the reason for the resurgence of anti-Semitism across the world and calls for the abolition of Israel, and all that flows from that in terms of anti-Western sentiment. This is the racism that *IS* allowed. And it is destructive and devolutional. Nothing good can come from it.

I link this official hatred on the Left, right down to the hatred of the body and of children being encouraged to hate and want to change the bodies that they are given at birth, with *ressentiment* and with the worrying decline in mental health. This will not bring a new dawn but a new darkness. The signs are everywhere. Here I would cite the Catholic writer Rémi Brague: 'Law is the deepest expression of our being. Like the laws of nature. What we are commanded to do is the highest level of our nature'.[28]

And always the *one* commandment remains, love *not* hatred, love your neighbour as yourself. *Thy will*, not my will.

Is this where your important notion of "forth-giveness" comes in? Of the libido going out to others, to the neighbour, not getting stuck in and against the self? This, as I understand it, is your key to mental health.

Yes! Do not focus on the lack in yourself (narcissism). It is there but do not overly notice it or worry about it. Go forth to others. The analyst can allow you to work through how you hold back in what Nietzsche called *ressentiment*,[29] or hatred of life, hatred of the other, and show the way to forth-flowingness. The latter belongs to the Real of life. Analysis exists to make this possible.

And let us not be in the least sentimental about love. Love means engagement with the other. Engagement, if necessary, in battle. I haven't changed. I still think love is an active engagement with the other, not merely a space to speak. You know the kind of thing where you are given your space to speak and that's it! Nothing more. There is no other. As if speaking in a space was all that mattered. *It means nothing unless it is heard and engaged with.* Even corporations allow you to speak! But very often do nothing. It is part of their "complaints procedure".

But can I ask with respect: are you yourself guilty of going against the Law? Wasn't that the whole basis of your teaching? Can I ask you to reflect on that now? Was that wrong?

> In part it was! The law of the land is always imperfect as it is based on hidden violence, enforced and legitimised by the State. But it protects the culture, the Good people, the institutions, the family, and *so on*. There is always an element of hypocrisy here in this law. It is required for public order. What I was attacking was raw power – the raw power of the super-ego, that was everywhere apparent in schools, in the Church, in families, and *so on*. You hear the legacy of that time still being reported upon today. There is a perverse, sadistic element that goes with raw power, the corruption of the Church.

Did you make a distinction between the law and the castrating superego?

> In retrospect, I did not make sufficient distinction. That was a grave error on my part. I saw a wall and I wanted to smash it. That was wrong.

Has that sort of thinking contributed to the darkness of the present times that you have referred to?

> Yes. Without doubt.
>
> That was the mistake of the *soixante-huitards*? It was forbidden to forbid.[30] They were reacting to stifling conformity of their childhoods in fifties France. But it led to violent extremism later with Baader–Meinhof, and *so on*. I was reacting to the stifling conformity of fifties Ireland. The terrible violence that followed here drew at least in part on older historical sources.
>
> I underestimated the degrees of displaced hate – displaced from early childhood demand. This was the driver and still is the driver, *now, without any walls*. This was a grave mistake then and now.

You never used the term "bourgeois". So, you didn't go further down this leftist route to revolution.

> No, that never interested me. I was more interested in the personal – what happened to individual people, rather than the slogan that became all the rage – 'The personal *is political*'. That was going down a reactive route and

I think Lacan was right when he told the rioting students that they were looking for a master.

I always really hated socialism as an ideology for the mass death that it created in Russia, China, Vietnam, and *so on*. And you know, unlike Nazism, the Communist crimes of mass death have never been worked through or accounted for in any way whatsoever. And some in your generation are getting nostalgic for socialism with more than a Green tinge. I have no doubt there are sincere socialists – good people, but it is the **violent ideology** that is wrong, wrong, and wrong again, TODAY. It's coming round again, and the younger generations know nothing about the horror of it, the immiseration of whole continents for decades. They know nothing, because the history is not studied.

Take, for instance, American journalist Anand Giridharadas who felt completely free to write this:

> *They're building a new country and you're not invited* … The darkness that you see now is a funeral for White Supremacy, a funeral for outdated, outmoded male power. It is the mourning of a time when certain Americans could claim to be the default American, not having to share. This year, there have been amazing shifts in mainstream white opinion, in way unthinkable 5 or 10 years ago. Thus, what we are witnessing in this darkness is backlash; it is not the engine of history. These people are not the future, they are the "barnacles on the future" that is going to happen with or without them. What we are trying to create has never been created before is the new kind of America, a democratic, multiracial superpower which looks like the [rest of] world. And we are actually getting there, and these people are terrified that they will actually have to share power. And day-by-day, hour-by-hour, we are getting there.[31]

'*With or without them*'. Be sure to note these words … With or without them.

I think I follow your argument. The media in cahoots with the Left are trying to divide us into black and white races …

Because NOW is an inflection point. The smooth plane of the curve changes sign from plus to minus. Today the sign changes *from personal to impersonal*; from surviving *human* to *trans-human*, from taken-for-granted kindness of ordinary people to the coming exceptional cruelty – you can be sure. Yes, black versus white.

All the signs are there. But we in the West have reached the state of super-indifference. To answer your earlier question, that is why I am back – super-indifference to the renewed possibility of mass cruelty.

But God, you're implying something even worse, it seems to me – old-fashioned Leftist violence combined with the totalitarian possibilities of the internet? The virus was the inflection point. Was it not Baudrillard indeed who suggested that the irony of the security state was that we have end up "internalising terror"? As with mad cow disease, you kill the whole herd as a precautionary measure. Or, you lockdown the whole economy initially for virus control, in preparation for severe Green policies that are already hollowing out the middle and lower classes, the one-time backbone of democracies.[32] You forbid people getting together, you keep them virtual. Baudrillard also refers to, 'the eclipsing of sovereignty [that] leaves unbridled power with the savagery that is no longer natural but technical'.[33]

> Yes. Sovereignty of nations, gone. The sovereignty of individuals, going or gone. It is fashionable to say that the self does not exist, that we are fully biochemical machines with only the illusion of self-control and that we should be controlled by other machines. This is such a dangerous notion because it is the elimination of *Homo sapiens* to make way for the trans-human. Add to that, pervasive "white ethno-masochism" among young white liberals in the West in the last few years. Destroy yourself before you are destroyed. Yes, it is part of the softening-up process towards extinction. Not natural but technical. Big tech controls all. All the elements are there to control the narrative. Above all control the narrative.

There is a pause. Neither of us speak.

I am trying to take in the enormity and the complexity of this.

So, let me see, you have come back because of the inflection point and its passing? We are already trans-human – we treat ourselves as machines – and we have given up the fight, the fight for our humanity, for the very short-term gain of material wealth (for some), convenience, security, and *so on*. The fight back is replaced by super-indifference and somnambulism.

You were wrong in some respect before when you were alive on earth, as you have admitted, you underestimated the reservoirs of hate. (Am I trying to reassure myself that he could be wrong again?) And one way or another you have been forgotten, perhaps twice forgotten. Remember how they treated you as if you had never existed, those younger analysts in Ireland who sought recognition from the IPA (International Psychoanalytic Association) in the eighties. They did not like the Christian thing. They claimed that analysis in Ireland began with them! So, you died, and they certainly buried you. That is the main reason why I felt a duty and a need to study you.

> All I can only say is that it does not matter in the least about me. It didn't matter then and it doesn't matter now. It the truth that matters, not *my* truth or falsehood. It never was *my* will be done. We all need to be freed from a million prejudices that prop up the ego with hate, resentment, and envy. Ultimately, that is what analysis should be about. *FREE* association. That was my work. That is my work. To allow the river to flow again and not be locked in hate! That was my message – *LET GO HATE*! Including self-hate. You could even say, it's a violent message!

Yes! Yes! I think that is a powerful message. People said that you were like an Old Testament prophet. Where are the prophets now when we need them. That is the Christian message allied to psychoanalysis. I get it! Where is the roar of the shofar? *If a shofar is sounded in a city, can the inhabitants fail to be terrified?* (Amos 3:6).[34]

Those younger analysts killed off their father. And in their smugness, they were not even aware of what they had done.

I am so grateful to you. I now have a direction. I now have a direction to my life. I just wanted to say that, although words are insufficient. I am so grateful. Thank you. Thank you so much.

★★★

She bows with her hands together. He clasps her hands briefly.

They part.

Notes

1 Hanaghan dies in 1967.
2 Levinas, E. 1981, p. 49.
3 Hanaghan, J. 1957.
4 www.irishtimes.com/news/social-affairs/taoiseach-warned-control-of-north-inner-city-dublin-on-verge-of-being-lost-1.4477389.
5 On an unstoppable rise since the 1970s: https://en.wikipedia.org/wiki/Illicit_drug_use_in_Ireland.
6 .www.cbsnews.com/news/opioids-drug-overdose-killed-more-americans-last-year-than-the-vietnam-war/.
7 Žižek, S. 2000, p. 8.
8 Lasch, C 1995.
9 Fanon, F. 1961.
10 https://babylonbee.com/news/man-waits-to-form-opinion-on-all-major-issues-until-corporate-brands-weigh-in.
11 https://.www.projectveritas.com/news/undercover-video-twitter-engineers-to-ban-a-way-of-talking-through-shadow-banning-algorithms-to-censor-opposing-political-opinions/.
12 https://kwwl.com/2021/01/13/pbs-lawyer-who-called-for-re-education-camps-for-republican-children-no-longer-with-network/.
13 Lacan, J. 1969–1970, p. 120.
14 Danto, A. 2005.
15 Bettelheim, B. 1984.
16 Lacan, J. 1975-1976, p. 14.
17 Laplanche, J. 1997.
18 Badiou, A. 2017, p. 95.
19 Hanaghan, J. 1931, p. 39.
20 Lacan, J. 1972–1973, p. 68.
21 Huxley, A. 1932, p. 126.
22 Ibid., pp. 124–125.
23 Ibid., p. 102.
24 Ibid., p. 43.

25 St Mary's College Oscott. "The Problem Of Evil In St Thomas Aquinas". 2017. http://oscott.net/problem-evil-st-thomas-aquinas/
26 Chesterton, G.K. 1908, p. 6.
27 Baudrillard, J. 1990.
28 Brague, R. 2014.
29 Nietzsche, F. 1967, p. 57.
30 Hargreaves, S. 2018.
31 www.msnbc.com/the-last-word/watch/the-january-6-insurrection-was-a-last-gasp-for-white-supremacy-99557445706.
32 Kotkin, J. 2021.
33 Baudrillard, J 2004, p. 120.
34 The simple meaning of this verse is that a shofar was sounded when enemies were converging on a city, which was terrifying. Alternatively, this refers to sounding the shofar in the month of Elul. The sound of the shofar reaches the core of every Jew – even those who seem distant and cold to Judaism are affected by the shofar. www.chabad.org/parshah/article_cdo/aid/3547999/jewish/On-the-Haftarah-The-Lions-Roar.htm.

References

Badiou, A. 2017. *The True Life*. Trans. Spitzer, S. Cambridge UK and Malden: The Polity Press.

Baudrillard, J. 1990. *The Transparency of Evil*. Paris: Éditions Galilée. Trans. J. Benedict. London: Verso, 1993.

Baudrillard, J. 2004. *The Intelligence of Evil or the Lucidity of the Pact*. Paris: Éditions Galilée. Trans. Turner, C. New York and Oxford: Berg.

Bettelheim, B. 1984. *Freud and Man's Soul*. London: Chatto & Windus.

Brague, R. 2014. "Christianity and Freedom". https://www.youtube.com/watch?v=CaVN_3TICiw

Chesterton, G.K., 1908. *The Man Who Thought He Was Thursday. A Nightmare*. London: Penguin Red Classic, 2007.

Danto, A. 2005. *Freud's Free Clinics. Psychoanalysis and Social Justice, 1918–1938*. New York: Columbia University Press.

Fanon, F. 1961. *The Wretched of the Earth*. Trans. Philcox, R. London: Penguin Modern Classics, 2005.

Hanaghan, J. 1931. *By Mortal and Immortal Seas*. Dublin and Cork: The Talbot Press.

Hanaghan, J. 1957, *Freud and Jesus*. Dublin: the Runa Press.

Hargreaves, S. 2018. "The Legacy of the Soixante-Huitards". *Quillette*. https://quillette.com/2018/05/02/legacy-soixante-huitards/

Huxley, A. 1932. *Brave New World*. England, St Albans: Granada Publishing Limited, 1977.

Kotkin, J. 2021. "Serfing the Planet. Green Policies Will Accelerate the Immiseration of the Global Working and Middle Class". https://www.spiked-online.com/2021/11/01/serfing-the-planet/

Lacan, J. 1969–1970. *Seminar 17. The Other Side of Psychoanalysis*. Trans. Grigg, R. New York: W.W. Norton, 2005.

Lacan, J. 1972–1973. *The Seminar 20. Encore: On Feminine Sexuality, the Limits of Love and Knowledge*. Fink, B. (Ed.). London: W.W. Norton, 1998.

Lacan, J. 1975–1976. *Seminar XXIII. Le Sinthome*. Trans. Price, A. London: Polity, 2016.

Laplanche, J. 1997. "The Theory of Seduction and the Problem of the Other". *International Journal of Psychoanalysis*, 78(4), 653–666.

Lasch, C 1995. *The Revolt of the Elites and the Betrayal of Democracy*. London and New York: W. W. Norton Company.

Levinas, E., 1981. *Otherwise Than Being Or Beyond Essence*. Trans. Linguis, A. Pittsburgh: Duquesne University Press, 1988

Nietzsche, F. 1967. *On The Genealogy of Morals and Ecce Homo*. Trans. Kaufmann, W., Hollindale, R. New York: Vintage.

Žižek, S. 2000. *The Fragile Absolute*. London: Verso.

7   Is it Righteous to Be?[1]

Should we exist? Do Levinas and Weil, in their different ways, ultimately (and unintentionally?) facilitate contemporary nihilism? In this chapter "white supremacy" and the questioning of "*my* place in the sun" (Pascal) are implied by the ethics of Levinas' *beyond* being, originary passivity, *ipseity* – pure self-exposure and recurrence, always already accusative. The key event for Levinas is not Christ but the interruption of *conatus essendi*. The example is given of maternity *qua* intimate proximity and substitution. Next, Weil describes the "blind mechanism" of affliction (*malheur*). At the foot of the Cross, affliction *is a nail*, but even here love remains a direction. Weil's ethical stance is represented by *amor fati* plus Grace – *waiting for God*. Does Weil's stress on "de-creation" and Levinas' persecution by the other come too close in their ethics to self-hatred and suicide?

'Oh God! Not another f★★★ing beautiful day', said Alice de Janzé under a brilliant Kenya sunrise, the moment before pulling the trigger and killing herself. That moment comes from the British movie called *White Mischief* (1987) based on true lives of ease, decadence, murder, and suicide among a group of wealthy colonialists, trapped and bored (to death) in East Africa during the early days of World War II.

It is tempting to think of this suicide in the context of the so-called end of Europe and its true life of ease, lasting into the 21st century, where cultural exhaustion, the inevitable curve of history, meets a radical ethical imperative: *just die*!

We must straightway invoke Freud's "short-circuiting" account of the death drive and how the organism desires to die it its own way, the ultimate (un)free choice – my right to end my life and to return to the inanimate state and how easy this opt out really is. For Freud, the default position is: 'the aim of all life is death … inanimate things existed before living ones'.[2] Death comes before life. What is secondary are 'decisive external influences', life or the life instinct, that cause 'ever more *complicated detours* before reaching its aim of death'.[3] Thus, for Freud, life only persists *in spite of* the death drive. Take away the complicated

DOI: 10.4324/9781003225010-9

detours – the sublimations, the reasons for living, the great effort at building life and creativity, the ethical substance of life lived in responsibility, responding to an "out there", the external influences; *take away the father* no less and death comes all too easily.

Apparently, some students have "suicide" as an option on their "to-do" lists. It is the father who leads us up the downward moving escalator of the death drive. He is the most decisive external influence. The father is the one who would willingly substitute himself for his (suffering) child. Again and again you hear fathers of sick children say this: I would give myself in exchange for my child. What do such strong sentiments, expressed or not expressed, communicate to the child? An unshakeable bond connected to being, to life, to persevering.

Freud introduced the notion of the death drive at a time when Europe was already dying, when a generation of so many young fathers and potential fathers had been lost in a devastatingly pointless war. On the level of language, Europe was already being deconstructed. The notion that it was "not righteous to be" was effortlessly gaining ground.

Cultural exhaustion and masochism plus colonial guilt were already consti-tuting the death of Europe, the collapse and deflation of Europe. As Bruckner follows Derrida revealing, 'our manifold unconscious complicity with horror, he [Derrida] has proven that crime is our most widely shared characteristic', and what Bruckner calls our "intellectual caste", that tiny but most influential permanent intellectual elite of opinion formers, 'is the penitential class par excellence, continuing the role of the clergy under the Old Regime. We have to call its members what they are: officials of original sin'.[4]

However, what was called for, what is being called for, is more than remorse, more than an awareness of original sin, which after all allows forgiveness, but something more like a pure culture of the death drive which has pitilessness and extermination at its heart. The post-structural logic is: Europe in its turn deserves no pity.

This is how it goes. There are so many examples.

Several black activists at Pomona College, associated with The Claremont Colleges, sent a letter to the college president asking administrators to "take action" against conservative journalists.

> Historically, white supremacy has venerated the idea of objectivity, and wielded a dichotomy of "subjectivity vs. objectivity" as a means of silenc-ing oppressed peoples. The idea that there is a single truth – "the Truth" – is a construct of the Euro-West that is deeply rooted in the Enlightenment, which was a movement that also described Black and Brown people as both subhuman and impervious to pain. This construction is a myth and white supremacy, imperialism, colonization, capitalism, and the United States of America are all of its progeny. The idea that the truth is an entity for which we must search, in matters that endanger our abilities to exist in open spaces, is an attempt to silence oppressed peoples. Conservatives

are, ignorant of interlocking systems of domination (intersectionality) that produce the lethal conditions under which oppressed peoples are forced to live.[5]

Is it righteous to be?

Mamadou Ba, head of the Portuguese "anti-hate" group SOS Racismo, spoke of the need to "kill the white man" at a recent online conference on "hate speech". Ba stated, 'it is necessary to kill the white man, murderer, colonial, and racist' to 'prevent the social death of the black political subject'. Allegedly, a quote from Algerian far-left anti-colonialist political philosopher Frantz Fanon, who openly advocated for violence during the French rule of Algeria in his seminal work *The Wretched of the Earth*.[6]

Similarly, Toronto Black Lives Matter co-founder Yusra Khogali, begs Allah for strength to kill white folks.[7] She went on to claim, 'whiteness is not humanness' and that white skin is sub-humxn [*sic*]; it is a 'genetic defect of blackness'. Whites have 'enzyme inhibitors that suppress melanin production', and melanin affects intelligence, memory, and creativity.[8]

Is it righteous to be?

Here is Pascal: "'This dog is mine', said those poor children; "that is my place in the sun. Here is the beginning and the image of the usurpation of all the earth'".[9]

We are not yet done with "othering". It extends to the most intimate places. Consider the wild celebratory mood in Ireland on 26 May 2018 when the "Yes" side won the abortion referendum by three-to-one majority. Peter Hitchens wrote in response,

> I'm interested in what kind of ideal society requires the easy disposal of unborn babies, regards making that action easier as a subject for public rejoicing, and loves it so much that it seeks to spread the idea to its neighbours.[10]

His atheist brother Christopher was against abortion for the simple reason that if the signifier "child" means anything substantial, so must the term "unborn child" also mean something substantial. And what should we make of Dr Wendy Savage for instance, at the heart of the BMA and an "ethics expert", who claimed effortlessly she had taken part in 10,000 abortions and who allows for sex-selection abortions and abortions up to full term?[11]

A UN report recently stated that around 126 million women are "missing" from the expected population in Asia and Eastern Europe.[12]

The young foetus may be just a ball of cells, but often the first photo in the baby album is the scan at x weeks. One father read the whole of *Great Expectations* to his child in the womb. Maybe the sharpest end of feminist power, namely abortion, abortion on demand, will soon emerge out of our collective repression as new technologies reveal that the so-called "ball of cells" is *demonstrably* a tiny human being with recognisable gestures and features.

The most dramatic relatively recent example of sharp-edged abortion is the little-known Gosnell case in Pennsylvania,[13] documented and made into a film by Ann McElhinney.

> And you know it's a really weird thing, here's a sanctuary city of Philadelphia – sanctuary city, right? Here's a Bhutanese refugee [Karnamaya Mongar] … No one investigated her death. Semika Shaw, a young African-American woman in Philadelphia, no one investigated, no one investigated.[14]

Is it righteous to be – *to be born*?
'That is my place in the sun'.
At one point recently, this became quite literally true when thousands of migrants fleeing Afghanistan and Syria arrived on "holiday islands" close to Turkey! Holiday makers complained that their place in the sun was ruined. As they were relaxing on sun loungers on the beach, just yards away scores of migrants set up camp, sleeping on cardboard boxes with rubbish strewn everywhere.[15]

Levinas

How should we now understand Levinas' most radical ethics *beyond* morality. Is it not enough to be remorseful and penitent and live? No. For Levinas, it is being itself that is condemned – is it righteous to *be*? Being is itself in question.

Such issues have recently reached a new intensity with the refugee crisis and fears of catastrophic climate change, and so Levinasian ethics continues to be relevant.

How should we now read things? First off, Levinas' privileging of the other is beyond ontology. The other is of a different register. Ethics is not politics. The former might dethrone the latter, and the latter comes down ultimately to a potential war of all against all, based on envy and greed and a level killing field.

In the introduction to *Totality and Infinity*, Levinas refers to being itself as *war*: 'the visage of being that shows itself in war is fixed in the concept of totality, which dominates Western philosophy'.[16] The grim determined impersonal face of being is dead set on its own advancement in individuals and groups.

For Levinas the transcendent bursts through the ontological, like a lightening flash. The ethical violence of the other is so strong it has to be tempered by the third that is the law that pacifies the potential violence of the utter proximity of the other. Levinas eschews Buber's "I–Thou" relation as being too reciprocal. Levinas asserts the radical asymmetry of the "I" blown apart by the other.

But this "being blown apart" cannot in any way be reduced to Azzam Tamimi, for instance, the British Palestinian academic and political activist, who is filmed in 2009 screaming for 'Jihad, Jihad, Jihad!' and commanding 'if they deny you water, if they deny your life, *explode in their faces*'.[17]

Ethics is beyond hate. Hate is our first reaction to the world. For Freud as well as for Levinas, it is a matter of self-preservation. For Levinas this hatred is built into the very structure of (impersonal) being. The notion, *conatus essendi* – perseverance in being – taken from Spinoza, is for Levinas the "law of being". But as *human* beings, the human beyond mere human*ism* is more than impersonal being: 'the human breaks with pure being, which is always a persistence of being. This is my principal thesis'.[18]

There is a pathway from ethics to politics. While politics always comes down to rationalising totalisations and calculations, justice ultimately depends and has always depended upon the *for-the-other* of ethical responsibility which is ultimate and non-negotiable: in summary, Athens underpinned, undercut by the biblical tradition. Or as Leo Strauss asserts, the conflict between the Bible and philosophy 'is the secret of the vitality of the West'.[19]

Levinas seeks the *source* of ethics – ethics as first philosophy – ultimate, exorbitant, hyperbolic, infinite. The ethics of ethics is way beyond any "ought" or superego, ego ideal command. And we would disagree with the term "perfectionist" as used by Hilary Putnam in *The Cambridge Companion*, as the source of ethics transcends any such descriptive term.

Israel of the Pentateuch stands. As Levinas says,

> Why worry about philology and history challenging the supposed date and origin of the sacred texts, if these texts are intrinsically rich in value? The sacred sparks of individual revelations have produced the light needed, even if they were thrown up at different points in history. The miracle of their convergence is no less marvelous than the miracle of a unique source.[20]

Just as ethics judges ontology and our egological *persistence* in being, our sense of our entitlement, and *so on*, the first five chapters of the Old Testament are timeless:

> Judaism is a non-coincidence with its time, within coincidence: in the radical sense of the term, it is an anachronism, the simultaneous presence of a youth that is attentive to reality and impatient to change it, and an old age that has seen it all and is returning to the origin of things.[21]

To want to conform to one's time and not to be "left behind", is an effect of (post)modernity, but the cost is high: 'it involves renouncing interiority and truth, resigning oneself to death and, in base souls, being satisfied with *jouissance*'.[22] This charge could be levelled at psychoanalysis today, having sold its soul to postmodern trends that are content with *jouissance* (however singularised), and asserted the so-called truth of desire itself as ethical.

In *The Anti-Oedipus Complex*, I attempt to underline the peril of ignoring the Origin:

> This is where the long march will ineluctably end: 'a machine [with] a set of cutting edges that insert themselves into the assemblage [institution, tradition, life form, Being, etc.] undergoing deterritorialisation …'. Thus, each is cut from within, like an abortion, a dilation and curettage

cleansing mechanism. Not surprising therefore that the cover picture on the Continuum paperback edition of *Anti-Oedipus* is a close-up image of an auger with its spiral cutting edge.[23]

Levinas also refers to: 'This time, *the blades* of reasonable history erode the very rock of Israel. This is what caused the erosion of the Absolute'.[24] Levinas is referring to the so-called Angel of Reason, the seductive double of Judaism. Over recent centuries: 'modern reason that transforms the world threatens Judaism to an unparalleled degree'.[25] However, Levinas states that the eternity of Israel, not at all carried away by illusions, is nevertheless,

> a function in the economy of being. It is indispensable to the work of reason itself ... [the modern world] invoked reason in order to have justice, and the latter surely needs a stable base, an interiority, or a person, on which to rest.[26]

Reason needs that stable unshakeable base. Levinas defended Judaism as, 'rigorously intellectual, rooted in textual study, rationalistic, anti-mystical, humanist and universalist'.[27] Reason *alone* does not in any way guarantee goodness. Quite the reverse. In 1793, the Jacobins announced a "Feast of Reason" and churches were turned into "Temples of Reason".[28]

One only has to recall those propaganda films circulated during the 1930s by the Nazis depicting the mentally ill and disabled lit from unusual angles in scenes of great distress with the voice-over appealing to the viewer in sympathetic tones that these "unfortunates" should be relieved of their suffering. Here is an article from the time.[29] One feels oneself drawn in by such "reasonableness".

My argument has been that psychoanalysis, the Jewish psychology, the psychology that welcomes antagonism, also requires that stable, anachronistic base on which to rest. It is not always a question of empathy or sympathy, those oftentimes clawing emotions, or even worse, reasoned "understanding", but instead a *here I am* [*hineni*]; *start speaking freely!* The analyst is a witness to the singularity of the other. The analyst must learn from Levinas – to be youthful and engaged, as well as old and disengaged. His/hers is an anachronistic base in touch with the unshakeable base of Judaism and Christianity.

It is not a question of empathy – if only we can empathise with the other, who is really the same as us; an enemy is only another whose story you are not yet ready to hear, and *so on*, goes the disingenuous phantasy of empathy that sustains a very fragile multicultural logic. Prior to (choosing) empathy is what Levinas refers to as an originary passivity, a passivity beyond the active/passive dichotomy of the ego, that leaves us utterly vulnerable to the other.

The crime of 28-year-old Usman Khan is exemplary in respect of the failure, the tragic inadequacy of empathy alone. Khan was attending an offender rehabilitation conference in Fishmongers' Hall on 29 November 2019 when he started attacking people with two knives taped to his wrists, killing two of the conference participants, Saskia Jones and Jack Merritt. He killed those most well disposed and most empathic towards him. Yet Khan, who had spent eight years in jail for planning to set up a terrorist training camp in Pakistan, was allowed to travel on his own from Stafford to London, even though it was well known he had become even more radicalised in prison.[30]

What gives the lie to most psychotherapeutic approaches is that the good-will of reasonableness and empathy mistakes the *radical* otherness of the other. Levinas goes further. My being in this world is already taking the place of another.

> The ego is the very crisis of the being of a being in the human domain … because I begin to ask myself if my being is justified, if the Da of my Dasein is not already the usurpation of somebody else's place.[31]

"My" ego is already a takeover of the singular stranger that I am to myself as well as the other out there. Try as I might, I cannot even empathise with myself!

The originary passivity of the self in its own body is the crucial datum for psychoanalysis. Without this radical passivity, there would be no psychoanalysis and no Levinasian ethics of ethics. Just think in terms of *Hilflosigkeit* or the primary helplessness of every human infant, the prototype of the traumatic situation and the ground of our ethical response. Freud emphasises the prematurity of birth of the human infant: 'it is sent into the world in a less finished state [than other primates]. As a result, the influence of the real external world … is intensified and an early differentiation between the ego and the id is promoted'.[32] Thus the ego, necessary as it is as a pragmatic agent in the world, becomes the problem, in its rigid fragility (neurosis) and constant *méconnaissance*, and, for our consideration here – an ethics *beyond* being.

Ipseity

Levinas gets to the point with his notion of *ipseity*. This is not identity as such which involves a predictable return to myself, but more a singularity in the Real, a *pre*-self, in–itself-ness, as it were, without separation out into a unity. It is self-enclosedness and concealment. It is driven only by a duty to itself which oppresses and contracts the soul. The other becomes the unmediated reference point *qua* exposure, devaluing the one-self. The subject become *sub-jectum*. It is the me that is in itself alone like 'one is in one's skin' – cramped, ill at ease – pure exposure to the other.[33] This structure without a name Levinas characterises as "recurrence" – a singular eddy of recurrence, being thrown back, or falling back on oneself, the breaking wide open of identity, without rest or peace. In fact, he says it is a 'condition of sacrifice', by virtue of its passivity, its susceptibility, its exposure to wounding and outrage, which motivates all efforts to escape.

Yet one is singled out, as Levinas says, 'being backed up against my own being and my own time … the whole weight of the universe is on my shoulders'. Even, 'the (French) grammar of *ipseity* is already accusative without the possibility of a nominative'.[34] Thrown into being – we are continually thrown into being. Far from being at rest or relaxation, itselfness is pure negativity in which, 'a subject is immolated without fleeing itself, without entering into ecstacy, without taking a distance from itself'.[35]

For Heidegger, as Levinas makes clear, Being is always cramped in its manifestation, definition or form – 'strangulation that is anguish'.[36] Thus, being restricted as a being gives rise to anxiety, understood as being-towards-death: the fatal (short circuit) hope to reach the deep of non-being. 'But, on the other hand, anxiety of the tightness [of ipseity] of the "going forth into fullness" is the recurrence of oneself, but without evasion, without shirking, that is a responsibility *stronger than death*'.[37] Against Heidegger, responsibility for the other is stronger than death.

Levinas is always at the extreme:

> The body is ... that by which the self is susceptibility itself. Incarnation is extreme passivity; to be exposed to sickness, suffering, death, is to be exposed to compassion, and, as a self to the gift that costs. The oneself is on this side of the zero of inertia and nothingness, in deficit of being, in itself and not in being, orphaned, without a place to lay its head, in the no-grounds, and thus without conditions. As such it will be shown to be the bearer of the world, bearing it, suffering it, blocking rest and lacking a fatherland.[38]

Recurrence. The coming around, the coming back to origin, occurs in the dead time or the meanwhile, 'which separates inspiration from expiration, the diastole and the systole of the heart beating dully against the walls of one's skin'.[39] Recurrence is pure dispossession of oneself *for* the other.

Levinas cites the Greek myth of Nessus' tunic as illustrative of recurrence. Fearing that Heracles had taken a new lover in Iole, his wife Deianira[40] gives him the "shirt", stained with the blood of the centaur Nessus. She had been tricked by the dying Nessus into believing it would serve as a potion to ensure her husband's faithfulness. In fact, it contained the venom of the Lernaean Hydra with which Heracles had poisoned the arrow he used to kill Nessus. When Heracles puts it on, the Hydra's venom begins to cook him alive, and to escape this unbearable pain he builds a funeral pyre and throws himself on it.[41]

The unbearable pain is on the hither side of the self, 'breaking up the principle of being in me'.[42] I cannot but help being summoned, being called, becoming a hostage to the other.

Levinas cites Otrepiev's dream in Pushkin's *Boris Godunov*.

> the false Dmitri catches sight of his future sovereignty in the equivocal laughter of the people: 'from above, Moscow appeared to me like an anthill, below the people were boiling and pointed to me and laughed. I

was overcome with shame and fear and in throwing myself down head-first, I awoke'. Laughter at the bottom of the gesture that points me out, shame and fear of the ego, the "accusative" where everything designates me and assigns me, awakening in a headlong fall – all this is the uncondi-tionality of the subject behind its sovereignty.[43]

Here is the cruel laughter directed at the dreamer being laughed *at* by the carnivalesque Moscovite chorus, creating a vertiginous loss of control, even paralysis, a kind of social death. The dreamer is isolated, alienated, and alone and trapped in this ipseity. He is pointed out, singled out, for shame and laugh-ter, mocking laughter, the butt of everyone's joke. As Zimmermann says, 'We see here the despairing interplay between the desire of the self, caught up in its own selfish intrigues, ultimately consuming and forging the destruction of its own being'.[44]

Is it righteous to be? Myself. Alone.

My place in the sun?

The origin of ethics is already outside me. Levinas describes an ethics of ethics. For him, the key event is *not* Christ on earth: 'For me the great event of history – but this is already or still an event of sacred history – would be the apparition of the human which would signify the interruption of the pure perseverance of a being in its being'.[45] The prematurity and thus defensiveness of the ego, the Darwinian struggle for survival, is blown apart by the infinite vulnerability of proximity.

In an earlier work, I paraphrased Levinas:

> [T]here is between being and nothingness, between being as what mani-fests (things, entities, essences, beings as what appear, as what disclose, what persist) and nothingness (the zero point, the void), between these two positions, there is fraternity or solidarity. Humanity, the excluded middle, excluded from everywhere, excluded by every discourse, occu-pies a "null site" between being and non-being. Before I can speak, I am affected by the other, I am accused by the other. Before I can choose to be ethical or unethical, I am chosen, by virtue of being human, by virtue of belonging. There is no escape![46]

Where in life itself do we observe the ethics of ethics? In prayer? 'At the same time there is, in this being closed up in oneself of suffering, the sigh or the cry which is already a search for alterity ... that it is the first prayer'.[47] Maternity? '[O]ur analysis will follow sensibility in its prenatural signification to the mater-nal, where, in proximity, signification signifies before it gets bent into perse-verance in being in the midst of a Nature'.[48] For Levinas, 'Maternity is the complete being "for the other"'.[49]

I have earlier referred to Hanaghan, who formulated the reversal of Freud's self-preservation drive in the originary cry of the infant for the mother. For Levinas, the maternal is the absolute materiality of ethics, *of proximity before being able to respond*, of a hyper-intimacy and hyper-dependency mediated by the placental villi that "extend" proximity to a huge surface area of contact, cell to cell, and exchange by diffusion. Recall also that the uterus/womb is associated with the notion of mercy: in Hebrew, the word for womb is *rechem* (רחם) and in Arabic it is *raHim* (رحم), which has the same root as the word for mercy, *racham* (רחמים) in Hebrew and *raHma* (رحمة) in Arabic.[50]

And the ethical turn? As we have seen, the other in the later Levinas is no longer "exterior", but closer to us than we are to ourselves. We are already hostage to the other. Agency has gone. This is an "inversion of being" whereby the subject is *constituted by the other* in the rear-view mirror.

However, 'The responsibility for the other is an immediacy antecedent to questions, it is proximity [and] [i]t is troubled and [only] becomes a problem *when the third enters*'.[51] The third is not just *another*, but *all* the others; it is knowledge, rationality, logos, justice, and *so on*. 'In the proximity of the other, all the others than the other obsess me, and already this obsession cries out for justice, demands measure and knowing, is consciousness'.[52] The anarchy of the one-for-the-other beyond being is not yet a problem and not a question; it only *becomes* a problem and a question when the third appears.

The ego has to come into play but now does so with a commitment and generosity because at the heart of subjectivity is an anarchy of the one-for-the-other that bespeaks fellowship, humanism beyond humanism, and an ethics beyond ethics.

> The relationship with the third party is an incessant correction of the asymmetry of proximity in which the face is looked at. There is weighing, thought, objectification, and thus a decree in which my anarchic relationship with illeity is betrayed but in which it is [also] conveyed before us.[53]

With the third, we shift a gear from the Real to the Symbolic – the Real of impossible proximity to the law which regulates justice.

The inhuman

In spite of the radical alterity in his description of the subject coming into being via substitution, via sacrifice for the other, being my brother's keeper, and *so on*, Levinas does not describe the *inhuman* as specific criminal acts. His radical emphasis on ethics to the point of self-annihilation exposes the "criminal" outcome of egoity and being in the world. The other liberates me from the "evil" of egoic being and turns me towards the Good beyond being.

The "there is" persists as the radical impersonal of being which we can neither avoid, nor assume, nor take responsibility for. It represents an unavowable suffering at the heart of existence which insinuates itself into being *and the other*. The other does not liberate me from being and the tragic destiny of being. Far from it, the proximity of the other leads almost inevitably to violence and racism.

Levinas refers to Lamentations as the core of his teachings:

> *To tend the cheek to the smiter and to be filled with shame* (Lamentations 3:30), to demand suffering in the suffering undergone (without producing the act that would be the exposing of the other cheek) is not to draw from suffering some magical redemptive virtue.[54]

And on the last page of *Otherwise than Being*:

> This weakness is needed. This relaxation of virility without cowardice is needed for the little cruelty our hands repudiate. That is the meaning that should be suggested … concerning the passivity more passive still than any passivity, the fission of the ego unto me, its consummation for the other such that *from the ashes of this consummation no act could be reborn*.[55]

No act could be reborn; therefore it is *not righteous to be*. After the Holocaust, it is not righteous to be. How else can the suffering undergone be intoned except via the radical *anti*-humanist gesture of Levinas' ethics where the Good is *beyond* being.

And from this perspective, Žižek says, quite ironically,

> '[W]hat Levinas, with all his celebration of Otherness, fails to take into account … [is] the radically "inhuman" Otherness itself: the Otherness of a human being reduced to inhumanity … the terrifying figure of the *Muselmann*, the "living dead" in the concentration camps'.

Žižek stresses how Agamben posits the *Muselmann* as an absolute witness to the horror and the one 'no longer able to say "Here I am" (and in front of whom I can no longer say "Here I am")'.[56] But Žižek goes further to interpret Levenasian meta-ethics as: 'this is not how a survivor of the *Shoah*, how one who actually experienced the ethical abyss of *Shoah* thinks and writes. This is how those *who feel guilty* for observing the catastrophe from a minimal safe distance think'.[57]

So, via a rather shameful psychoanalytic reductionism, Levinas' ethics *pace* Žižek, boils down to *his* "guilt of the survivor". And, surely, *we are all survivors* of the camps. Recall Bauman's extrapolation from modernity suggesting, 'Modern civilization was not the Holocaust's *sufficient* condition; it was, however, most certainly its *necessary* condition. Without it, the Holocaust would be unthinkable. It was the rational world of modern civilization that made the Holocaust thinkable'.[58] For Foucault, Nazism was a manifestation of "bio-power" which is 'the administration of bodies and the calculated management of life'.[59] Bio-power controls the reductive biology of 'propagation, births and mortality, the level of health, life expectancy and longevity, [and] all the conditions that can cause these to vary'.[60]

Is this austere way of thinking – condemning *all* science – gaining ground today? Is there simply a straight line from the mastery of science and treating people as objects for the purposes of legitimate study and human improvement, to the death camps? Therefore, we *all* share in the shame and guilt of the survivors. Surely Levinas and what he evokes by way of a meta-ethics shatters the reifying temptations of science by precisely installing the self-reflective shame of the survivors. There is thus a large question mark placed over (European) being *per se*, over the "ontology of power" (the usurpation of all the earth) and hope, the only hope perhaps in Levinas consists in the percolation of the anarchic Good *beyond* being *into* being, but then only by chance, as it were, as demonstrated in a key text for him, namely *Life and Fate*.[61]

As Catherine Pickstock complains, 'in some ways Levinas appears to offer an ethic for nihilists', not least because he presents 'no means of teleological discrimination between acceptable and unacceptable instrumentalizations'.[62] Such a lack of means is particularly dangerous today as we move rapidly towards the *unacceptable* instrumentalisations of 5G total surveillance, referred to elsewhere in this work. However, Pickstock appears to overlook his powerful defence of the Torah and the Pentateuch.

Affliction, de-creation, and Simone Weil

To include Weil[63] and Levinas in the same chapter is already problematic. One should caveat such a juxtaposition as provisional, cautious, and respectful of the otherness of each to the other. Perhaps they are incomparable. Levinas was certainly critical of Weil's wholesale rejection of her Jewish heritage (in which she was not raised) and her outright rejection of Yahweh. He was sceptical of her desire for mystical union with God which he regarded as merely a pursuit of personal salvation.[64] As Boulous Walker says, 'Levinas is critical of the mystical tendency, to confuse what he sees as the primacy of the ethical relation with the other, with a relation with the sacred, or God'.[65]

Weil was a mystic, a Christian Hellenist believing that, 'the wisdom of Plato is nothing other than orientation of the soul toward grace'.[66] Whereas Levinas' orientation is ethical, primary, and towards the other, more strictly, the face of the other. However, as Levinas says, the face of the other is the trace of God.[67] Indeed, when one says good-bye to the other, *adieu*, we are also saying *à Dieu*. The other is made in the image of God. The otherness of the other draws us towards God.

In the realm of marginalisation and suffering, affliction (*malheur*) has a special place, which is irreducible and Real.

> 'To acknowledge the reality of affliction means saying to oneself: "I may lose any moment … anything whatsoever that I possess, including those things that are so intimately mine that I consider them as being myself"'.[68]

André Gide referred to Weil as 'the patron saint of all outsiders'. The afflicted are outside. Affliction takes possession of the soul and stains it with 'the mark of slavery'.[69]

Affliction is an uprooting of a life, the physical pain of which chains down our thoughts and affects, indeed every aspect of life – social, psychological, physical. It is humiliation and social degradation. Affliction makes God seem truly absent as horror submerges the soul.

Weil was afflicted throughout her life with terrible migraines. However, in a Benedictine monastery, in the midst of a severe migraine, she claimed she was able to leave her flesh huddled in a corner and rise to the ecstasy of the music. On another occasion, when she was reciting George Herbert's poem on love, she felt God came down to her. She claimed that God had sought her, before indeed she had read the mystics. She had direct experience of the divine and these experiences happened *at the height of personal affliction.*

At the utter low point, the soul seems incapable of love, yet the soul has to keep on loving in the emptiness. Or, at least, as Weil says, a *fraction* of the soul must continue *wanting* to love, in the vain hope that God will come to reveal the beauty of the world, the Good beyond being. Here, in this radical Christian formulation, the most *sub-jected* subject is a passive subject á la Levinas, and a hostage to the other as God.

The afflicted are despised and the soul comes to identify with its affliction, being ashamed of shame. Victims are treated with revulsion and contempt. Weil asserts, 'Men struck down by affliction are at the foot of the Cross' (73). Christ accursed on the Cross is God at the greatest distance from God, God forsaking God at Gethsemane. The key moment for Christians (the key moment for humanity) was Christ being afflicted, dying like a criminal, like a slave. Yet Weil asserts a supreme paradox,

> The cry of Christ and the silence of the Father together make the supreme harmony, that harmony of which all music is but an imitation, that to which our harmonies, those at once the most heartbreaking and the most sweet, bear an infinitely far away and dim resemblance.[70]

In a similar fashion, the deepest truth is that, 'the void is the supreme plenitude but man does not have the right to know it … Even Christ did not know it at a certain moment'.[71]

Weil is suggesting that humanity who crucified Christ is part of the 'blindness of the mechanism of necessity', the operational tectonics of the universe, which causes affliction, the ground zero of being (Levinas) and rendering of the afflicted as anonymous things. The mechanism of the created world order grinds on, radically indifferent to human suffering. 'A blind mechanism,[72] heedless of degrees of spiritual perfection, continually tosses men about' (73), challenging us to keep our eyes *still* turned towards God.

Man is evil, not because of his egotism, his narrow self-interest, or narcissism, but because of his being *per se* – his refusal or reluctance to give up his "I" in favour of the impersonal sacred. As Levinas implies, man is not righteous in being. Man is 'only a thing, a stone that falls'.[73] This is Spinoza's assertion. We are like a falling stone that might have the illusion of thinking that it is controlling its fall.

Blind mechanistic necessity throws men down into affliction. Mechanism is distance, mechanism is evil – everything is obedient to the total blindness and infinite cold of the machinic, 'mechanically harsh matter' (75), which is the way the world works down to the smallest particle. Affliction truly opens up, reveals this vast Real beyond every illusion, *where God seems perfectly absent* having retreated into his Godself.[74]

This mechanism for Weil is perfect obedience (to God), wherein lies its sublime beauty, needing to be seen in slow motion to capture the silent gravity – the roar of the oceans, the collapse of a glacier, the mathematics of the sciences, orbits of planets, and *so on*. Consider the lilies, beautiful because of their docility and passive obedience. For Weil, '[O]ne must learn to feel in all things, first and almost solely, the obedience of the universe to God' (78). Thus, ultimately for Weil, 'joy and suffering are two equally precious gifts ... to be savored to the full' (78).

Perversion?

Suffering as a gift!? Blessed are the poor, etc., the paradoxical saying must never be passed over lightly. Or, as Žižek asks: is this the perverse core of Christianity? Suffering is a gift to the pervert. God sets out to torture us. And the pervert gives themselves over with pleasure/*jouissance* to be the pure object of the torture of the other. God sets up the law, so perversely we want to transgress it.

> [I]f it is prohibited to eat from the Tree of Knowledge in Paradise, why did God put it there in the first place? Is it not that this was a part of His perverse strategy first to seduce Adam and Eve into the Fall, in order then to save them? That is to say: should one not apply Paul's insight into how the prohibitive law creates sin to this very first prohibition also?[75]

God becomes neo-Stalinist and simpletons–Christians are duped without agency into becoming perverts, instruments of the totalitarian Other's will. And with what he calls the perverse 'logic of reimbursement':[76] you can sin because you can always get forgiveness as part of a divine insurance package.

With her preparedness for de-subjectivisation, de-creation, and kenosis, was Weil simply a masochist, forcing the other to exist?

Was Weil an anorexic forcing the (M)other to exist? She was born prematurely. Her mother was ill with appendicitis when she was just 6 months. She was suddenly weaned and became ill and became difficult to raise. Later she complained with a (perverse?) smile that she had been poisoned in infancy, presumably by the change in the milk at that time.[77]

Likewise, was Levinas' ethics masochistic a questionable surrender to the other? No. Drichel, for example, argues that Levinas instead offers us an "ethics of surrender".

> I argue that ... masochism or narcissism defend *against* relational vulnerability – a defense that manifests as a form of "ethical impairment".

Levinas's ethical for-the-other existence, by contrast, is predicated upon a defense *of* relational vulnerability – as the condition of possibility for ethical subjectivity.[78]

Neither Weil nor Levinas seeks defensive masochistic consolation, worse still horrific "pleasure" (*jouissance*) in any way (from the Father/Other). To suggest otherwise detracts from the singularity of each thinker. To reduce either to psychopathology seems more than a cheap shot, trivialising in that very ironic postmodern way when "depth" becomes impossible. As Anna Freud, who was consulted about Simone Weil, observed very respectfully, 'I do not think we should characterize this case as clinical. We should try to see the world as she did, in order to fathom what she felt and said … We should indeed be careful in the naming of this sickness'.[79]

When Weil asserts that affliction is a nail, 'whose point is applied at the very centre of the soul … *blind, brutal and cold*' (81, emphasis added), she is asserting an absolute truth of the Real, exploding any psychopathological medicalisation games. God is infinitely distant in this one point. The creature 'struggles like a butterfly pinned alive into an album' (81). Critically, for the tenacity of faith (not pathology), Weil insists against despair and giving up, *love remains a direction*.

What Weil calls de-creation (*décréation*) means surrender, becoming nothing, becoming *im*personal, so that the light of God can pass through us. She has the conception of love as radical self-sacrifice. There are at least two instances in the Bible. One is in Genesis where God created the world then withdrew. God expressed his love for us by withdrawing from creation, making room for us, making space, time, and matter – imperfect things. Secondly, by sacrificing His Son on the Cross for our redemption.

Clearly de-creation cannot be suicide, but openness beyond the ego "active passivity" (126) or "non-active-action" (Bhagavad Gita). *Hupomone* is key: being steadfast; *amor fati*; not being moved by misfortune and the absence of God. In a Platonic sense, Weil understands the gap between the order of necessity of the impersonal world on the one hand, and the good on the other. Weil's constant refrain is the reward granted for motionless attention to the order of the universe, including evil – to be the "obedient clay" in the hands of the maker, 'Thy will be done'. 'There is only waiting [*attente*], attention, silence, immobility in suffering and joy' (126). *Be still and know that I am God* (Psalm 46:10).

Masochism *per se*, therefore, is not necessarily a perversion. Masochism enables one to endure suffering and accept fate when it cannot be changed. The psychoanalytic prejudice that masochism is solely and exclusively, a 'sexual perversion in which satisfaction is tied to the suffering or humiliation undergone by the subject',[80] is to deny the possibility of non-perverse sublimated masochism where *jouissance* is *not* the primary aim.[81] Maybe, masochism enables the subject to creatively and courageously "bind" suffering in order to bear unavoidable pain.

Weil and Levinas, however, point to the Real beyond even any possibility of binding. As McCullough, commenting on Weil, says: 'No one, however perverse, could possibly find genuine affliction attractive or choose to become afflicted. Not even Christ was fully able to "choose" it [Weil] points out but prayed in dread that the cup be removed from him (Mark 14:36)'.[82]

Levinas makes clear that suffering, especially physical suffering, 'entails the impossibility of detaching oneself from the instant of existence. It is the very irremissibility of being … there is an absence of all refuge'.[83] With no possibility of retreat, we are backed up against being. In one of his major works, *Totality and Infinity*, Levinas states that, 'The whole acuity of suffering lies in the impossibility of fleeing it … being cut off from every living spring'.[84]

Although Levinas is talking about physical suffering and pain and its absolute proximity to the sufferer, Freud, in his addendum C to *Inhibition, Symptoms and Anxiety*, links physical and mental pain. He says, 'Yet it cannot be for nothing that the common usage of speech should have created the notion of internal, mental pain and have treated the feeling of loss of object as equivalent to physical pain'.[85] Physical pain is marked by a narcissistic cathexis, whereas mental pain is marked by an intense object cathexis, in other words, a cry to the other. Freud continues, 'The continuous nature of the cathectic process and the impossibility of inhibiting it [its proximity in Levinas's terms] produce the same state of mental helplessness'.[86]

Radical helplessness implies that ultimately suffering remains *outside and beyond any integrating process or theory*. It cannot be assimilated, appropriated, or grasped because it is a suffering *for nothing*, to no purpose, for no meaning. Levinas states: 'Suffering is pure undergoing',[87] more passive than any free choice of stoical receptivity, prior to any openness of being, any assumed passivity – suffering is pure submission. Meaninglessness, malignancy, waste, and absurdity, at the heart of suffering, explode the whole notion of redemptive suffering. Weil would not disagree, but would make the ultra-paradoxical assertion that at that terrible point there is also God *absolutely present*. And she lived this absurdity.

Suffering is exposure, being open, without any possibility of holding back. Lacan pointed to the gap in being. Levinas refers to "diachrony", which prevents the ego from joining back with itself in the same. The ego arrives just too late to re-cover and bind, unable to stop leaving itself wide open and exposed to outrage, wounding, sickness, ageing, and *so on*. This pre-original passivity is the obscure *source* of our later proneness to feeling exploited or victimised (at work, in relationships, etc.). I feel victimised by the other. I am already ontologically primed for this affliction.

If you refuse to take the leap of faith demanded by Weil, that is to love "iron" necessity, you will still experience affliction and become uprooted and disoriented, pinned up against the wall of being. However, if you have gone just some way down the route of faith, you will fare better. Those who have faith recover more quickly.[88]

However, this risk aversion approach – religion is good for your mental health – is just "mediocre" for Weil, who argues that it is the mediocrity of man which *wills* the good (values moral action, good works, and *so on*), and mediocre man loathes the passive *contemplation* of the good. She believes that the good cannot be reached by any muscular effort (of being, ego, will, etc.), salvation is not achieved through desire. She compares the will to the effort the peasant makes when he gets rid of weeds. 'It is a negative effort since it is, according to her, not the [work of the] peasant but the sun and water that make wheat grow'.[89] Here, she defiantly and radically rules out the moderate reasoned Aristotelian sense of virtue.

Nothing less than perfect obedience will do, leading to the putting aside of the "I". God comes to the one who refuses to give attention to things *other* than God. Likewise, to avoid illusion, we are encouraged, 'to prefer real hell to imaginary paradise'.[90] Affliction *without* consolation helps to attain total detachment, that is, the only reality. 'The duty to love the Good, in Weil's thinking, implies the self-annihilation of the human creature who is nothing compared to the Good and whose end is therefore to become nothing'.[91] Likewise, hope is irrelevant for Weil. We can only hope not to disobey. Hope is harmful because it is associated with a lack of detachment.

For Weil, it seems, the Good order of creation is the better off without humans! Her insight that man is mediocre preferring to give love to social groups when he can say 'we' instead of 'I', explains much evil in the world. Man is prepared to die for a cause, a "we", but is much more afraid to become nothing, to lose his "I" out of love for God. God wants us to become nothing.

Weil may express surprise that Christianity has not taken on Stoic piety for the universe. Most Christian theologians have not been able or, perhaps, do not wish to reconcile the love of God with the misfortune that the universe inflicts. This would also explain why (mainstream) Christianity has not integrated the Stoic *amor fati*. Christians believe that God loves us in spite of affliction, which becomes hard to sustain given such abjection fearlessly described by Weil. This is where the feint-hearted stop believing. Whereas Weil, *yet again scandalously*, believes that affliction is the expression of God's love, because misfortune de-creates us, and only *mystical* "knowing" can see this as God's mercy. Only mystical "knowing".

God gives being; being must be surrendered to God; *à-Dieu*.

★★★

Taking just Levinas and Weil as two examples of, let us venture the term, "ethical cleansing" – sacrifice, substitute yourself for the other on the one hand; de-create yourself so the light can shine freely with no shadow, on the other. What perfect simplicity, messianic purification! Both eliminate human agency. *The subject must not exist.* Accept this nihilism! Nihilate yourself …

With only a small parallax shift, we should be clear, millions could die. Recent polemics in America bring this distopian posibility closer.

For the *white* person, it is not righteous to be. Schools in the US have classes on "white privilege". Increasingly, mere humility is not an option, it is not good enough. It has to be non-being. Consider Patricia MacCormack and her beyond zero of the human.[92] She anticipates, or actively embraces, issues like human extinction, vegan abolition, atheist occultism, death studies, a refusal of identity politics, deep ecology, and the apocalypse as an optimistic beginning.

Disintermediation is required. Untangle the truth from the mainstream. The only way to begin to understand the contemporary is to go for the extremes, not the mainstream. Rational consensus argument teaches us nothing in the days of social media. The consensus is a compromise formation; the extremes reveal the latent content of the dream/nightmare of the approaching posthuman dystopia, amidst the very noisy crumbling of the West becoming buried under the weight of its own shame and guilt.

'Can you keep yourself safe?', the psychiatrist says to the suicidal patient. This is increasingly the question today for the very edgy, panicky posthuman orphaned subject who wonders even if she has a right to exist, especially if she is very young. And collectively we can no longer keep ourselves safe because if you look beyond the screen, everything begins to feel scary. Even this word "scary", its infantile nature, signals our orphaning.

Are you tempted to take your own life? Or, are you tempted to take *another* life? Have you ever felt like hurting someone? The subconscious lust for hate and self-destruction is on fire, burning across American cities during the summer and autumn of 2020.

We should recall *Forbidden Planet* from 1956.

Dr. Morbius: In times long past, this planet was the home of a mighty, noble race of beings who called themselves the Krell. Ethically and technologically they were a million years ahead of humankind, for in unlocking the mysteries of nature they had conquered even their baser selves … abolished sickness and insanity, crime and all injustice. Then, having reached the heights, this all-but-divine race *perished in a single night*, and nothing was preserved above ground.

Commander Adams: But like you, the Krell forgot one deadly danger – their own subconscious hate and lust for destruction.

Dr. Morbius: The beast. Even the Krell must have evolved from *that* beginning.

Commander Adams: And so those mindless beasts of the subconscious had access to a machine that could never be shut down. The secret devil of every soul on the planet all set free at once to loot and maim. And take revenge, Morbius, and kill!

Dr. Morbius: My poor Krell. After a million years of shining sanity, they could hardly have understood what power was destroying them.

Our task here now, as psychoanalysts, is to understand quite what that hidden power is and its absolute proximity.

Nearly a century ago, Chinese author and poet Lu Xun imagined the deadly threat posed by the absolute proximity of the inhuman.

> Imagine an iron house without windows, absolutely indestructible, with many people fast asleep inside who will soon die of suffocation. But you know since they will die in their sleep, they will not feel the pain of death. Now if you cry aloud to wake a few of the lighter sleepers, making those unfortunate few suffer the agony of irrevocable death, do you think you are doing them a good turn?[93]

'Silence', the poet concluded, 'was tempting but inexcusable; awakening even the few might also save the others'. Remember the well-rehearsed story, 'First they came for the gypsies, and I did nothing. Then they came for …'

It is only the father who wakes us to reality, and enables and *affirms* our being and our place in the sun.

Notes

1 A title by Levinas. Levinas, E., 2001.
2 Freud, S. 1920, p. 38.
3 Ibid., p. 39.
4 Bruckner, P. 2006, pp. 20–21.
5 Moran, R. 2017.1
6 www.breitbart.com/europe/2020/11/24/euro-anti-hate-group-boss-discussed-necessity-of-killing-whites/.
7 www.breitbart.com/big-government/2016/04/07/black-lives-matter-co-founder-ask-allah-help-not-kill-men-white-folks/.
8 https://pjmedia.com/trending/2017/02/09/toronto-black-lives-matter-co-founder-so-racist-even-huffpo-turns-on-her/.
9 Pascal, B. 1670.
10 Hitchens, P. 2016.
11 Adams, S. 2017.
12 UNFPA (United Nations Population Fund). www.unfpa.org/gender-biased-sex-selection.
13 Kliff, S. 2013.
14 Davis, D. 2018. In 2010 when the FBI raided the clinic of a Philadelphia abortion doctor, Kermit Gosnell, what investigators found was truly horrifying.
15 www.dailymail.co.uk/news/article-3099736/Holidaymakers-misery-boat-people-Syria-Afghanistan-seeking-asylum-set-migrant-camp-turn-popular-Greek-island-Kos-disgusting-hellhole.html.
16 Levinas, E. 1961, p. 21.
17 http://hurryupharry.org/2019/08/18/freedom-of-expression-on-palestine-suppressed/ (not available anymore).
18 Levinas in Critchley, S. and Bernasconi, R. (eds) 2002, p. 264.
19 Strauss, L. 1981, p. 203.
20 Hand, S. (ed) 1989, pp. 255–256.
21 Ibid., p. 256.
22 Ibid., p. 257.
23 Weatherill, R. 2017, p. 51.
24 Levinas cited in Hand, S. op. cit., p. 256.

25 Ibid., p. 255.

26 Ibid., p. 256.

27 Levinas cited in Critchley S. and Bernasconi, R. (eds) 2002, p. xx.

28 See Gray, J. 2018, p. 79.

29 Quinn, D. 2018 cites the Associated Press reporting "Nazis Plan to Kill Incurables to End Pain". https://twitter.com/DavQuinn/status/1329168593125330948/photo/1.

30 "Fishmongers' Hall: Usman Khan Unlawfully Killed Cambridge Graduates". www.bbc.com/news/uk-england-london-57260509.

31 Hand, S. 1989, op. cit., p. 85.

32 Freud, S. 1926, p. 154.

33 Levinas in Critchley, S. and Bernasconi, R. (eds) 2002, p. 242.

34 Alphonso Lingis introducing Levinas in Levinas, E. 1981, p. xxxvi.

35 Levinas, E. 1981, p. 108.

36 Ibid., pp. 194–195, n10.

37 Ibid., p. 195, n10.

38 Ibid., p. 195, n12.

39 Ibid., p. 109.

40 Translated as "man-destroyer" or "destroyer of her husband".

41 https://en.wikipedia.org/wiki/Shirt_of_Nessus.

42 Levinas, E. 1981, p. 114.

43 Ibid., p. 195.

44 Zimmermann, M. 2009.

45 Levinas, E. 2001, op. cit., p. 119.

46 Weatherill, R. 2011, p. 68.

47 Levinas, E. 2001, p. 57.

48 Levinas, E. 1981, p. 68.

49 Ibid., p. 108.

50 See for instance: http://augustinecollective.org/mercy-of-the-womb/.

51 Levinas, E. 1981, p. 157 emphasis added.

52 Ibid., p. 158.

53 Ibid.

54 Levinas, E. 1981, p. 111.

55 Ibid., p. 185.

56 Žižek, S. 2006, p. 112.

57 Ibid. Emphasis added.

58 Bauman, Z. 1989, p. 13.

59 Foucault, M. 1980, p. 139.

60 Ibid.

61 Grossman, V. 1980. Levier: *Éditions L'Âge d'Homme*. Trans. Robert Chandler. London. Harville Press, 1995.

62 Pickstock, C. In Davis, C., Milbank, J., and Žižek, S. 2005, p. 309.

63 We will limit our discussion on Simone Weil to her post-revolutionary period which can be dated quite precisely, when, in 1934, she proclaimed: 'From human beings, no help can be expected'. Cited in Abosch, H. 1994, p. 85.

64 Reed, R. 2013, p. 25.

65 Boulous Walker, M. 2002, p. 312.

66 Simone Weil, cited by Panichas, G. 1994, p. xix.

67 Levinas, E. 1963.

68 Cited in McCullough, L. 2014, p. 25.

69 Weil, S. 1951, p. 67. Page nos. in bracket refer to this text.

70 Weil, S. 1957, p. 199.

71 Lowtoo, B. 2009, p. 55.

72 Maybe the Deleuzian "desiring machines".

73 Ibid. Weil, S. 1957, p. 193.

74 We will take this Gnostic theme up in the next chapter.

75 Žižek, S. 2003, p. 15.
76 Ibid., p. 171.
77 Oxenhandler, N. 1994.
78 Drichel, S. 2019.
79 Cited in Abosch, H. 1994, pp. 129–130.
80 Laplanche, J. and Pontalis, J.-B. 1974, p. 244.
81 Of course, *jouissance* is essentially undefinable and therefore cannot be excluded.
82 McCullough, L. 2014, p. 24.
83 In Hand, S. op. cit., pp. 39–40.
84 Levinas, E. 1961, p. 238.
85 Freud, S. 1926 (1925), p. 85.
86 Ibid., p. 86.
87 Levinas, E. 1991, p. 92.
88 1998. Duke University Medical Centre. "Having Religious Faith Can Speed Recovery from Depression in Older Patients". *Science Daily.* www.sciencedaily.com/releases/1998 /05/980504125233.htm.
89 Lowtoo, B. 2009.
90 Weil, S. 1947, p. 53.
91 Lowtoo, B. 2009, p. 74.
92 MacCormack, P. 2020.
93 www.newyorker.com/news/daily-comment/chinas-iron-house-struggling-over -silence-in-the-coronavirus-epidemic. 12 February2020.

References

Abosch, H. 1994. *Simone Weil. An Introduction.* Trans. Kenny, K. New York: Penbridge Books.

Adams, S. 2017. https://www.dailymail.co.uk/news/article-4327606/Let-mums-abort -babies-wrong-sex-says-ethics-boss.html

Bauman, Z. 1989. *Modernity and the Holocaust.* Cambridge: Polity.

Boulous Walker, M. 2002. "Ethically Eating: Emmanuel Levinas and Simone Weil". *American Catholic Philosophical Quarterly* 76, no. 2, 295–320.

Bruckner, P. 2006. *The Tyranny of Guilt. An Essay on Western Masochism.* Trans. Tendall, S. Princeton and Oxford: Princeton University Press, 2010.

Critchley, S and Bernasconi, R. (eds) 2002. *The Cambridge Companion to Levinas.* Cambridge UK and New York: Cambridge University Press.

Davis, C., Milbank, J., Zizek, S. 2005. *Theology and the Political. The New Debate.* Durham and London: Duke University Press.

Davis, D. 2018. https://www.dailysignal.com/2018/10/05/the-true-story-of-kermit -gosnell-and-his-victims/

Drichel, S. 2019. "Emmanuel Levinas and the 'specter of masochism': A Cross-Disciplinary Confusion of Tongues". *Psychoanalysis, Ethics and History* 14. https://www.tandfonline .com/doi/abs/10.1080/24720038.2019.1550999?journalCode=hpsp21

Foucault, M. 1980. *The History of Sexuality, Vol. 1, An Introduction.* New York: Vintage, 1999.

Freud, S. 1920. *Beyond the Pleasure Principle. SE 18,* 3–66.

Freud, S. 1926 (1925). *Inhibitions, Symptoms and Anxiety. S.E. 20,* 77–178.

Gray, J. 2018. *Seven Types of Atheism.* London: Penguin Random House.

Grossman, V. 1980. *Life and Fate.* Levier: Editions L'age d'Homme. Trans. Robert Chandler. London. Harville Press, 1995.

Hand, S. (ed) 1989. *The Levinas Reader.* Oxford: Blackwell.

Hitchens, P. 2016. http://hitchensblog.mailonsunday.co.uk/2018/05/its-hour-come -round-at-last-reflections-on-the-abortion-referendum-in-ireland.html

Kliff, S. 2013. https://www.washingtonpost.com/news/wonk/wp/2013/04/15/the -gosnell-case-heres-what-you-need-to-know/

Laplanche, J and Pontalis, B. 1974. *The Language of Psychoanalysis*. London: Hogarth.

Levinas, E. 1961. *Totality and Infinity*. Trans. Linguis, A. Pittsburgh: Duquesne University Press, 1969.

Levinas, E. 1963. "La Trace de L'Autre". Trans. Lingis, A. *Tijdschrift voor Philosophie*, 605–623.

Levinas, E. 1991. *Entre Nous: Thinking-of-the-Other*. Trans. Smith, M. and Harshaw, B. London: Athlone Press.

Levinas, E., 2001. *Is it Righteous To Be? Interviews with Emmanuel Levinas*. Ed. Robbins, J.. Redwood City, CA: Stanford University Press.

Lowtoo, B. 2009. *Love for God's Necessity: The Ambiguity of Simone Weil's Hupomone*. Faculteit Katholieke Theologie, Universiteit van Tilburg. http://arno.uvt.nl/show.cgi?fid=96578

MacCormack, P. 2020. *The Ahuman Manifesto. Activism for the End of the Anthropocene*. London and New York: Bloomsbury Academic.

McCullough, L. 2014. *The Religious Philosophy of Simone Weil. An Introduction*. London and New York: I. B. Tauris & Co. Ltd.

Moran, R. 2017. "Student Activists Demand College 'Take Action' Against Conservative Journalists". http://www.americanthinker.com/blog/2017/04/student_activists_ demand_college_take_action_against_conservative_journalists.html

Oxenhandler, N. 1994. "The Bodily Experience of Simone Weil". *L'Esprit Créateur* 34, no 3. John Hopkins University Press, 82–91.

Panichas, G. 1994. *Simone Weil: A Reader*. Wakefield, Rhode Island: Moyer Bell Ltd.

Pascal, B. 1670. *Pensees*. Harmonsworth: Penguin Classics, 1966.

Pickstock, C. 2005. "The Univocalist Mode of Production". In Davis, C., Milbank, J., Zizek, S. 2005, 281–324.

Reed, R. 2013. "Decreation as Substitution: Reading Simone Weil through Levinas". *The Journal of Religion* 93, no. 1. University of Chicago Press Journals. https://www.journals .uchicago.edu/doi/abs/10.1086/668103?mobileUi=0&journalCode=jr

Strauss, L. 1981. "Theologie et philosophie. Leur influence reciproque". In Heim, C. (Trans.) *Le temps de la reflexion*. Paris: Gallimard, 1981.

Weatherill, R. 2011. *Forgetting Freud? Is Psychoanalysis in Retreat?* San Francisco: Academica Press.

Weatherill, R. 2017. *The Anti-Oedipus Complex. Lacan, Critical Theory and Postmodernism*. London and New York: Routledge.

Weil, S. 1947. *Gravity and Grace*. Trans. Crawford, E. and von de Ruhr, M. London and New York. Routledge, 2002.

Weil, S. 1951. *Waiting for God*. Trans. Craufurd, E. New York: G.K. Putnam' Sons. Harper Perrenial Modern Classics. 2009.

Weil, S. 1957. *Intimations of Christianity among the Ancient Greeks*. Trans. Chase Geissbuhler, E. London: Routledge & Kegan Paul.

Zimmerman, M. 2009. "Karol Wojtyla and Emmanuel Levinas on the Embodied Self: The Forming of the Other as Moral Self-disclosure". *The Heythrop Journal*, 988.

Zizek, S 2003. *The Puppet and the Dwarf. The Perverse Core of Christianity*. Cambridge, MA: MIT Press.

Žižek, S., 2006. *The Parallax View*. Cambridge, MA: The MIT Press.

8 Tired to Death in an Evil World

This chapter envisages an exhausted, depressed, minimalist God grown weary by the savagery of His creation. The apparent vicissitudes of God's love and hate for humanity are imagined in a series of scenarios. Starting in Poland after World War II, a rabbi finds God close to death. After Nietzsche, there are only *traces* of God and our mocking laughter at the "madman". Steiner warns that now we have no way to register tragedy and suffering. At the beginning, God gave the Commandments and His greatest gift, His Son, and *then went silent*. He had said and given everything. *And you shall see my back* (Exodus 33:23). Returning to the Old Testament, the rage of God on Sinai was not out of envy but love. The foundational trauma of the Law has always been the source of murderous Jew hatred, returning again today. Thus the call: *Leave Egypt behind and liberate the spirit!* The Gnostic call to secret knowledge (given God's withdrawal [*Tsimtsum*]), enables the hatred of being itself *qua* alienated: we are strangers on the earth. Was Lacan a Kabbalist? The divine sparks (*objet a*) leftover from the pleroma? Modern Gnosis has *not* been overcome. Instead, death becomes God. The world is evil and full of anguish. Finally, for Kojève influencing Lacan, the slave must become a warrior for thanatic "freedom". Divine violence against the (mythological) violence of the Law. No! Law helps us to walk.

At the end of George Steiner's, *The Death of Tragedy*, he tells a short story. He was taking a train journey in Poland some years before. As the train passed a gutted ruin on the side of a hill, one of the Poles in his compartment told him the story that it had once been a monastery and the Germans had turned it into a prison for captured Russian soldiers in the last years of the war. As the Germans began receding from the east, no food reached the prison. The guards pillaged what food they could from the land, but soon the police dogs turned dangerous with hunger. The Germans loosed the dogs on the prisoners. The dogs ate several of them alive. When the garrison fled, they left the survivors locked in the cellar. Two of them managed to keep alive by killing and devouring their companions. Finally, the advancing Soviet Army found

DOI: 10.4324/9781003225010-10

the two men, gave them a meal, and then shot them. Soon other travellers in the compartment recounted incidents as bad or worse. Then there was silence. Shortly, an older man recalled a medieval parable:

> In some distant village in central Poland, there was a small synagogue. One night when making his rounds the Rabbi entered and saw God sitting in a dark corner. He fell upon his face and cried out – Lord God what art thou doing here? God answered him *neither in thunder nor out of a whirlwind*, but with a small voice – I am tired Rabbi, I am tired I am tired and to death.[1]

Clearly, muses Steiner,

> God had grown weary of the savagery of man. Perhaps he was no longer able to control it and could no longer recognise His image in the mirror of creation. He had left the world to its own inhuman devices and dwells now in some other corner of the universe so remote that His messengers cannot even reach us.

Steiner's point is that our sense of the tragic 'requires the intolerable burden of God's presence'.[2] Without God, we are left with monstrosities. Indeed, without God, we *demand* monstrosity. And monstrosities are what we get.

Nietzsche was incandescent. Recall the madman who was one of God's messengers, running into the marketplace with his lantern lit in spite of full daylight, crying: 'I seek God! I seek God!' People laughed and joked.

The madman jumped into their midst and pierced them with his eyes.

> Whither is God?' he cried; 'I will tell you. *We have killed him* – you and I. All of us are his murderers … Is not night continually closing in on us? Do we not need to light lanterns in the morning? Do we hear nothing as yet of the noise of the gravediggers who are burying God? … God remains dead. And we have killed him … How shall we comfort ourselves … who will wipe this blood off us? What water is there for us to clean ourselves?[3]

If our sense of the tragic requires God's presence and God's presence means the registers of truth, beauty, and justice – the 'intolerable burden' in Steiner's words, has been lifted. We are left with not so much a "God-shaped-hole", but no detectable hole at all. No hole, no burden, no loss! No way of sensing loss. We could be fooled into believing that there is no loss, just a seamless world out there. Whereas, in truth, maybe the scale of loss is enormous and immeasurable.

The madman's cry in the marketplace, or God in the synagogue, is a message from the God who no longer exists which echoes the cry of Christ – *My God, my God. Why hast thou forsaken me?* (Matthew 27:46). God has forsaken God. This cry, repeated in every incarnation of suffering, should disabuse anyone who thinks that Christianity might be the soft option with the Father shielding us from the Real of death. God, it seems, against our childish Oedipal wishes, has no power to intervene. He is entirely power-*less*. Maybe, *He* is the blind watchmaker[4] after all who set everything going and then left the scene. Our little planet is drifting … unchained … plunging, 'Are we not straying through an infinite nothing? Do we not feel the breath of empty space? How shall we comfort ourselves, the murderers of all murderers?'[5]

Nietzsche's madman is still laughable. We continue to laugh *at* him. The laughter is infectious. It puts a vast sea of indifference between us and the Lacanian Real. Indeed, Martin Amis recalls, 'If Nietzsche is right, and *the joke is an epigram on the death of feeling*',[6] it is allied to *jouissance*, a *jouissance* of mockery and contempt, forbidden by political correctness – no stigmatising of madness – but outside this illusory utopia, it seems to be everywhere, behind the serious business of living and producing; and the direct opposite of the laughter of human solidarity and proximity which keeps the Real in mind.

Nietzsche's madman was being laughed out of town when the planet was gearing itself up for its Primal monstrosity (World War I) that changed every civilised coordinate, and that was before the Second and the Third monstrosity. The mocking laughter became a pathetic *self*-mocking laughter that has given up on anything good.

God's shadow could still be found in some caves, but Nietzsche wanted even the shadow vanquished, lest it continue to "darken our minds". Was Nietzsche deeply Christian? It is suggested that 'Nietzsche hated Christianity with all the intensity of someone who had once been caught up in its workings'.[7]

Baudrillard joined in the mockery, when after the attack on the Twin Towers when nearly 3,000 Americans were killed, he blamed America. 'For it is that superpower which by its unbearable power, has fomented all this violence which is endemic throughout the world, and hence that (unwittingly) terroristic imagination which dwells in all of us'.[8]

Baudrillard states, 'God is *not* dead, he has become hyperreal',[9] by becoming diffused in New Age spirituality which costs nothing – Tai Chi, yoga, mindfulness, druids, angels, God as "she", an "energy" in the universe, etc. All very at ease with the secular virtual. The (real) catastrophe that Baudrillard evokes, his negative theology, asserts we have long since passed beyond the end. But no one notices.

Levinas points to the "hidden intentionality" caught sight of by the phenomenolgical movement, that informed Western thinking with its increasingly complacent autonomy and immanence, thus *having no need of God*, in fact making democratic secularists *allergic* to Otherness or the Real. According to Levinas, there is no more than just "the trace" of God left in the ravaged face of the other. Being *per se*, is the elephant in the room, elephantine, clumsy.[10] Being tramples things, like the rich in Scott Fitzgerald's *The Great Gatsby*:

> They were careless people, Tom and Daisy – They smashed up things and
> creatures and then retreated back into their money or their vast carelessness,

or whatever it was that kept them together, and let other people clean up the mess they had made.[11]

Tied to *this* body with *this* contingent consciousness we are already and ineluctably "the rich", condemned to see only *through a glass darkly* (St Paul. 1 Corinthians 13:12). To *be* is to be rich, clumsy, and ignorant. Thus, being is usurpation. Being is normal perversion. To be is to *be perverse* – Original Sin. Being is contradiction – good and evil. The subject is divided. Christianity itself is divided: between the bourgeois property-owning Christians who confess their sins while trying to live a good and virtuous life *within* the burden of being, as against the mystics, aware of the perverse nature of being itself, eschewing the egoic world to live radically *otherwise*, following the New Testament. While the latter are often regarded as the only true Christians, subversive of the former who are deemed hypocrites and Pharisees, the true picture is always more complex.

Levinas refers to an "irrecusable order", one that cannot be questioned: irrevocable, persecutory, extreme, a visitation. Levinas asks, 'What then can be this relationship with an absence radically withdrawn from disclosure and from dissimulation?' He refers to Sartre's notion of the other as 'a pure hole in the world'. A trace, he tells us, 'in the strict sense disturbs the order of the world'. He suggests that the criminal who wanted to wipe away his fingerprints nevertheless leaves some traces and has therefore not committed the perfect crime. He has disturbed the order. Recall Chesterton's God who is a criminal. He has been and gone. Always past. Levinas quotes Plotinus: '[E]xistence is a trace of the One', in its absolute separateness and past-ness, 'the past of the other, in which eternity takes form ... more remote than any past and any future which still are set in my time'. He concludes, 'The revealed God of our Judeo-Christian spirituality maintains all the infinity of his absence, which is the personal order itself. He shows himself only by his trace'.[12]

He has spoken. Now silence

God is tired, with his head in his hands. God is in retreat. God is sick to death. God is dead. But, as Rémi Brague points out, God *has* spoken and given his Son and he has gone silent. Or, has *been silenced* by us who will not, will never hear word from a "divine" source. All authority in our time is deeply suspect unless it is technical-scientific. Whereas in the Old Testament it is clear that God "spoke" – words, visions, revelations, and *so on* – in spectacular fashion, as it were, in the New Testament comes the era of grace, and Brague quotes St John of the Cross: 'For by giving us as He has done, His son, His unique Word – there is no other – He has spoken and revealed all things at one time in one Word. There is no need to speak further'.[13] The Old is a prefiguration of the New: 'God has clearly said what he wanted to say and there is nothing more to say to us'.[14] Thus, Christians are responsible for God's plight! In fact, the three Abrahamic religions believe themselves to be final and definitive. For instance, Muhammad is the *Seal of the Prophets* (Koran 33; 40), the last of the prophets. Jews refer to the Talmud as the eternal Law of Moses. Christianity fulfils the Old Covenant. It is in the nature of religion itself, to be definitive, to have the last word, to be Revelation. Brague cites Pascal: 'God speaks well of God'.[15]

Pascal was made afraid by the silence of the infinite spaces, what he referred to as 'the whole universe in its dumbness'. He says of 'blind', 'wretched' man: 'Let him regard himself as lost'.[16] 'I have tried to find out whether God left any traces of himself'.[17] Man has rashly probed into these infinities of nature, 'as if there was *some proportion between themselves and her*'.[18]

The father of economics, Adam Smith, adds just less than a century later, 'the very suspicion of a fatherless world, must be the most melancholy of all reflections'.[19] Hume, who was Smith's mentor, Smith and Hume being the 'engine of the Enlightenment',[20] speculated that the world was unfinished, created by a young god, then abandoned. According to Brague, this was possibly the first time, circa 1800, "the death of God" entered the language.[21]

Swiss-French political thinker, activist, and writer on political theory and religion, Benjamin Constant, proposed the parable of the god who died. In the parable,

> we feel destined for something about which we haven't the slightest idea; we are like watches without dials, whose gears … turn and turn until they are worn out, without knowing why, telling themselves always: since I turn I therefore have a goal.[22]

At a similar time, German romantic writer Jean Paul's "Speech of the Dead Christ from the Universe that There Is No God" in 1796, was celebrated throughout Europe.

> I traversed the worlds, I ascended into the suns, and soared with the Milky Ways through the wastes of heaven; but there is no God. I descended to the last reaches of the shadows of Being, and I looked into the chasm and cried: 'Father, where art thou?' But, I heard only the eternal storm ruled by none … Then came into the temple a heartrending sight, the dead children who had wakened in the churchyard, and now cast themselves before the sublime form on the altar saying: 'Jesus! have we no father?' – And he replied with streaming tears: 'We are all orphans, I and you, we are without a father'.[23]

Between Jean Paul and Nietzsche, Gérard de Nerval dreams that the earth has become undone, the stars are extinguished – he had in mind the Apocalypse of St John,

> I thought I saw a black sun in the deserted sky and a globe or red blood above the Tuileries. I said to myself: "the eternal night is beginning, and it

is going to be terrible"... I thought that the earth had left its orbit and that it was wandering in the firmament like a dismasted ship....[24]

As Brague also notes, the black sun is not just hidden, it is not there, thus the earth has *no* orbit, *no* destination. This is not just anti-Ptolemaic, anti-heliocentric, but also anti-Copernican! In Lacanian terms, there is no Other of the Other.

God's silence is challenged again and again in desperation. *O my rock, be not deaf to my cry, lest, if thou answer me with silence, I become like those who go down to the abyss. Here my cry for mercy* (Psalm 28:1). *Thou hast seen all this, O Lord, do not keep silent. O Lord be not far from me* (Psalm 35:22). *Rest not, O God; O God be neither silent or still* (Psalm 83:1). *O God of my praise, be silent no longer* (Psalm 109:1). *Why stand so far off Lord, hiding thyself in time of need?* (Psalm 10:1). *Why does thou countenance the treachery of the wicked?* (Habakkuk 1:13). *Our sanctuary, holy and glorious ... has been burnt to the ground and all that we cherish is ruin. After this O Lord, wilt thou hold back, and wilt though keep silence and punish us beyond measure?* (Isaiah 64:11). *I called for thy help, but thou dost not answer; I stand up to plead but thou sittest aloof.* (Job 30:20).

Levinas, on behalf of Jews, is very concerned about the ontological status of Revelation, the ongoing communication between Heaven and Earth in what he calls 'the desert of today's religious crisis'. With the destiny of the West in mind, the question of Revelation remains critical. How can we make sense of the "exteriority" – outside history – of the signs and truths of Revelation's encounter with reason? And in these days with 'the news of the end of metaphysics, the triumphs of psychoanalysis, sociology and political economy ... signs without signifieds', we wonder if we are not indeed 'witnessing the magnificent funeral celebrations held in honour of a dead god'.[25] The pagan funeral celebrations of laughter and derision.

Some would argue that Levinas himself is part of the funeral celebrations. Radically antinomian – *You must regard yourselves as dead to sin and alive to God, in union with Christ Jesus* (Romans 6:11). For Levinas, the violence of the infinite, the transcendental Good, breaks into finite consciousness, but in a way that is inconceivable, seemingly entirely anti-dialectically: as God tells Moses, *And you shall see my back, but my face shall not be seen* (Exodus 33:23). As we indicated above, we can catch a "trace" of God when he is gone. God has withdrawn leaving only a trace.

At the very opposite end of the spectrum of the Neoplatonic contemplation of the mystical *ichnos* and the intimate beauty of the world around us, comes Talmudic ethical justice – not the One but the Other *qua radical, impossible Other*. According to Agata Bielik-Robson,

> Levinas, chooses the most antagonistic possible model of the encounter between transcendence and immanence and thus risks that it will result in catastrophic consequences for the soul: the breaking of the psychic vessel resulting in dispersion, disorientation, paralysis, or even death.[26]

Furthermore, 'the trace appears as a site of the permanent catastrophe which scatters divine sparks, mixed with broken shells (kelipoth), throughout the universe'.[27] Give up therefore any hope in communing with such an absent God. The Truth as a lightning strike, not possible to integrate into the Symbolic universe of meaning.

Here Bielik-Robson is referring to the Lurianic Kabbala. Not so much an absent God, but a God who has withdrawn, the tired God in a cave, contracted, leaving the "world", the Lacanian Real, to dereliction for some and not for others.

The lightning strike of Revelation. Maybe however we should not fail to be impressed by the catastrophic shock of the divine – anything less violent reduces/diminishes the Otherness of God's Wrath, the shattering violence of creation and the silence that haunts it. The aporia, the gaping hole of the disaster, remains in sharp contrast to the ontological commonplaces of reassurance. Bielik-Robson's question is precisely how is divine violence really different from the pagan sacred violence of the Same and the One, not the Other? Levinas would be bound to stress that divine violence is beyond the ontological, beyond mundane being as such, having to do with the transcendental Good of a violence that is *non*-violent, a Good beyond being. Thus, to say the very least, as an aporetic "concept", it can offer us *no* hope, *no* guidelines for help in our everyday creaturely existence. Whereas Bielik-Robson wants to 'argue in favour of the *dialectical* solution, practiced by the tradition in order to be able to bear Revelation, abide in it and talk about it',[28] rather than getting stuck in the non-space of a radical apophasis.

It is the selfish world of pride and confidence that forgets God, has no need of God, that provokes the legendary *jealousy* of the God of Israel. Thus, normal life will be torn through, haunted by, apocalypticism – a spiritual fire that enervates complacent life, shaking its foundations.

> *They roused my jealousy with a god of no account, with their false gods they provoked me ... I will heap on them one disaster after another ... The sword will make orphans in the streets and widows in their homes ... If only they had wisdom to understand this and give thought to their end!*
>
> (Deuteronomy 32: 21–29)

The reason for such jealousy is clear: *I am the Lord, that is My name; I will not give My glory to another god, nor My praise to any idol* (Isaiah 42:8). There is *one* God; the others are false. Period. *I will be He whom I will be* (Exodus: 3:14). There can only be a *strict* monotheism, as God is one – i.e. utterly consistent within Himself. One divine substance, in that everything called divine has the same properties. Thus, there can be no pluralistic sharing with other so-called gods.

When He says, *I shall be jealous for My holy name* (Ezekiel 39:25), He is not demonstrating insecurity or envy in any way, but merely his total strength and sovereignty. Monotheism means unity and totalitarianism. In fact, God here is at His most human and personal. He is nothing but fully engaged to the point of rage. He is thus a necessary counterpoint of dark excess, demanding justice, in radical dialectical contrast to the Christian love in the New Testament vis à vis the Jewish law. The agape love which suspends the law is necessarily accompanied by the arbitrary cruelty which also suspends the law. Žižek suggests that these apparently irreconcilable extremes are a parallax problem: 'There is no "substantial" difference between the God of love and the God of excessive arbitrary cruelty ... it is one and the same God who appears in a different light only due to a parallax shift in our perspective'.[29]

God appears as radically Other with an anger that can only be understood as a loving anger, divine violence against injustice. A rage against the perversion of His creation. As in the emblematic story of the Golden Calf, the enduring symbol of decadence and materialism, the worship of the Golden Calf breaks the second commandment regarding the prohibition against idolatry. Moses, returning from the mountain with the tablets containing the Ten Commandments given by God on Mt Sanai, sees the Golden Calf and the people celebrating.

> He flung the tablets down, and they were shattered to pieces at the foot of the mountain. Then he took the calf they had made and burnt it; he ground it to powder, sprinkled it on the water, and made the Israelites drink it.
>
> (Exodus 32:19, 20)

Moses then ordered his fellow Levites to slaughter thousands of those who had participated in the idolatry. God told Moses that he intended to eliminate the Israelites, but Moses pleaded that they should be spared, and God eventually relented. Moses returned to Sinai to receive replacement tablets after fasting and praying for another 40 days.

Christ does not merely represent God, He *is* God. Christ is not just an excellent and a good person, like Socrates, Buddha, Muhammad, Gandhi, Mandela, etc., he does not just *resemble* God, He *is* God. Thus, when Christ dies on the cross, we come to the appalling conclusion that God dies too. Christ's atheistic cry: *why has thou forsaken me?* is our cry also. Thus, man's alienation from God – God's radical exteriority and unfathomableness – coincides with God's alienation from Himself, with His cry from the cross. The movement from divine substance to the finite human subjectivity of Christ must also occur *within* God. God objectivises Himself on earth. When Christ dies God dies and both become Holy Spirit. Thus, the inevitable modern atheistic conclusion will be:

> [T]here is no way back [to the divine], all there is, all that "really exists" are from now on individuals, there are no Platonic Ideas or Substances whose existence is somehow "more real". What is "sublated" in the move from the Son to Holy Spirit is thus God himself: after Crucifixion, the dead of the incarnated God, the universal God returns as a Spirit of the community of believers.[30]

Thus, the Incarnation is the Badiouian Event for Christian believers. The Event that *they* believe in. Nothing beyond that.

It ends with Christ's Passion. After that, *that* God will remain silent. Revelation is done. In A Letter to the Hebrews: 1–3, the author is clear in the first verses:

> *When in former times God spoke to our forefathers, He spoke in fragmentary and varied fashion through the prophets. But in this the final age He has spoken to us in the Son whom he has made heir to the whole universe, and through whom he created all orders of existence: the Son who is the effulgence of God's splendor and the stamp of God's very being and sustains the universe by His word of power.*

Thus, what was said in fragments is completed in Christ. God has given everything! He has given everything *in his Son*. Christ does not bring a message; Christ *is* the message. Christ is the Gift that transcends itself. It overflows continuously what has been given. What more could be given than God's sacrificial entrance into history? There is *no* eternal return, no coming around again. God appeared in history *once*. We are *in the* Gift of the Incarnation *before* it is present to us. It is already *more*. Thus, the reason there is silence, that there is nothing more to be said, nothing that can be said in so many words, nothing to add, is because *God is The Answer*.

God's silence means *man can speak*. As Brague says,

> To set Christ's silence *against* human liberty is the most radical perversion one could conceive of, because this silence has precisely for its goal to allow man to speak and to permit him to respond in full knowledge to what is offered him.[31]

Responding in *full knowledge to what is offered him* because liberty *without* this divine Revelation and its full knowing is finally slavery and death. Freedom is key – the Grand Inquisitor notwithstanding.

He has stopped speaking in words that we can hear. *He* has banned images (Exodus 20:4), self-cancelling Himself as He is beyond our understanding and beyond any questioning or complaining.

His mighty response to Job (Job 38) comes out of the whirlwind:

[2] Who is this that darkens counsel by words without knowledge?
[3] Gird up your loins like a man,
   I will question you, and you shall declare to me.

[4] Where were you when I laid the foundation of the earth?
   Tell me, if you have understanding.
[5] Who determined its measurements – surely you know!
   Or who stretched the line upon it?

⁶ On what were its bases sunk,
 or who laid its cornerstone
⁷ when the morning stars sang together
 and all the heavenly beings shouted for joy?

⁸ Or who shut in the sea with doors
 when it burst out from the womb? –
⁹ when I made the clouds its garment,
 and thick darkness its swaddling band,
¹⁰ and prescribed bounds for it,
 and set bars and doors,
¹¹ and said, 'Thus far shall you come, and no farther,
 and here shall your proud waves be stopped'?

¹² Have you commanded the morning since your days began,
 and caused the dawn to know its place,
¹³ so that it might take hold of the skirts of the earth,
 and the wicked be shaken out of it?
¹⁴ It is changed like clay under the seal,
 and it is dyed* like a garment.
¹⁵ Light is withheld from the wicked,
 and their uplifted arm is broken.

¹⁶ Have you entered into the springs of the sea,
 or walked in the recesses of the deep?
¹⁷ Have the gates of death been revealed to you,
 or have you seen the gates of deep darkness?
¹⁸ Have you comprehended the expanse of the earth?
 Declare, if you know all this.

We are speechless. There are no words.

★★★

Jewish suffering

In "To Love the Torah More than God", Levinas is moved by an anonymous text, a fictional document written during the last few appalling hours of the Warsaw Ghetto resistance, by one Yossel, son of Yossel Rakover of Tarnopol.[32] He is about to die. He has witnessed all the horrors. His children are dead. He is his family's last surviving member. Levinas asks the age-old question: 'What is the meaning of the suffering of the innocent? Does it not witness to a world without God; to an earth where only man determines the measure of good and evil?' Finding himself alone without a comforting God – 'what kind of strange magician did you project as the inhabitant of your heaven' – Yossel, son of

Yossel, under an empty heaven, feels the weight of all of God's responsibilities on *his* shoulders. Following the story, Levinas summarises,

> The moment when God withdraws himself from the world and veils his countenance, he has sacrificed humankind to its wild instincts and because those instincts dominate the world, it is natural that those who preserve the divine and the pure should be the first victims of this domination. It is the hour when the just person has nowhere to go in the outside world; when no institution affords him protection; and even the comforting sense of the divine presence experienced in the childlike person's piety, is withdrawn; when the only victory available to the individual lies in his conscience, which necessarily means, in suffering.

Levinas emphasises that this story represents the specifically Jewish meaning of suffering where victims find themselves in a disordered world, that is, where goodness does not succeed in being victorious. Quoting from the same anonymous text,

> To be a Jew means to be an everlasting swimmer against the turbulent, criminal human current … I am happy to belong to the unhappiest people in the world to the people whom the Torah represents the loftiest and most beautiful of all laws and moralities.

As professor of English and religion Regina Mara Schwartz comments: 'An absent God becomes most immanent internally. God is no protector or saviour but is internalized as a moral principle that guides action'.[33]

Is *He* possible asks Levinas? This absent, infinitely remote God? Or is *He* just a metaphysical construct? The anonymous author answers almost blasphemously, suggests Levinas: 'I love Him, but I also love His Torah even more … And even if I had been deceived by Him and, as it were disenchanted, I would none the less observe the precepts of the Torah'. He loves the Torah because it shows *categorically* that, 'You cannot possibly be the God of those whose deeds are the horrible expression of a militant absence of God'.

The fact the Torah exists, has existed, means that the brutal world is not all. And the brutal world is judged.

As Levinas reminds us, this is not an 'emotional communion' with an 'incarnate God', but instead, *a meeting of minds*. He continues, 'The guarantee that there is a living God in our midst is precisely a word of God that is not Incarnate'. The author contrasts, "our" God as a God of vengeance – 'Our Torah is filled with death penalties for venial sins', this "virile" God, leads the judges to be considered murderers; yet, by comparison, 'The God of the gentiles has commanded to love every creature made in his image and in his name our blood has been poured out for over 2000 years'. Here is Levinas' paradox:

> The true humanity of man and his virile tenderness come into the world with the severe words of a demanding God; the spiritual becomes present,

not by way of a palpable presence, but by absence; God is concrete, not by means of incarnation but by means of the Law … filling us with higher thoughts.

This God, *qua* veiled, is as far removed from the 'palpable communion' with the divine as well as 'the desperate pride of the atheist'. This God demands an *adult* human! Not a child seeking comfort and consolation. Levinas ends, 'To love the Torah more than God – this means precisely to find a personal God against whom it is possible to revolt, that is to say, one for whom one can die'.

And Schwartz ends her commentary with a strong warning:

> What the gift of justice does, on the other hand, is present one with the harsh reality that only acts of justice performed by the subject, and only by him, can help to create a just world and only this can relieve despair. There is no other way out. And this is what makes the covenantal demand of justice ultimately political: while Revelation is a radical rupture into the status quo, it does not offer a miraculous solution to human pain.[34]

World-shaking transition

Thus, the "Jew" became *the* bad conscience of Western history. Kafka said, 'He who strikes a Jew strikes down mankind'. Steiner tries to fathom the unique horror of the Holocaust. He acknowledges of course that his own feelings are implicated. However, it remains an unspeakable horror. Pressing beyond the secular explanations – Nazi racial theories, petit-bourgeois bitterness against (Jewish) elites, financial collapse, over-hasty Jewish assimilation, Nazi and Stalinist anti-Semitism, and *so on* – Steiner seeks a different register, the register of the Real beyond the Symbolic and the Imaginary.

He is thinking of the immensity of the world-shaking transition from polytheism to the Mosaic conception of ONE God, in real time, in real historical time. What we must recapture in some way, he says,

> as nakedly as we can, is the singularity, the brain-hammering strangeness of the monotheistic idea … The abruptness of the Mosaic revelation, the finality of the Creed at Sinai, tore up the human psyche by its most ancient roots. The break has never really knit.[35]

Again, we are speechless. This time *by command*. Command: not to speak; not to imagine; but to believe, to love, and to obey an unfathomable abstraction and real absence. Steiner cites Schoenberg in *Moses und Aron*:

Inconceivable because invisible
because immeasurable
because everlasting
because eternal

because omnipresent
because omnipotent.[36]

No fiercer exigence, immense and relentless, 'hammers on human conscious-ness, demanding that it transcend itself, that it reach out into a light of under-standing so pure that it is itself blinding'.[37] This decisive eclipse of pagan polytheism, of human freedom among the gods is *unforgivable*. Christianity, he acknowledges, was something of a compromise. However, the seething resentment against *this* particularly Jewish ethics beyond ethics, this unattain-able ideal, 'a way of making good the *mauvaise foi* … By killing Jews, Western culture could eradicate those who had "invented" God, who had, however imperfectly, however restively, been the declarers of His unbearable absence'.[38]

Steiner stacks up the enormity of this moral demand that brooks NO com-promise. The Book of Prophets, the Sermon on the Mount, the parables of Jesus all serve 'the extremity of their call': *give up your life*! 'Men had enforced upon them, ideals, norms of conduct, out of all-natural grasp'.[39] Steiner refers to 'the blackmail of transcendence … the insistence of the ideal continued, with a terrible tactless force'.[40]

Thus, the *murderous loathing* built up against Judaism, so closely associated with perfection and utopia. At least, three times – Sinai, primitive Christianity, messianic socialism, the West is brought close again to the Ideal of living together. Then came the Holocaust – 'a lashing out against intolerable pres-sures of vision'. Self-mutilation. Extirpation: 'It [the Holocaust] enacted the suicidal impulse in Western civilization. It was an attempt to level the future, to make history commensurate with the natural savageries, intellectual torpor, and material instincts of an extended man'.[41] Steiner refers to it as a Second Fall – not only just the leaving the Garden of Eden, but destroying it, *scorched earth, burning the Garden* as we leave, lest we continue to remember. The murderous loathing continues.

Gnosis

Let us return to the *first* Fall. As Conor Cunningham helpfully reminds us, 'one can venture that it was not the breaking of God's instruction that caused the Fall. Instead, it seems that it was the very idea of *knowledge apart from God* that was the Fall'.[42] It was the notion of a separate Gnosis that was heretical. How could knowledge exist independently of God, who created everything? Gnosis is first and foremost knowledge for the elect, for the elite.

Irenaeus of Lyons describes a typical early Gnostic opponent of Christianity, probably Valentinian. He says, this person, 'thinks that he is neither in heaven nor on earth, but rather that he has entered into the Pleroma ('Perfection'), and has already been joined to his "angel". He walks around with a pretentious and supercilious air'.[43]

A radical dualism arose in opposition to early Roman Christian orthodoxy in the 2nd century CE. Against the notion that the created world was all good because it was created by a loving God, Gnostics believed the *material* world to be irredeemably fallen. If the material world is evil then the body also is evil; only the soul, the spirit, can save us. Jesus, for instance, was just spirit. The resurrection of His *body* was an impossibility. Attaining esoteric knowledge is Gnosis. The template may have been the Platonic division between Idea (reason) and matter (necessity). The way out of the cave was to enter a mystical realm of knowing and be free.

The claim here is that our age is essentially Gnostic, whether we care to know it or not. What this comes down to is that we favour world destruction. The material world is an error, a mistake. Its final disappearance should be understood as a liberation.

However, the need for destruction of the dysfunctional world is not just a Gnostic ideology, but extends back to Jewish apocalypticism, in for instance the Book of Revelation. The term "apocalypse" itself, or "*apokálypsis*" in Greek, means "lifting of the veil" or, in dynamic terms, a shattering primal revelation of what must remain repressed. In other words, the apocalypse brings Gnosis.

John Gray asserts that, 'Modern revolutionary movements are continuations of medieval millenarianism. The myth that the human world can be remade in a cataclysmic upheaval has not died'.[44] He cites the Jacobins, the Bolsheviks, Mao, and Pol Pot. Today, there are multiple possibilities, from the deep Greens to the Transhumanists. Surely, the internet, Google, where all knowledge is available instantly is revelatory, apocalyptic, and is already causing the shattering of all bonds, of all orientations, all commitments, and *so on*. And only those elites (Gnostics) who *know* will survive. The rest will remain ignorant serfs.

As Lacan observes: 'Here we are then, up against the wall, up against the wall of language'. He tells us that the analyst and patient are on the same side of the wall, and that, 'There is nothing that is anything but outer darkness to us beyond this wall'.[45] Lacan asks, 'What am "*I*"'? The answer. '*I* am in the place from which a voice is heard clamoring, "the universe is a defect in the purity of Non-Being"'.[46] Only a Gnostic can have *this* knowledge. For Lacan, being *per se* is a trap organised by the Symbolic (Other) into which we are at first thrown, then seduced, and which we should properly reject with, 'a solid hatred address to being'.[47] Gnostically speaking, the Symbolic register is experienced not as an opening onto God's world for every child led by the Father, but quite the opposite, an oppressive Weberian "iron cage" of a fateful reality where beings are destined for misery, suffering, and death.

The Gnostic therefore aims messianically at the destruction of the old order enabling the return to the primordial pleroma of non-being and infinite *jouissance*. Leave Egypt behind and liberate the spirit from the machine-like function of rationality. Only Gnostics despair for the "world dungeon". An implacable refusal to make concessions to the status quo marks out the Gnostic sensibility. Burn the Garden! It is a botched creation!

However, there is within the total negation of the evil world system by the Gnostic, a remnant that remains *unalienated* and escapes the trap of being (wherein we are dead to life already without knowing it). The only way to go for the initiate, it is alleged, is not quite into nihilism *per se*, but via the death drive, to *jouissance* or intense joy.

To be alien, to be alienated, a stranger on earth – to accommodate to this strangeness all too well and all too easily by succumbing to the desire of the (m) Other, one becomes an exile via the allegedly suffocating Oedipal family. The way back is via embracing that strangeness in the strange world to repudiate it in the most radical, revolutionary terms.

There has been a primitive disaster. Wilfred Bion said as much.[48] The great divine fire (pleroma) has exploded or been almost completely quenched by the corrupted world, created by a demiurge, and all we are left with are smouldering embers which we must identify and blow on to rekindle life with the divine fire.

We should make the contrast. The Christian understanding is that God's great joy continues to imbue the universe with the brightest light, but we have become too alienated, too fallen, too limited, seeing only through a glass darkly (Corinthians 13:12). Our task is to recover that simplicity of joyful illumination, not by destruction, but through prayer and understanding beyond understanding – a different *Gnosis* if you will, that we are created and forgiven in *imago Dei*.[49]

Lacan inverts the ladder of normative desire, which according to Professor of Jewish Studies, Agata Bielik-Robson, celebrates Jewish mysticism,

> The unique theme of Jewish Gnosticism, which is of particular interest to us here, is *life*: the Great Life full of infinite joy, which, due to some cosmic cataclysm, gets lost and exiled into the alien universe of matter, time, and death, where it errs and wanders in the form of a distorted remnant, endangered by self-oblivion, until it becomes recalled and awakened.[50]

Translated into Lacanian psychoanalytic terms, the once infinite *jouissance* "without limits" (in Kabbalistic terms: *Ein Sof*) is lost, limited, and thus negated/repressed. It becomes the wandering drive – *Trieb* – which Lacan calls the drift of *jouissance*. The drive attaches erroneously to the [maternal] objects of the world which fixate it. However, it is awakened by the psychoanalyst to its true destiny – the non-existent, non-objectifiable, ineffable *objet a*. Then, it no longer suffers in the world run by the seemingly iron rule of necessity (*hermaimene*). The *trieb*, as it were, recalls its "otherworldly" origin, gives up on the 'sheeplike conglomerations of Eros' and 'turns back' on 'the inverted ladder of desire';[51] even if the drive cannot fully return to the lost pleroma, which, in Lacan's terms, is "the impossible", it can nonetheless partly regain its joyful peace, by becoming self-sufficient and self-sustained, with no desirous attachment to any object.[52]

The inverted ladder, the scorched earth of the Garden, the negation of original negation by the Other, and *so on*: the Other forbids and thus negates the original pleromatic *jouissance*, by introducing language. The (small) other of this Other negates the negation, and brings in the restorative moment of *jouissance*, partly regained. As radical Jewish philosopher Jacob Taubes suggests: 'I can imagine … an apocalyptic: let it go down. I have no spiritual investment in the world as it is'.[53]

Lacan distinguishes between *ex*-sistence and *sub*-sistence: the former is linked to the Symbolic and the latter is what remains of life in the Real. The non-investment in the alien world that Gnostic adherents would like to leave as scorched and destroyed, should be brought about by rage emanating from the Real. As Bielik-Robson says: 'Love for the Real can only manifest itself as hatred for being – the rule which the Gnostic tradition perceives as definitive for its antinomian practices of challenging the law and order of the seemingly harmonious and benign creation'.[54] Lacan wishes to recover the pure hatred for being, *primally* repressed behind the Christian teachings of Aristotle and St Thomas and all their alleged misinterpretations and misrepresentations via the big Other.

Ironically, such a virulent hatred of being, hatred of God, could only have been generated or provoked by the extreme formative power of the monotheistic matrix itself and its shattering, puncturing, and transformative break with what went before, namely, the notion of the harmonious weaving of the pagan sacred. Radically and fatally in Lacan's view, and the view of Gnostic heretics, the developmental vagaries of the "Othering" of the psyche – attaching the psyche to the Other – leaves only scattered remnants, sparks no less, to be mobilised against that Other and its expropriating alienating seduction via language. Lacan refers to the sparks of the original *jouissance*, as *objets a*, traces of the Real with an auratic uncanny quality, to which we are nevertheless ineluctably still secretly attracted, around which desire secretly still circulates.

Analysis will blow on these dying embers, these precious remnants of the divine, thus fanning the flames of desire, but *not, absolutely not*, at the behest of the Other.

Thus, Bielik-Robson rehearses Lacan as a Kabbalist.[55] The first phase of *Ein Sof* or "without limits", or the "not-All", refers to the "undifferentiated state" of primary narcissism – the child fused to the mother in "autistic *jouissance*", the pre-relational "mineness". The second stage, the *Tsimtsum*,[56] God's contraction or exile creating a space for creation. This cut, Lacan associates with the paternal – the first invasion of the Other and its severe judgement leading to the ego ideal. Finally, the Fall into the world of objects with just the shattered remnants of the divine, the *objets a*, amidst wholesale loss by expropriation like the turning of a glove inside out. This third stage is the "breaking of the vessels" (*Sh'virat Ha-Kelim*), unable to contain the explosive power of the divine light, allowing the libido to be squandered in the alienated desire of the Other. But some remnants remain, which cannot be experienced directly because they are part of the original pleroma. The last phase is the connecting of the sparks, the shattered fragments of desire so that they can (re)form the ONE *qua* desire, uniquely one's own unalloyed joy.

Lacan challenges Freud: *I question his God: 'Che vuoi?'*[57] This is the volcanic God's terrifying question: *What does He want from me?* Phantasy is deployed to fill out this anguished void in being. Thence emerges the psychoanalytic question par excellence and Lacan presses its Otherness right back to the Old Testament. Such is His power: *He* is the only One who can say *I Am That I Am* (YHVH), taking all Being for Himself. The question for us remains: how can any of His subjects claim 'I am' too?

A frenzy of (self-)destruction in response is inevitable. Monotheism could be destroyed at this very point. The *Kol Nidre*, the Day of Wrath, signifies the periodic moment of (psychotic) crisis, annulling any vows made to God. The sound of the shofar makes the Israelites tremble in awe, awakening God from His slumber to take up once again His terrifying living presence.

As Bielik-Robson concludes:

> But this awakening happens only in a vertiginous flash. The alliance, which is being renewed, is not struck between the Living God and the Israeli tribe, as the official story goes. It is struck between the Dead/ Murdered God, now only summoned back from the dead for merely a critical moment. For the [rebellious] sons can live only if He does not live any longer ... which is the only "way out" that Judaism invented in order to negotiate the "hatred for God" and his ontological order of the law/ language/being.[58]

We believe that we can only live *without Him* – His contraction (*Tsimtsum*), His tiredness, His weary retreat, His silence - He is a hidden God – *Deus Absconditus*: *Indeed, You are a hidden God, You God of Israel, the Saviour* (Isaiah 45:15). The tired, dejected God of our medieval parable is the God now wandering and lost himself. Maybe, suggests Harold Bloom, 'there are (at least) two *kenomas*, two cosmological emptinesses, our world and 'the wandering God of the Abyss, not only cut off from us, as we are from Him, but as helpless without us as we are without Him'.[59]

God departed in time. Having given His Word and his life, He left, leaving a black hole, an abyss, the desert of the Real, an appalling darkness to which we are here attempting to bear witness. Then there is the Hegelian God who consents to his own *kenosis* thereby encumbering the world with a sense of guilt and a terrible and scandalous loss. One way or another, behind the very fragile scenes we construct, there is this horrendous loss.

The *Tsimtsum* brings about the radical self-limitation of the infinite. Leaving us haunted by radical doubt about the efficacy of the world, recurring disgust about the suffering and evil of human war and greed – World War I, and the Holocaust, the Gulags, the extinctions, and *so on*. There can be *no* safety nets, *no* longer any ontological dependence on the divine, *no* foundation, *no* truth as presence. Remember what Sebald said about the Holocaust? No serious person ever thinks about anything else.[60]

Derrida spoke of, 'The disappearance of the Good-Father-Capital-Sun'.[61] The world thus radically degraded becomes a mere contingent collection of dead fragments in chaotic disarray, with just the broken vessels that contain God's emanative light. It is the end of all Platonic Forms and eternal universals. For those who have the courage to face the dark, for the Gnostic, creation is limited to the sparks of the divine with no guarantee of rekindling the divine fire.

In 1984, the Romanian scholar of religion and magic, Ioan Culianu, declared about a decade before his mysterious murder,

> [G]nostics have taken hold of the whole world, and we were [/*are*] not aware of it. It is a mixed feeling of anxiety and admiration, since I cannot refrain myself from thinking that these alien body-snatchers have done a remarkable job indeed.[62]

For Culianu, this was another moment of high jocularity. In Gnostic thinking the signifier "alien" is overdetermined – our bodies rendered alien, evil, strange, uncanny, other, unknown. Yet, most of us are entirely unaware of our alienated state. We think we know ourselves, are in command and control of our lives!

Overcoming Gnosticism?

Historian and humanities professor Benjamin Lazier suggests that

> Whereas gnosticism's first overcoming was Augustine's work reasserting [Catholic] orthodoxy's hegemony, only a partial success. Its second, and for [philosopher and historian] Hans Blumenberg "final" overcoming was the work of an ethos of human self-assertion best instantiated by the scientific program of Francis Bacon.[63]

However, our hyper-technical and scientific mastery over the world pressed eventually into the service of mass death and ecological destruction during the early and middle part of the last century became a dire existential threat. Hence the wide appeal of Gnosis as trans-mundane and revelatory, a "religion" for the modern and postmodern.

The Gnostic denigration of the world could make any inquiry into the world, any improvement in world conditions, merely a part of the evil genius. Gnosticism is *Entweltlichung*, "deworldification", similar to the unbinding involved in Freud's death drive. Deworldification is 'an evacuation or making-absent from the world. To come loose from the world, *an annihilation of that which binds to the world*'.[64]

Thus, the Gnostic heresy, seemingly overcome at the end of the Middle Ages, surfaced again in interwar Europe. The *third* overcoming of Gnosis, according to Blumenberg, was attempted by the pioneering work on Gnosticism of Hans Jonas, whom he suggests almost defined what is meant today by Gnosis and tried to tie down and thus limit its proliferation of meanings, believing in '*something* rather than nothing' and the possibility of 'transcendence awakened in immanence'.

As Lazier has it, the story outlined by Jonas begins with the Heideggerian, 'ground of Being, or the Divine, [who] chose to give itself over (tzimtzum) to chance and risk endless varieties of becoming'. This avoids the 'troubling questions' around the awful failures of divine providence, and *so on*. The story continues,

> with the "first gyrations of matter", and the advent of transcendence from the "opacity" of purist immanence. Jonas imagined the coming-to-be of an inner worldly transcendence … [which] did not deny God, and still more, discovered traces of an absent divine in the order of worldly things.[65]

Referring to the Holocaust, Jonas declared, 'I believed I owed it to those shadows that something like an answer to their long-gone cry to a silent God be not denied to them'. He was speaking in memory of his mother and Dorothea, the wife of Rabbi Leopold Lucas, on the occasion of receiving the prize in his name in 1984 at Tübingen University. Both women perished in Auschwitz. He chose to talk about God *after* Auschwitz. Not only did God not help the afflicted, *God could not help*, having ceded sovereignty to the world. He adds,

> By forgoing its own inviolateness, the eternal ground allowed the world to be. To this self-denial all creation owes its existence and with it has received all there is to receive from beyond. Having given himself whole to the becoming world, God has no more to give: *it is man's now to give to him*.[66]

Jonas takes as exemplary in this respect Etty Hillesum, a young Dutch Jewess, who when deportations in Holland began in 1942, volunteered to work in the hospital in Westerbork concentration camp, to help fellow Jews, and where she herself died late in 1943. Jonas quotes from her diaries in which she says she does not find God, but constructs God for herself, to whom she makes promises but asks for nothing in return:

> I shall try to help you, God, to stop my strength ebbing away, though I cannot vouch for it in advance. But one thing is becoming increasingly clear to me: that You cannot help us, that we must help You to help ourselves … Alas, there does not seem to be much You Yourself can do about our circumstances, about our lives. Neither do I hold You responsible. You cannot help us, but we must help You and defend Your dwelling place in us to the last.[67]

He compares this to the answer given in the Book of Job which extols God's plenitude of power, whereas Jonas, by contrast, invokes God's voidance of power but in the positive light of "becoming" – as a liberating gift.

As an inversion of premodern orthodoxy, a snatching of victory from the jaws of death-of-God defeat, as it were, the liberating gifts, sparks of the divine are set in the context of the naked truth of the Real, the permanent catastrophe of the destruction of the meaningful cosmos. With this "overcoming" of Gnosis, paradoxically, the crypto-theologists, according again to Bielik-Robson, believe that this 'takes over the whole richness of theological meanings and it will be now the role of the World to answer'.[68]

This different theology of the "hidden God", developed mostly by Walter Benjamin and Gershom Scholem, replaces the "mystery of power" with the "mystery of promise". Therefore, these hidden-God theologies will prevent the world sliding into nihilism; instead, the possibility of a "world regained". For Blumenberg, for instance, a small, a modest Epicurian *Libenswelt*, will require an "active forgetting". The divine becomes dialectical *crypto*-theologically productive of meaning in history – 'all these moments point to a revolutionary break with the Greco-Christian cosmos of the Neoplatonic harmony, *yet without just leaving it in ruins*'.[69]

Instead, it is a world made of infinitely mysterious and unknown singular beings and this mystery is *not* the mystery of power, hierarchy, and omnipotence but the mystery of yet-to-be-fulfilled *promise*. Thus, for Derrida, there is, there remains ultimately, an 'irreducible religiosity ... of promise and justice'.[70] Not harking *back* to the Passion but *forward* to the promise of the future – a radical otherness as open possibility. The hidden God remains as a spectre, a halo, a setting sun as against the '"naked truth" of *factum brutum*'.[71] As against Nancy and Blanchot, for example, where there are no "hiding places" for the dead God.

Death becomes God

However, the ruins still threaten, deworlding continues apace, as the memory of the Passion fades and as the Western world continues to crumble from within and from without. Not so much the "death of God" but the *god of Death* is emerging from the shadows. We will tarry with the negative a little longer.

Just as Basilides has Jesus laughing as another poor wretch (Simon the Cyrene?) takes his place on the cross and was crucified in error,[72] *we* have *The Life of Brian*[73] and *Father Ted*.[74] Are these "blasphemies" yet more mocking laughter at the site/sight of the catastrophic death of Christianity in postmodernity and a quasi-avowal of atheism or Gnosticism?

After all, from the Lacanian-Gnostic point of view, life-enhancing identifications, as seen from the Anglo-American perspective on psychoanalysis – those that accord with enlightenment principles, give life, and open us to the unfolding world and its creativity – are seen by the Gnostics as precisely the opposite – as life-denying, death-dealing alienation. As R.D. Laing used to say, the Stone Age baby meets 20th century living! Massive alienation required. To oppose this and save/retrieve your real unalienated life, as it were, an esoteric language is required – a secret knowledge, accessible to only the very educated few, impossibly obscure, to reveal the new pathway.

Dis-alienation involves embracing the "double negative": the negation of that originary negation of life by the Law of the big Other. And all the while one risks descent into the abyss of meaninglessness and nihilism, beyond our newly confident liberated finitude in which God dwells at some unknown and incommunicable remove.

Some burden for the freed slaves! But one to be enthusiastically and indeed *ethically* enjoined – maybe even enjoyed – but at what cost? A reinvention of the wheel seems required, with God departed, and the baseline is the naked truth of *factum brutum*. At every moment of the day we hear secular prayers – *Live Life*! Every kind of wretched banal positive behavioural command. Celebrate your life! *Your* life – treasure it! Love yourself! Sooth yourself! Discover your beautiful soul within! Shouted with joy over the abyssal void without God.

This was already inscribed within what Žižek refers to as the "perverse core" of Christianity. He cites that pivotal moment with the son of God praying to an absent God in an appalling atheistic moment when Jesus understands that God has forsaken him. In Lacanian terms, at this critical instant, *there is ALREADY no Other*. What dies on the Cross is the big Other, the disintegration of what we believed guaranteed the meaning of our lives. For the Gnostic, this is the good news; it means that you are now radically alone *in freedom from the appalling weight of tradition*.[75] Thus, the only true atheism goes via Christianity and the realisation that *God* died on the Cross and the silence since is just that – SILENCE! Period.

Recall Argentinean writer, Alejandra Pizarnik's haunting words – 'Everything makes love with silence'. Žižek understands *this* song, the song of silence, unsung as it were, unanswered, failed lovemaking, as the radical defeat of all our efforts, as the terrifying noumenal domain of the Real.[76]

Gnosis continued ...

According to a Cathar prayer, 'We are not part of this world and the world is not of us'.[77] The Bogomils of Bosnia, one of the most important heretical movements of the Middle Ages, appealed for the virtues of early Christianity and the Gospels, while rejecting the Old Testament. They taught that to be united with God, they must disregard the material world. They believed that the material world was created by the devil, and they condemned close contact with matter, including eating meat, drinking wine, and marriage. They were praised even by their enemies for their impressive austerity.

The Greek word *kosmos* means order. Therefore, evil must be just a localised affair. Even the Camps in all their horror were set under the beautiful infinity of the stars. Evil on earth in the sensible world is an exception. In Manicheism, for example, the world is a mechanism to liberate, purify, and renew the Light held captive by the world.[78]

Nevertheless, Freud's first theory of anxiety involved an excess of drive and then Lacan suggested that anxiety is the only affect that does not lie,[79] a factor indeed in all neuroses. Similarly, for Gnostics the world is characterised by anguish. 'Pain and anguish cover things like rust covers iron … anguish can become as thick as fog. Anguish is the raw material of the world … the way a plank is made *of* wood'.[80] Anguish is the warp and woof of the world (with no father to provide the "narrow footbridge" between anxiety and death).[81]

No father, no mother, only abandonment. 'The soul is abandoned in the world like an aborted foetus in the formless void'.[82] Tossed or thrown into the world by violent propulsion, shipwrecked, cast up onto the shoreline. The world is *not* our habitat; we are too good for this world.[83] We are the flower on the dung heap of the world.

We should be clear, to refuse the big Other is to sever the connection between the Old Testament and the New; the Law and faith; leaving an austere ultra-Paulinism, an antinomianism, with the link severed between creation and redemption. Thus dualism: creation and flesh become evil created by the demiurge. This is heresy against the orthodoxy of the Catholic Church where fallen creation is redeemed by the overflowing generous willingness of Christ to suffer with us and all creation.

Radicalism is "recovered" in so-called "hot" messianism asserted in different ways by Heidegger, Taubes, Agamben, Badiou, and Žižek. They begin with a blank slate, as it were, and 'the happening of strangeness',[84] and the "double nothing". Being there in *this* world signals that we are between two nothings: the nothing of "thrownness" and the nothing of "projection". As Critchley points out, 'Heidegger insists that Dasein does not load guilt onto itself. *It is in its being already guilty*'.[85] With *no* Covenantal Ground, Heidegger asserts no pre-moral source for any ethics – guilty before the other, as in Levinas, before being able to assume guilt. Thus, uncanniness, anxiety, and dread are registers of naked nullity which is Dasein's "facticity", being's groundless and accidental arrival in the horror of the world. Dasein is, 'called back to its thrownness so as to understand this thrownness as the null basis which it has to take up into existence'.[86] These are the high stakes of authenticity – the authenticity of nothing. Being nothing is what is authentic. Being nothing.

I recall a so-called "Tough Love" video of a weekend workshop for adolescents in trouble. It was confrontative, breaking every defence of the participants, who were reduced to tears as they were forced to confront their pasts in dysfunctional families. On the third day, each participant faced the enigmatic leader of the group.

- Who are you?
- I am … x or y … (through tears)
- No you are not. You are nothing, from nowhere. Nothing.
- Okay. Okay … (trails off)
- What are you?
- Okay, I am nothing. I am nothing.
- What are you? Repeat please.
- Nothing.

- Say, *I am nothing.*
- I am nothing.
- Say, *I am nothing.*
- I am nothing.
- Repeat.

Recall also, Lacan's 'zone between two deaths'.[87] Jacques-Alain Miller refers to the subject who 'discovers in its absolute nakedness the truth of his desire'.[88] Being prepared to die in this life in non-relation to the Symbolic or any idealism, for the sake of desire (authenticity),

> Lacan lauds Oedipus at Colonus who calls down curses before dying, and he associates him with Antigone, walled up alive, who has not given in at all. Both have rejected the right to live in order to enter the "in-between-two-deaths", – *entre-deux-morts* – that is immortality.[89]

In line with the radicalisation of Paul, Lacan excoriates, 'the terrible Father of the primal horde (Freud's *Totem and Taboo*), Luther's God with 'his eternal hatred against men, a hatred that existed even before the world was born'; the Father of the law who, as for St Paul, leads to temptation: "For me, the very commandment – Thou shall not covet – which should lead to life has proved to be death to me. For sin, finding opportunity in the commandment, seduced me and by it killed me"'.[90] The Old Testament Law equals death to life.

Thus, we have arrived at the "God of Death", whose ghostly presence has hovered over the West in its failure to truly overcome Gnosticism. Apparently, it was the German-American philosopher Leo Strauss who remarked on the margin of his copy of *Sein und Zeit* that in Heidegger, unlike in Nietzsche, it is not that God is dead, but *Death herself becomes God*.[91] What we see here is the "divinisation of death" over and very much against the Judeo-Christian Revelation. In Hegel, death fulfils the same traumatic function that Revelation did in shaking the soul in "fear and trembling" in the presence of the transcendent God. With Hegel, it is death who is the absolute Master.

In Lacan's famous formula, desire is the desire (of the desire) of the other. Thus, desire in itself is decentred, i.e. empty – *nothing* but the other's desire, a fight to the death for pure prestige. A fight to the death for recognition by the other. Desire is always the desire for recognition, thus a purely *social* reality. Self-consciousness wants to see itself outside itself, in another self-consciousness. The slave craves recognition from the Master. And the Master craves recognition from the slave and thus dialectically becomes a bit of a slave himself by demanding recognition from what after all he regards as still an animal for his fear of death.

It is the slave who takes the long view of death by turning from the Real, to language, rational thought, and the world of the spirit. As against the Master, who didn't blink when faced with the absolute negativity of death head-on, purifying himself from all earthly attachments. But he now lives in the shadow of death. The slave, in contrast, gradually transforms wild nature into civilisation through work and he becomes human. Death governs the natural world negating singularities, peculiarities, life in itself, and *so on*. The *non*-natural world of spirit – reason, thought, language, and work, and *so on* – performs the same deathly negating function (the symbol is the murder of the thing) but at one remove, by depriving it of life of its particularities and uniqueness, instead creating concepts and universals. Hegel favours the slave in his civilising work together with the possibility of the Christian resurrective capacities of the spirit. The slave matures by "working through" or sublating his traumatic encounter with death.

Since Hegel, the *deathly negating* effect of the spirit, representation, and *so on* has taken centre stage, most noticeably and influentially with Kojève who aligns Hegel with Heidegger: with this death or deadly effect now front and centre. According to Kojève, the slave rather than shunning and deferring death through language, thus progressing history onwards and upwards, as it were, must rather turn around and realise his full *living* life by a fight. He must face death full on. He 'must become a Warrior – that is, he must introduce death into his existence, by consciously and voluntarily risking his life, while knowing that he is mortal'.[92] The slave must become a master or else he just becomes the hated slavish bourgeois, alienated Nietzschean 'Last Man', who has betrayed his desire (Lacan) by remaining inauthentic (Heidegger). Unable to face death, he lives a dead inauthentic life, erroneously believing he is alive.

Kojève reverses Hegel, turning around his ascent to idealism back into the materialist Real, going therefore from the Symbolic to the Real, inspiring a passion for the Real on the radical Left in his French followers from Bataille to Lacan, creating what Bielik-Robson calls a "thanatic strain" with Gnostic overtones:

> [B]y voluntarily accepting the danger of death in a Struggle for pure prestige that Man appears for the first time in the natural World; and it is by resigning himself to death, by revealing it through his discourse, that Man arrives finally at absolute Knowledge or at Wisdom, in thus completing History.[93]

This double negativity – facing death head-on, always preferring the negative – inevitably ends in impasse, paralysis, deadlock – the same existential impasse that Hegel ascribed to the 'stupid and idle' way of life of the Master.

> Nothing works any more, nothing tarries, nothing progresses; everything that would want to emerge from this abyss of negativity, has to be immediately corrected and returned to its neantising matrix, as indeed in the Blanchotian *pas au dela* which is always a *faux pas*, a false step, an error – seemingly out of the night, but in fact always only deeper into the unconquerable *nyx*.[94]

Borsh-Jacobsen summarises the Kojèvian dismissal or deconstruction of the Freudian ego, the self, identity, etc.:

> what is crucial here is Kojève's redefinition of subjectivity in terms of radical negativity … fascination with negativity in all its forms. Indeed, the philosophy of the subject becomes in Kojève's hands a philosophy of negativity, or better, of the subject *as* negativity. Why is that? Because consciousness, in Kojève's "anthropological" reading of Hegel, can be a truly human consciousness only when it negates itself as an animal body, when it accepts to risk its own life for no reason, in a gratuitous "struggle to the death for pure prestige". In other words, the very essence of consciousness is to be found in negativity, death and suicide: quite paradoxically, the Kojèvian [Lacanian] subject becomes a subject only when it vanishes, when it negates itself in order to be something *other* than it is. Hence the themes of death, of the Other, of desire, of desire of the desire of the Other, of lack-of-being, of absence-to-self, of transgression and so forth – themes that have literally dominated the French philosophical scene ever since.[95]

As is well known, this was a strategic move by Lacan to secure the future of psychoanalysis within the intellectual elite in his alleged "return to Freud". The subject is empty, discovered only via the other, ex-posed, the ego an illusion, and *so on*. To paraphrase the well-known phrase from Marx – all that was apparently solid melted into air – Freud's substantial claims are emptied of content, not least by Borsh-Jacobsen himself, who, contra Lacan, favoured a return to hypnosis and the early Freud.

Becoming mainstream

Thus, radical Christianity which rejects the Old Testament, rejects Sinai and the Law, linked with Žižekian–Lacan with his privileging of the death drive as the lighter fuel for the radical fight of our lives against alienating bourgeois capitalist consumption, is moving at some speed from the academic margins to the mainstream. The new generation of opinion formers and influencers are now well schooled in intersectional politics and activism, pushing at all the open doors of defeated, exhausted, cowardly conservatism that will conserve only nothing. The "solid hatred of being" can be openly declared in myriad ways without fear. And the rage seems to be endless.

> Let the cities burn!
> Defund the Police
> Silence is violence
> Heads bashed bloody against the Great Wall of Steel[96]
> Whiteness – a malignant, parasitic-like condition[97]
> Exterminate all the brutes[98]

Salt water has replaced Zyklon B[99]
Humans are biohazards, machines are not[100]
Human-*less*, contact-*less* technology
The Decomposition Directive[101]
Our souls are dead[102]
Insult. Ignore. Incite[103]
Your vote was a hate crime[104]
Zio tears replenish my electrolytes![105]
Divine violence against mythological violence[106]

However, Critchley could not be clearer when he says that *with Paul we do not escape the law*:

> If the law was not fully within me, as the awareness of my fallenness and consciousness of sin, then faith as the overcoming of the law would mean nothing ... [if] we throw out the Old Testament, then we attempt to throw away our thrownness and imagine that we can distance ourselves from the constitutive flaw of the law, from our ontological defectiveness ... [imagining] ourselves perfected without stain or sin.[107]

According to the Jewish Halakha, it is the law that helps us to walk. According to Rémi Brague, the law set out in the Torah enables us to *be*, to properly be. Those who do not obey the higher law fall victim to a lower law. By way of an example, those who do not obey the laws of figure skating, fall, and are forced to obey the lesser law of gravity. **In abandoning the law of reason, one falls under the law of nature**.

Likewise with Kant, if we renounce moral law, we admit the law of penchants, i.e. the pathological.[108] There is a Freudian version. Those who do not heed the reasonableness of the moral law, will fall under the irrational "law" of the superego. Thirdly, failing to conform to the control of the superego, they will fall prey to the law of the Kleinian mirror of the id, namely the archaic tyrannical superego.

The law can only be transcended if we firstly identify our self-centred phantasies and how they arose in childhood, then surrender each in turn using the law as our guide, in this way to become truly free from the law. As Milbank suggests: 'St. Paul first of all in history proposed a step beyond a divided subjectivity in thrall at once to the law, and by the same token to its own obsessions and illusions'.[109] The law is our most precious guide. There is no other way to identify our demons.

★★★

Melancholia (Lars von Trier) is billed as a 'beautiful film about the end of the world'. The film is set in a remote chateau where Justine (Kirsten Dunst) and her husband arrive two hours late for their elegant wedding reception, hosted by Justine's sister Claire (Charlotte Gainsbourg) and her rich husband John

(Kiefer Sutherland). Justine's melancholy dreamy sadness indicates that she is not really present for the occasion. Her estranged parents played by Charlotte Rampling and John Hurt add to the *Festen*-like atmosphere of the party. The wedding is a fiasco, with family tensions mounting and relationships fraying. And all the while, the planet Melancholia is ominously on track to collide with Earth. It is Claire, supposedly the calm sister, who succumbs to panic; for Justine, the apocalypse will be a relief – 'the world is an evil place'. The film is haunted by the melancholy mood, symbolised by the slow-moving hallucinatory montage of moonlit images set out at the beginning in the slow-motion characteristic of depression. We know that many in the world are indeed affected by what used to be called melancholia; this condition and the world have already collided! Maybe, therefore, we should regard the film as an allegory for mankind's silent extinction.

Notes

1 Steiner, G. 1961, pp. 352–353.
2 Ibid.
3 Nietzsche, F. 1882, pp. 181–182.
4 God as the intelligent watchmaker was first suggested by William Paley in 1802. In Richard Dawkins use of the analogy, he is blind. See Dawkins, R. 1986.
5 Nietzsche, F. 1882.
6 In Amis, M. 2002, p. 247.
7 Fraser, G. 2014.
8 Baudrillard, J. 2002, p. 6.
9 Baudrillard, J. 1994, p. 4, emphasis added.
10 Referred to at length in Chapter 5.
11 Fitzgerald, S. 1926, p. 170.
12 Levinas, E. 1963b, pp. 345–359.
13 Brague, R. 2013, p. 85.
14 Ibid., p. 86.
15 Ibid., p. 89.
16 Pascal, B. 1670, p. 89.
17 Ibid., p. 88.
18 Ibid., p. 90.
19 Cited by Brague, R. 1999, p. 191.
20 Rasmussen, D. 2017.
21 Brague, R. 1999, 192.
22 Ibid., p. 192.
23 Part of the translation by Erika Casey comes from Casey E. and Casey T. (eds) 1992.
24 Brague, R. 1999, op. cit., p. 192.
25 Levinas, E. in Hand, S. 1989, pp. 192–193.
26 Bielik-Robson, A. 2014, p. 13.
27 Ibid., p. 12.
28 Ibid., p. 4.
29 Žižek, S. 2006, p. 187.
30 Žižek, S. 1997–2001.
31 Brague, R 1999, pp. 113–114.
32 Levinas, E. in Kolitz, Z. 1995, pp. 27–32. https://web.ics.purdue.edu/~akantor/readings/levinas_love_the%20_torah.pdf.
  Also, In Levinas, E. 1963a, 143.

33 Schwartz, R. in Davis, C., Milbank, J., and Žižek, S. 2005, p. 121.
34 Ibid., pp. 122. She also adds: 'When reformers gave up the doctrine of transubstantiation (even as they held onto revised forms of the Eucharist), they lost a doctrine that infuses all materiality, spirituality, and signification with the presence of God'. Schwartz, R. 2008, back-cover summary.
35 Steiner, G. 1971, p. 37.
36 Ibid. in translation.
37 Ibid., p. 38.
38 Ibid., p. 41.
39 Ibid., p. 43.
40 Ibid., pp. 44–45.
41 Ibid., p. 46.
42 Cunningham, C. in Davis, C., Milbank, J., and Žižek, S. (eds) 2005, p. 96.
43 Williams, M.A. 1996, p. 116.
44 Gray, J. 2018, p. 73.
45 Lacan, J. 1953, in Lacan, J. 1970, p. 260.
46 Lacan, J. 1960, in Lacan, J. 1970, p. 694.
47 Lacan, J. 1972–1973, p. 99.
48 Bion, W. 1967, p. 101. Extending Freud's notion of coming upon an ancient civilisation, 'we were exposing evidence not so much of a primitive civilisation as of a primitive disaster'.
49 According to the Congregation for the Doctrine of the Faith: 'In general, the Gnostics believed that salvation is obtained through an esoteric knowledge or *gnosis*. Such *gnosis* reveals to the Gnostic his or her true essence, i.e., a spark of the divine Spirit that lives inside him or her, which has to be liberated from the body, which is extraneous to his or her true humanity. Only in this manner, the Gnostic returns to his or her original being in God, from whom he or she was alienated due to a primordial fall ... [H]ow could it be possible for the salvation mediated by the Incarnation of Jesus, his life, death and Resurrection in his true body, to come to us, if the only thing that mattered were liberating the inner reality of the human person from the limits of the body and the material, as described by the neo-Gnostic vision?' https://www.vatican.va/roman_curia/congregations/cfaith/documents/rc_con_cfaith_doc_20180222_placuit-deo_en.html#_ftn6.
50 Bielik-Robson, A. 2019, pp. 21–22.
51 Lacan, J. 1977, pp. 104–105.
52 Bielik-Robson, A. 2019, p. 22.
53 Taubes, J. 2004, p. 103.
54 Bielik-Robson 2019, op. cit., p. 28.
55 Ibid., p. 31ff.
56 *Tsimtsum* is a term used in Isaac Luria's Kabbalistic doctrine that God began the process of creation by "contracting", to allow for a conceptual space in which finite and seemingly independent realms could exist.
57 Lacan, J. 1958–1959. 19 November 1958.
58 Bielik-Robson, A. 2019, pp. 38–39.
59 Bloom, H. 1996, p. 244.
60 Cited in Amis, M. 2020, p. 306.
61 Derrida, J. 1981, p. 165.
62 Cited by Lazier, B. 2003, p. 619.
63 Ibid., p. 620. See also Blumenberg, H. 1966.
64 Jonas cited on p. 623. Italics added.
65 Lazier, B. 2008, pp. 61–62.
66 Jonas, H. 1984, p. 12 italics added.
67 Ibid., pp. 12–13, n8. Jonas is citing Ascherson, N. 1984, pp. 8–12, esp. 9.
68 Bielik-Robson, A. 2020. In Styfhals, W. and Symons, S. (eds) 2020, p. 66.

69 Ibid., p. 68, italics added.
70 Derrida, J. 1999, p. 234.
71 Bielik-Robson, A. 2020. In Styfhals, W. and Symons, S. (eds) 2020, p. 70.
72 Kelhoffer, J. 2014, p. 80.
73 A British Monty Python film, directed by Terry Jones, satirising the life of Jesus, made in 1979.
74 A very popular British Channel 4 sitcom (1995–1998) satirising the priests and nuns of the Irish Catholic Church, created by Irish writers Graham Linehan and Arthur Mathews.
75 It is worth remembering that for Chesterton, on the contrary, this is the unparalleled *strength* of Christianity. It can contain this atheistic core at the most perilous moment in Christ's life.
76 Žižek, S. 2006, p. 155.
77 Cited in Brague, R. 1999, p. 83.
78 Ibid., p. 64.
79 See Harari, R. 2001, p. 105.
80 Brague, R. 1999, p. 67.
81 See Chapter 2.
82 Basilides cited in Brague, R. 1999, p. 68.
83 Ibid., p. 69.
84 Heidegger, M. 1959, p. 158.
85 Critchley, S. 2012, p. 193. Italics added.
86 Heidegger, M. 1962, p. 287.
87 Lacan, J. 1959–1960, p. 320.
88 See J.-A. Miller's commentary on Seminar 7. Miller, J.-A. 1986.
89 Ibid.
90 Ibid.
91 Bielik-Robson, A. 2015, p. 2.
92 Kojève cited in Bielik-Robson, A. 2015, p. 6.
93 Kojève, A. 1973, p. 124.
94 Bielik-Robson, A. 2015, p. 9.
95 Cited in Oakley, C. 1995, p. 428.
96 President Xi indicating the fate of opponents in a speech celebrating the centenary of the Chinese Communist Revolution. 'Anyone who dares try to [bully China] will have their heads bashed bloody against the Great Wall of Steel forged by over 1.4 billion Chinese people'. July 2021. https://www.bbc.com/news/world-asia-china-57648236.
97 Moss, D. 2021.
98 *Exterminate All the Brutes*. Raoul Peck on HBO. April 2021.
99 "Labour Momentum Speaker Franco Berardi and the New Nazis", posted at Harry's Place 23 September 2018. Now deleted.
100 Anuja Sonalker on self-driving cars.
101 Briefly, the "Disintegration Directive", also known as the "Decomposition Directive" (officially *Richtlinie* 1/76 or the *Zersetzung*) was the approach that the East German secret police (the *Stasi*) took from 1976 onwards to crush dissent. Less severe and controversial than the earlier prison and Gulag methods.
  https://threadreaderapp.com/thread/1373761707500257280.html.
102 Haitiwaji, G. and Marchadour, E. 2021.
103 Provocation of the deplorables after the Trump defeat. 17 November 2020.
104 Spray-painted on the Jefferson Davis Monument during anti-Trump protests: wp.me/p5hgNQ-1l4N #RVA. 983. 369 Comments.
105 "Chicago Dyke March Uses Neo-Nazi Slur for Jews".
  www.israelnationalnews.com/News/News.aspx/232534.
106 See Benjamin, W. 1978, p. 300.
107 Critchley, S. 2012, p. 203.

108 Brague, R. 2009, pp. 11, 12.
109 Milbank, J. 2005. "Materialism and Transcendence" in Davis, C., Milbank, J. and Žižek, S. 2005, p. 421.

References

Amis, M. 2002. *Koba the Dread*. London: Jonathan Cape.

Amis, M. 2020. *Inside Story*. London: Jonathan Cape.

Ascherson, N. 1984. "In Hell". *New York Review of Books* 31, no. 13, July 19, 8–12.

Baudrillard, J. 1994. *Simulacra and Simulation*. Trans. Glaser, S. F.. Ann Arbor: University of Michigan Press.

Baudrillard, J. 2002. *The Spirit of Terrorism*. Trans. Turner, C. London and New York: Verso.

Benjamin, W. 1978. *Reflections: Essays, Aphorisms, Autobiographical Writings*. Trans. Jephcott, E. New York: Schocken Books.

Bielik-Robson, A. 2014. "The Antinomian Symptom: Lévinas's Divine Comedy of Violence". https://www.academia.edu/29174083/The_Antinomian _Symptom_Lévinas_s_Divine_Comedy_of_Violence

Bielik-Robson, A. 2015. "The thanatic strain. Kojève and Rosenzweig as two readers of Hegel". Routledge: *Journal for Cultural Research* 19, no. 3, 274–290. http://dx.doi.org /10.1080/14797585.2015.1021990

Bielik-Robson, A. 2019. "Solid Hatred Addressed to Being: Lacan's Gnostic Uses of Judaism". In Tourage, M., Valentini, P. (Eds.) 2019, 15–46. https://www.academia .edu/42653995/_Solid_Hatred_Addressed_to_Being_Lacan_s_Gnostic_Uses_of _Judaism.

Bielik-Robson, A. 2020. in Styfhals, W., Symons, S. (Eds) 2020. "The God of Myth is not Dead – Modernity and its Cryptotheologies". 51–80. https://www.academia.edu /41943391/_The_God_of_Myth_Is_Not_Dead_Modernity_and_Its_Cryptotheologies _A_Jewish_Perspective

Bion, W. 1967. *Second Thoughts. Selected Papers on Psycho-Analysis*. London: Maresfield.

Bloom, H. 1996. *Omens of the Millennium*. New York: Riverhead Books.

Bloomberg, H. 1966. *The Legitimacy of the Modern Age*. Trans. Wallace, R. Cambridge, MA: The MIT Press.

Brague, R. 1999. *The Wisdom of the World. The Human Experience of the Universe in Western Thought*. Trans. Fagan, T. Chicago and London: University of Chicago Press, 2003.

Brague, R. 2009. *The Legend of the Middle Ages*. Trans. Cochran, L. Chicago and London: University of Chicago Press.

Brague, R. 2013. *On the God of the Christians*. Indiana: St Augustine Press.

Casey, E., Casey, T. (Eds.). 1992. *Jean-Paul. A Reader*. John Hopkins Press. http://50watts .com/Jean-Paul-Speech-of-the-Dead-Christ

Critchley, S. 2012. *Faith of the Faithless. Experiments in Political Theology*. London and New York: Verso.

Cunningham, C. 2005. "Nothing Is, Something Must Be: Lacan and Creation from No One". In Davis, C., Millbank, J., Zizek, S. (Eds.) *Theology and the Political*. Durham and London: Duke University Press, 72–101.

Davis, C., Millbank, J., Zizek, S. 2005. *Theology and the Political*. Durham and London: Duke University Press.

Derrida, J. 1981. *Dissemination*. Trans. Johnson, B.. Chicago: University of Chicago Press.

Derrida, J. 1999. "Marx & Sons". In Sprinker, M. (Ed.) *Ghostly Demarcations: A Symposium on Jacques Derrida's "Specters of Marx"*. London: Verso, 1999.

Dworkins, R. 1986. *The Blind Watchmaker: Why the Evidence of Evolution Reveals a Universe without Design*. London: Norton & Co.

Fitzgerald, S. 1926. *The Great Gatsby*. London and New York: Penguin Books, 1990

Fraser, G. 2014. "Nietzsche's passionate atheism was the making of me". *The Guardian*, February 5th. https://www.theguardian.com/commentisfree/2012/feb/05/passionate-atheism-me-christianity-nietzsche

Grey, J. 2018. *Seven Types of Atheism*. London: Penguin Random House.

Haitiwaji, G and Marchadour, E. 2021. "'Our Souls Are Dead': How I Survived a Chinese 'Re-education' Camp for Uighurs". *Guardian*, Jan 12. https://www.theguardian.com/world/2021/jan/12/uighur-xinjiang-re-education-camp-china-gulbahar-haitiwaji

Hand, S. 1989. *The Levinas Reader*. Oxford: Blackwell.

Harari, R. 2001. *Lacan's Seminar on "Anxiety". An Introduction*. Trans. Lamb-Ruiz, J. New York: Other Press.

Heidegger, M. 1959. *Introduction to Metaphysics*. Trans. Manheim, R.. New Haven: Yale University Press.

Heidegger, M. 1962. *Being and Time*. Trans. Macquarrie, J., Robinson, E.. Oxford: Blackwell.

Jonas, H. 1984. "The Concept of God after Auschwitz: A Jewish Voice" *The Journal of Religion*, 67, no. 1 (Jan., 1987), pp. 1–13 Chicago: The University of Chicago Press. http://www.jstor.org/stable/1203313

Kojève, A. 1973. "The Idea of Death in the Philosophy of Hegel". Complete Text of the Last Two Lectures of the Academic Year 1933–1934. Trans. Carpino, J. J. *Interpretation. A Journal of Political Philosophy* 3/2, no. 3, 114–156. https://interpretationjournal.com/wp-content/uploads/2018/02/Vol_3-2-and-3-3_Kojeve_The-Idea-of-death-in-the-Philosophy-of-Hegel.pdf

Kolitz, Z. 1995. *Yossel Rakover Speaks to God: Holocaust Challenges to Religious Faith*. New Jersey: KTAV Publishing House Inc.

Kelhoffer, J. 2014. *Conceptions of "Gospel" and Legitimacy in Early Christianity*. Tübingen: Mohr Siebeck.

Lacan, J., 1953. "The Function and Field of Speech and Language in Psychoanalysis". In Lacan, J. (Ed.) *Ecrits. The First Complete Edition in English*. London and New York: W.W. Norton, 197–268.

Lacan, J. 1958–1959. *Seminar 6. Desire and its Interpretation*. Trans. Gallagher, C. Dublin. http://www.lacaninireland.com/web/wp-content/uploads/2010/06/THE-SEMINAR-OF-JACQUES-LACAN-VI.pdf

Lacan, J. 1959-1960. *Seminar 7. The Ethics of Psychoanalysis*. Paris: Les Édition du Seuil, 1986. Trans. Porter, D. London: Routledge. 1992.

Lacan, J. 1960. "The Subversion of the Subject and the Dialectic of Desire in the Freudian Unconscious". In Lacan, J. (Ed.) *Ecrits. The First Complete Edition in English*. London and New York: W.W. Norton, 671–702.

Lacan, J., 1970. *Ecrits. The First Complete Edition in English*. Trans. Fink, B. London and New York: W.W. Norton, 2002.

Lacan, J. 1972–1973. *The Seminar 20. Encore: On Feminine Sexuality, the Limits of Love and Knowledge*. Fink, B. (Ed.) London: W.W. Norton & Co. 1998.

Lacan, J. 1977. *Écrits: A Selection*. Trans. Sheridan, A. London: Tavistock Publications.

Lazier, B. 2003. "Overcoming Gnosticism: Hans Jonas, Hans Blumenberg, and the Legitimacy of the Natural World". *Journal of the History of Ideas* 64, no. 4, 669–670.

Lazier, B. 2008. *God Interrupted: Heresy and the European Imagination between the World Wars.* Princetown and Oxford: Princetown University Press.

Levinas, E. 1963a. *Difficult Freedom. Essays on Judaism.* Trans. Hand, S. Baltimore: John Hopkins University Press.

Levinas, E. 1963b. "The Trace of the Other". In Lingis, A., (Trans.) *Tijdschrift voor Philosophie.* Chicago and London: University of Chicago Press, 345–359.

Millbank, J. 2005. "Materialism and Transcendence". In Davis, C., Millbank, J., Zizek, S. 2005. *Theology and the Political.* Durham and London: Duke University Press, 393–426.

Miller, J.-A. 1986. "The Seminars of Jacques Lacan". https://www.lacan.com/seminars2.htm

Moss, D. 2021. "On Having Whiteness". *Journal of the American Psychoanalytic Association* 69, 355–371. https://doi.org/10.1177/00030651211008507

Nietzsche, F. 1882. *The Gay Science.* para. 125. Kaufmann, W. (Ed.). New York: Vintage, 1974.

Oakley, C. 1995. "Mikkel Borch-Jacobsen Talks to Chris Oakley". *Free Associations* 5, no. 4, 423–452.

Pascal, B. 1670. *Pensees.* Trans. Krailsheimer. A. New York and London: Penguin Classics, 1966.

Rasmussen, D. 2017. *The Infidel and the Professor: David Hume, Adam Smith, and the Friendship that Shaped Modern Thought.* Princetown and Oxford: Princetown University Press.

Schwartz, R. in Davis, C., Milbank, J., Zizek, S. 2005. *Theology and the Political.* Durham and London: Duke University Press.

Schwartz, R. 2008. *Sacramental Poetics at the Dawn of Secularism.* California: Stanford University Press.

Steiner, G. 1961. *The Death of Tragedy.* London: Faber and Faber.

Steiner, G. 1971. *In Bluebeard's Castle. Some Notes towards the Redefinition of Culture.* New Haven: Yale University Press.

Styfhals, W., Symons, S. (Eds.) 2020. *In Genealogies of the Secular. The Making of Modern German Thought.* Albany, NY: State University of New York.

Taubes, J. 2004. *The Political Theology of Paul.* Trans. Holänder, D. Stanford: Stanford University Press.

Tourage, M., Valentini, P. (Eds.). 2019. *Esoteric Lacan.* London: Rowman & Littlefield.

Williams, M.A. 1996. *Rethinking "Gnosticism": An Argument for Dismantling a Dubious Category.* Princetown University Press.

Zizek, S. 1997–2001. "Only a Suffering God Can Save Us". http://www.lacan.com/zizshadowplay.html#_ftn13

Žižek, S. 2006. *The Parallax View.* Cambridge, MA: The MIT Press.

9   The Irreducible Datum

This chapter considers the "fatal strategies" (Baudrillard) of the death drive that Lacan makes the aim of his clinic. The bad omens of today and of more than a century ago (World War I) act as the backdrop. According to Lacan, subjected to the automatisms of the Symbolic and the drive itself, we are "written-off", crushed from the beginning. Masochism is key – "the first phase of misery". Furthermore, consider the myth of the lamella, 'creeping over your face' (Lacan/Žižek) and the "Body without Organs" (Deleuze). Technological rationality is the death drive at work in modernity. There are two conceptions of the death drive in psychoanalysis. 1) Freud–Klein version: death drive as merely destructive pathology, extending to biological apoptosis – human cells die when isolated. 2) The radicalism of Lacan and the French Left: *there is nothing outside the text*. Therefore, the Lacanian challenge is: find desire; find *your* life – *demand the impossible*! But Roudinesco warns the Lacanians about their "inhumanity".

Recall Philip Larkin's poem[1] about the young men, taking such care to leave the gardens tidy that summer, and their *innocence*, ahead of what was soon to be the Original Sin, or the Primal Scene of the century. As Furedi has it, '[t]he traumatic upheavals unleashed during the course of this four-year-long conflict (WW1) called into question the moral and intellectual premises of Western culture and civilisation. For many, the war served as the ultimate symbol of moral exhaustion and Western decline'.[2] The out-workings of this demoralisation and decline will be traced out below under the twin headings of guilt and the (Lacanian) celebration of desire.

In August 1914, Kafka began writing *The Trial*, the same month that the Great War started. According to George Steiner, 'Kafka prophesied the actual forms of the disaster of Western humanism which Nietzsche and Kierkegaard had seen like an uncertain blackness on the horizon'.[3] And in his essay, "The Great Ennui", Steiner looks at the confident, liberal century *before* the Great War as the *source* of the inhuman: 'the crises of our own time that compel a redefinition of culture, are to be found in the long peace of the nineteenth

DOI: 10.4324/9781003225010-11

century … at the heart of the complex fabric of civilisation'.[4] And are we not in roughly the same position today after the long period of peace in Europe at least since 1945, lulled into a false sense of security with two generations at least who have not known war first-hand? The storm clouds of the political extremes are gathering again accelerated by the de-sublimative effects of the (un)social media.

On being written-off

The well-known Lacanian cliché about the death drive, 'Have you acted in conformity with the desire that is in you?',[5] Lacan tells us is a "last judgement" on your life. 'The only thing you can be guilty of is having given ground to your desire'. There is ethical purity here – conforming to desire and not compromising or ceding ground at all. Are you ready to die for your desire?

However, this *guilt* at having given ground to your desire has another older meaning of course – guilt at having given ground, or yielded, to desire – being led astray by desire as sin or temptation to sin, recalling the universal myth of the Fall. Wrong turns taken, and, today, the wrong turns are proliferating with new "hate crimes" and unknown, yet to be discovered, "sins". One way or another desire is at the centre of ethics.

We are no longer called upon to sacrifice our lives tragically for anything anymore – for God, our country, or our own desire. Today's is a hedonistic ideology – suit yourself; be yourself. Your goal is happiness, grabbing pleasure wherever you can get it. However, desire – pure desire – irrupts, interrupts, destroys – you only have *one* life, one destiny. Ask an old left-wing politician who has made too many compromises over the years with the status quo in order to stay in power: is *this* what you fought for in your youth – cutting welfare to pay off the national debt? Haven't you ceded too much? Or, maybe there is the unbearable question that poses itself, as you lie awake restless in the early hours: what have you done with your life? Has it been worthwhile? As Lacan says, this giving ground, 'is always accompanied by in the destiny of the subject *by some betrayal*'.[6] For Lacan, this is the *ethical* question. Maybe, you have ceded to the demands of others, i.e. betrayed your own singular desire? And Lacan makes his opposition to Aristotle clear; there will always be a bourgeois compromise with power.

In the context of the secular postmodern, all is radical uncertainty and pure accident – quantum physics, Bohr, Heisenberg, relativity – indeterminacy at the infinitesimal level leading to the radically chaotic nature of the Real, beyond the traditional laws of nature. The self is a fetishistic illusion; there is no self awaiting realisation. To coin that wonderful phrase from Kundera, this is "the unbearable lightness of being". Being that is so incredibly free. '[T]he absolute absence of burden causes man to be lighter than air, to soar into heights, take leave of the earth and his earthly being, and become only half real, his movements as free as they are insignificant'.[7]

Maybe such lightness or dizziness caused Catherine Millot to worry for Lacan for an instant:

We had climbed to the summit of Etna. At the edge of the huge crater among the gas and smoke, I suddenly became anxious and overwhelmed at the crazy idea that he might throw himself in, as Empedocles had done and pull me with him.[8]

By contrast, recall the old psychoanalytic joke[9] about the terribly anxious man who was preoccupied with himself because he was convinced he was just a grain or a seed. He went to a psychiatrist who convinced him after many sessions that he was really a man not a seed. He left the psychiatrist's office pleased to have his real identity as a man stabilised. He strolled along the street until he met a chicken. In panic he ran back to the psychiatrist's office in a state of near collapse, shouting at the psychiatrist – 'Okay, I know, I know, that I am a man, *but does the chicken know?*'

The joke needs updating. There are allegedly no longer any chickens to fear or avoid on the one hand, and the grain, on the other hand, is not obligated in any way to become a man. Whatever he wants to be must conform only to the desire that is in him, i.e. have nothing to do with any repressive normalisation as a man. His analyst might say these days it is safe to live as a grain or a seed in an equal, inclusive, pluralist world with all traditional chickens consigned to history.

To continue the Lacanian deployment:

> The ultimate lesson of psychoanalysis is that human life is never "just life": humans are not simply alive, they are possessed by the strange drive to enjoy life in excess, passionately attached to a surplus which sticks out and derails the ordinary [normative] run of things.[10]

The key word is "drive". Its strangeness consists in its tendency to fixate and get stuck and circulate around a particular object seemingly forever – the repetition compulsion – ultimately a very conservative pointless repetition, very often observed as being caught in a loop of guilt and pain. No longer a passionate metonymical search for the (lost) object of desire, but often being caught prematurely in *loss* itself and the seeming endlessness of it due to the libidinisation of the loss and pain that spells a life of suffering which is excessive and immune to relief. Thus, instead of translating Freud's *Wiederholungszwang* as repetition compulsion, Lacan prefers repetition *automatism* to avoid any psychological overtones. Lacan's stance is about the structuring effect of the Symbolic order: 'it turns out that the symbolic order can no longer be conceived of there as constituted or created by man but must rather be conceived of as constituting him'.[11]

Thus, the death drive with its automatism comes from some structuralist "beyond"; it is thus determining of human nature rather than determined by human motivation however extreme. Thus, the subject seems compelled via the authoritarian operations of the signifier. The subject is always already de-natured and automated. Maybe a way of detecting the operation of the death drive *clinically* is the degree to which the subject *seems* automated or robotic in his speech and behaviours. Clearly this Lacanian approach represents a move against Freud's 'paganism' – the alleged cosmic conflict between the life and the death instincts.[12] According to Žižek, 'there is only one drive, the libido, striving for enjoyment, and the "death drive" is the curved [repetitive] space of its formal structure'.[13] There is an excess of negativity peculiar or unique to human existence, a kind of basic fault of self-sabotaging. The death drive is the name of a basic malfunction, the stickiness of the drive. But also, 'humans are not simply alive, but possessed by a strange drive to enjoy life to excess of the ordinary run of things – and "death" stands simply and precisely for the dimension beyond "ordinary" biological life'.[14] Lacan says as much, 'It is not a perversion of instinct, but rather a desperate affirmation of life that in its purest form we can find of the death instinct'.[15] This Kantian shaking off the human with all of its compromises to prevent a greater evil is reflected in the chorus at the beginning of Anouilh's *Antigone*. 'The machine is in perfect order; it has been oiled ever since time began, and it runs without friction. Death, treason and sorrow are on the march'.[16]

Thus, the ordinary harmony and homeostasis of the pleasure-reality principle oscillation of everyday life has something of the same repetitive nature of the death drive – the nine-to-five job, the pension after 40 years in the rat-race, etc. – against the exuberant *real life* of living (dangerously) – the ethical act of striking out for freedom, not counting the cost; as per the 1968 slogan: "*Soyons Réalistes, Demandons L'Impossible*" ("Let's be realists, demand the impossible").

There is some foundational ontological fault, like the gap in the order of Being, which enables the subject to be. Lacanians understand the death drive as a violent striking out for freedom, against the clamour of the Real, clearing a space for the act of creation *ex nihilo*. As we have said, the death drive as "freedom" is the high point of a Lacanian analysis. The death drive is not (necessarily) the blind pointless will to self-destruction, but the violent energy required for the (revolutionary) Act-Event to blast a way through an ontological stasis. As Zupančič makes clear, 'After the act I am not the same as before. In the act the subject is annihilated and subsequently reborn'.[17] Something or some act breaks the One of the smooth peaceful sea of Nirvana. Something emerges from the One nothing – the drive – contrasted with the tedious "wheel of life". Authentic human autonomy is a life that exceeds life beyond measure, an anti-adaptational seizing of the day. As Alejandra Pizarnik says of the singularity of her poetry, 'Like every profoundly subversive act, poetry avoids everything but its own freedom and its own truth'.[18]

Likewise, the view of the most ardent Brexiteer staking everything on the sovereignty of Britain? Desire, authentic national autonomy, emerging out of the immovability and confident elitism of the EU, surely the Brexit vote is a good example of the near suicidal ethical Act. There will be no more business as usual.

Business as usual is the repetition compulsion of, let us say for example, the Remainers, stuck in the inexorability of Symbolic order. The compulsion to continue in the same old way, Lacan would call, 'the mask of the symbolic order'.[19] After all, the signifier as such, 'whose first purpose is to bar the subject, has brought into him the meaning of death … This is why every drive is virtually a death drive'.[20] And that is why there is a certain fatality in the "declinist" view of Britain's position. There is no way out but to stay in.

Primarily, Lacan links suicide with narcissism – 'the terms death instinct and primary masochism – depend in my view, on the fact that man's death, long before it is reflected … in his thinking, is experienced by him in the earliest phase of misery that he goes through', birth, prematurity, and weaning. Lacan continues, 'Thanks to Freud we can think of them as expressing the first vibration of the stationary wave of renunciations that scand the history of psychical development'.[21] He continues, 'we see the primordial ego, as essentially alienated, linked to the first sacrifice as essentially suicidal. In other words here we see the fundamental structure of madness'.[22] The subject is crushed from the beginning long before he knows it.

The ominous "first vibration" was noted by Freud who observed his grandson's repetitive game, where the child makes an object appear then disappear repeatedly, accompanied by the fort/da phonemes. '[T]he child thus begins to become engaged in the system of the concrete discourse of those around him by reproducing…his *Fort!* and *Da!*"[23] Lacan rejects what he calls the outdated notion of primary masochism being used, 'to explain repetitive games [in general] in which subjectivity simultaneously masters its dereliction', seeing in it rather, 'the moment at which … the child is born into language … Thus the symbol first manifests itself as the killing of the thing',[24] the birth of the Symbolic order. Thus, vital being is overwritten by the signifier or the Symbolic chain, which precedes him and lasts long after his death. The Symbolic is more deathly than mere biological death. We are written-off while we are alive. It is a blind automatism. Žižek points to the radical nature of this postmodern discourse: 'an animal excoriated by an insatiable parasite (reason, logos, language)'.[25] Thus, the death drive operates from *beyond*, hollowing out being, the being of an animal no less.

Every drive presses beyond satisfaction, need, and ordinary pleasure, and tilts towards the excess which Lacanians call *jouissance*. Paradoxically, *jouissance* in turn threatens the Symbolic whose deathly negation created it and could yet destabilise it and destroy it. Any conceptual contradiction/confusion about the death drive is covered by the unconscious where opposites can coexist; to the extent of an apparent *reversal* of the life and death drives. What we ordinarily thought (in our allegedly alienated state) was giving life, normal life, was on this register *giving death*! What we thought was utterly destructive was in truth the bursting through of life risking everything.

Lacan summarises Freud's grim Real: 'it is explicitly around masochism, conceived only in the dimension of the search for this ruinous jouissance, that Freud's entire text revolves'.[26] As Lacan has it,

> this [*jouissance*] dimension is introduced as soon as the historical chain is isolated, and the history presents itself as something memorable and memorized in the Freudian sense, namely something that is registered in the signifying chain and dependent on its existence.[27]

Thus the Symbolic, machinic process engenders the dangerous surplus that could turn around and destroy it. The death drive is not just found in the signifier but also in what might destroy it. This underlines Freud's claim that the death drive is omnipresent, in for instance the superego *and* the id, as the former borrows its energy from the latter.

For true adherents, the death drive acquires a mythical status, especially with the notion of the lamella and its asexual undeadness inspired by the endlessly replicating Protista whose substance never dies.

> Let us imagine it, a large crepe moving about like the amoeba, ultra-flat for passing under doors, omniscient in being led by pure instinct, immortal in being scissiparous. Here is something you would not like to feel creeping over your face, silently while you are asleep, in order to seal it up.[28]

Or as Žižek says, 'flayed, skinned body, the palpitation of raw, skinless red flesh'.[29] Lacan contrasts this eternal life of the lamella with the finite life of sexual beings, who, from the moment of conception have death on the horizon. Lacan refers to 'immortal … irrepressible life, life that has no need of an organ, simplified, indestructible life'.[30] Thus the death drive is the drive – the pure drive of life, for the pre-Symbolic state prior to our own history. The first loss is the loss that occurs at conception (Lacan says birth) – '*man that is born of woman has but a short time to live*' (Job 14:1). In his myth, the lamella that flies off at the moment of conception, the originary lack of the finite creature in the Real is displaced onto the Symbolic-Imaginary register as the lack in the signifying system, where the game of lack is played out incidentally and by displacement around the phallus – who has it and who hasn't it. But the *real* longing remains beyond the normative phallic economy, the longing for pure life. The game of lack, the game of alienation, an "animal excoriated by a parasite", echoes the Gnostic orientation outlined in the previous chapter. The parasite being the Judeo-Christian orientation and the terrifying abyss of the inscrutability of the big Other – never knowing what He wants from us. It is this parasite-God who traumatically invades our harmonious lives and drives us to mass hate on the one hand and to inner journeys of spiritual rebirth on the other.

Jagodzinski understands techno rhythmic pulsation as precisely the function of the body-as-machine akin to Deleuze and Guattari's "Body without Organs" (BwO) – 'immortal irrepressible life of *zoe* that needs no organ … the attempt to regain that which has been originally lost'.[31] In the pulsation of the techno-rave one becomes lost (again) in the mOther.

Two versions

As a variation on the theme of the Symbolic register, Lacan, following Heidegger, linked science and technological rationality specifically with the death drive. Cut off from tradition, cut off from Being, from blood, soil, and belonging by modernity, and globalisation, the subject of science as subject of the signifier is already dead (already sacrificed) while still living. This is why we should be suspicious of neuro-psychoanalysis, interesting as it is *qua* science, because it is the opposite of psychoanalysis proper. Lacan saw that the domain of the Real – the domain of death – is extended by means of science. Miller echoes this concern as he parodies Heidegger by proposing that the analyst should be 'the shepherd of the Real'.[32] The reference to Heidegger is: 'Man is the shepherd of being. It is in this direction alone that *Being and Time* is thinking when ecstatic existence is experienced as "care"'.[33] The editor of *Basic Writings*, Farrell Krell, explains care in this Heideggerian sense as being involved with 'one's birth, life and death, projects, inclinations, insights, illusions – awareness of my proper Being',[34] all of which are foreclosed by the scientific method and capitalism in their deracinating effects. At the same time, new scientific discoveries, new technical discoveries right up to the iPhone, are surely examples of scientific *desire* pushed to the extreme. Indeed, we call them "breakthroughs"!

However, with a slight shift in parallax, the death drive becomes just mundane pathology, the foundational basis for mental illness. We could not miss the critical parallax between *two* versions of the death drive. The heroic/tragic/ecstatic alluded to above; the one favoured by Freud and Klein that sees the death drive in quasi-scientific terms, as an extreme of the drive leading to violence, dissolution, and the silence and peace of the inorganic, or at least mental torpor, unless it is redirected by the life drive into ordinary aggression. This common-sense notion of the death drive, observable every day, has great clinical relevance.[35] For Freud, the death drive is linked with biology as every organism possibly retains a desire to return to the inorganic state, to rest in peace, as we have noted. Or, as a destructive/self-destructive impulse beyond ordinary assertive aggression, a kind of narcissistic rage, a compensatory omnipotence, so visible in our post-Oedipal times.

As Freud makes clear:

> We may regard the self-destructiveness as the expression of a "death instinct" which cannot fail to be present in every vital process ...
>
> And elsewhere in his conversation with Einstein, Freud makes clear that, 'some portion of the death instinct remains operative within the organism and we have sought to trace quite a number of normal and pathological processes and phenomena to this internalisation of the destructive instinct.[36],[37]

Furthermore, Laplanche and Pontalis make the central point: recognising in the death instinct,

> a new conceptual departure: the death instinct makes the destructive tendency, as revealed for example in sadomasochism, into an irreducible datum; it is furthermore the chosen expression of the most fundamental

principle of psychical functioning; and, lastly, insofar as it is "the essence of the instinctual", it binds every wish, whether aggressive or sexual, to the wish for death.[38]

While Freud is sanguine and stoical, it is clear that this orientation sees the death drive as entirely connected to severe mental illness, not least the perversions of the superego which enjoys suffering (of the melancholic, the obsessional), so much so that the more you obey it and cede to its demands, the more you feel guilty. Nowhere is this clearer today than with the increasing demand to be politically correct: the more you conform the more you have to virtue signal as the new evolving superego clings onto you.

In addition, I have already made reference to the key biological phenomenon of *apoptosis* – programmed cell death.[39] And here it is tempting to note a biological confirmation of the specifically object relations' assertion, contra Lacan and Freud, that *relating* is primary and biological. 'Modern biological findings show that cells, *on their own and isolated*, die for want of signals from their neighbours to keep them alive'.[40] In ordinary tissues, cells are *kept alive by (chemical) communication*. Communication is key; thus, contra Lacan, object relations are key. However, all cells are genetically programmed to die under some circumstances, particularly cells that are isolated. This is termed "apoptosis". Thus, 'Protista and cancers cells are immortal – they have lost the ability to die, but their very "aliveness" is death bearing'.[41]

Who cares?

As a Platonic philosopher reminded me, Lacan's ideological position is extreme. All the foundations are destroyed, leaving something close to a cognitive futility, undecidability, impossibility, and *so on*. Recall the neutron bomb, a tactical nuclear weapon strike that kills everything that is alive while leaving the infrastructure looking unchanged. Here we are: *being without being*, or being otherwise than being, in the manner of Beckett in *The Unnamable*: 'I can't go on, you must go on, I'll go on'. Or, the Silicon Valley slogan: "Fail early, fail fast, and fail cheap": their formula for creativity, creative desire, whereby failing does not have such a final quality. Like Schrödinger's cat that can be and not be at the same time.

As Lacan says in *Seminar XX*, 'The discordance between knowledge and being is my subject'.[42] Earlier he had made it clear that, 'I am thinking where I am not; I am where I do not think'.[43] There is therefore in this radical discourse, *no community between being and thinking*; each negates the other. Thus thinking, speaking, intelligibility, and *so on*, are enabled only via a violence done to Being. Being itself is dumb[44] and lacks all Logos; it is language that imposes a structure on Being. Being, or the Real, is too much of a fullness, therefore it has to be reduced or lacked so that thinking can take place. 'The symbol is the murder of the [Real] thing'.[45] Thus the Lacanian notion of the subject is already 'thin, empty and weightless'.[46] Now the signifier has to cover all that was formerly meant by mental life and indeed mental illness. In the near nothing, which is my life and the life of our patients, I can't go on, becomes: *from nothing to something as nothing.*

Thus, the insubstantiality of the text is all we are left with. If we follow Baudrillard: 'We are afraid of language since we have been told about the signifier and all that. The signifier has introduced terror into language. "The unconscious is structured like a language" – nothing has wreaked such havoc as that kind of proposition'.[47]

There is nothing outside the text. Now, even *within* the text, there is a war between names, as one name negates another. Names are violent because they are imposed upon the Real. Thus, every name is a point of contestation, where a fight can break out. And truth becomes a fight with the untruth (disinformation, fake news, etc.) or a fight with the non-sense that exceeds it. Thus, all names, truths, and *so on* compete for attention via omnipresent slogans lest they be reabsorbed into the Real. 'Our starting point, the point we keep coming back to, since we will always be at our starting point, is that every real signifier … signifies nothing'.[48] The nothing that must be as something. We are on the edge of nothing with little or nothing to show for it, because every time we think we have something worthwhile we are told – look it is an illusion, it's nothing. Right up to life itself – whatever it amounts to it is really nothing. It is nothing now and nothing after death. While, of course, this is "French Theory", it filters down from academia and informs worldview more widely.

Writing in *Le Monde* recently, the historian and leading authority on Lacan, Élisabeth Roudinesco,[49] deplores the loss of prestige suffered by psychoanalysis now that 'its heroic age is past'. She argues for a return to "humanist" psychiatry, suggesting that 'psychoanalysis has entered an endless phase of decline'. She complains that its practitioners use 'incomprehensible language in their writings intended only for their inner circle'. Their works of "dense theory" are printed in small editions not exceeding a few hundred copies. She notes that the psychoanalytic movement in France has splintered into 19 associations with a majority of women members, who often know nothing about each other. They organise conferences, enjoy belonging to an association, but younger analysts have difficulty setting up their practices because clients have become scarce as psychoanalysis attracts fewer and fewer patients. She concludes by suggesting that maybe analysts have become humiliated by the success of the many 'abject rantings discrediting Freud', and have largely 'abandoned public debate, turning a blind eye to any undertaking critical of them'.

Recall the days when Michael Ignatieff hosted discussions on late night Channel 4, with analysts such as Bruno Bettelheim, Hanna Segal, Adolf Grunbaum, Andre Green, Robert Young, Elizabeth Spillius, Juliet Mitchell, and others, published in the *Voices* series,[50] and discussed in *The Listener* weekly magazine which itself ceased publication in 1991 after 62 years

Roudinesco's observations remind one of literary critic John Carey's provocations. On a visit to Dublin, in discussion with Irish literary critic Declan

Kiberd, Carey dared to suggest that Joyce's *Ulysses* was a treatment for insomnia. Carey was reheating a theme from his *The Intellectuals and the Masses*,[51] about the response of the English literary intelligentsia to the new phenomenon of mass culture more than a century ago. The education acts of the 1870s created a mass reading public with mass circulation newspapers. Literary intellectuals were hostile to these developments, regarding universal education as a mistake. As Carey suggested, 'they resented the "semi-literate" masses, despised their pretensions to culture and detested newspapers'.[52] They created 'modernist literature which cultivates obscurity and depends on learned allusions, comprehensible only to the highly educated'.[53] Carey noted similar developments in the other arts.

Kiberd himself was to say something similar on the fortieth anniversary of May 1968.

> Those who failed to make a revolution in the world settled instead for making one in language. They retreated from the streets and factories to university arts' facilities. There they propounded extreme forms of post-structural theory in a specialist jargon, which no normally intelligent person could (or should) ever hope to understand.[54]

The "incomprehensible language" and "specialist jargon" of the Lacanian groups was in part an elitist response to the newly emergent mass therapy culture during the 1970s and 1980s including Anglo-American psychotherapy post-Freud. The Lacanian intent, never stated, was to exclude the therapy-hungry masses from such high culture and esoteric doctrines. When a colleague attempted to purchase a copy of Lacan's *Écrits* in a small Parisian bookstore back in the seventies, the owner of the shop strongly discouraged him on account of the supreme difficulty of the text.

Of course, there is so much that is of great value in Lacan. But here again we can usefully follow Carey approving of Orwell's observation to the effect that, in Joyce, Orwell detects a gradual death of feeling and its replacement by literary cleverness. In *Dubliners*, for instance, there is an identification with the suffering of the people, whereas in *Ulysses*, Stephen Dedalus is "intolerable" and Leopold Bloom does not evoke much pity even when his situation is pitiful.

So, when Roudinesco invokes (a return to) "humanist" psychiatry, before it is too late with the psi world now dominated by science, drug therapies, turning away from the subject, and *so on*, this term "humanist" is very problematic for the post-structuralists. For them, care and improvement are sometimes synonymous with the death drive itself, with hints of crushing normative and adaptive assumptions of alienation. On the other hand, maybe many patients might say, give me just some normal alienation so I can live! As Borch-Jacobsen complains, '[W]as it really a psychoanalyst's role to transform his office into the scene of a grandiose Greek tragedy [following desire, pure life, etc.] Wouldn't this completely belittle patients' request for solace and finally drive clients to despair?'[55]

There is the joke about the analyst who dies and goes to Heaven. An angel there offers to show him around. So, here's the room for the Freudians; here's the room for the Kleinians, and *so on* for the Winnicottians, Jungians, attachment theorists, etc. Then the angel says with much fuss, 'sh … sh … ', as they approach a high wall. 'Why keep quiet', he asks? Because behind the wall are the Lacanians, and they think they are the only ones.

The death drive unbound

Pascal Bruckner confirms that Europeans are growing timorous and self-devouring: 'the Old World is in danger of dying, like Rome, of obesity, and ectoplasm that grows larger as it loses its substance'.[56] A self-lacerating guilt lives side by side with 'living the life' – living the *pure* life or, as people declare, 'this is *my life*'. There are deadly side effects (as rights conflict) as we abandon any real notion of the social good. As Miller says, in almost a Thatcherite moment, 'The collective is nothing but the subject of the individual'.[57] And even the social good conceals the death drive, 'as we wait for it to drag us to our destruction',[58] and especially when we raise the question: 'for the good of whom?'[59] There is no such thing as society!

The deeper reason for the alleged "endless phase of decline" of psychoanalysis, beyond the academic language and terminology, beyond scientism and reductive materialism, beyond pharmacology, and *so on*, is the anti-Christian, anti-humanist orientation of the new atheistic religion to which politicised psychoanalysis now belongs almost by default, *which knows no evil*, or to be more precise, knows evil only as *out there* – in capitalism, the Symbolic, the white man, religion, and *so on*.

Instead of the burden of responsibility and realistic personal guilt we have inherited from earlier centuries, gaining insight, becoming reflective, forming therapeutic alliances, renouncing impulses, improving relations, and *so on*, Lacanian psychoanalysis has largely dispensed with all that emotional "work on the self", in exchange for a return to the pre-Christian Greco-Roman polytheism and the heroic affirmation of the death drive. Here there was/is no real question of good and evil.

It is no longer just elites, artists, and *so on* that really know this kind of freedom. It is now available for all. The silent masses, still mired in the old ethics to some degree, are catching up but may be worried about what real freedom without scruples and total openness actually entails.

Meantime, in the fractal universe there are thoughts without a thinker, maybe unthinkable terrifying thoughts whose depths have not yet been plumbed. This must be the web: thinking without thinking, thinking free of thinking – obscene, sometimes unimaginably so, on the dark web for instance. Who can now say it is bad or evil? Maybe it is art. A young boy is groomed on the web. He meets the man who groomed him who then kills him. The grieving family are sent videos of the killing at intervals anonymously during the following months. Transgressive art? In 2014, Petr Pavlensky nailed his scrotum to the cobbles in Red Square. The year before he had wrapped himself naked in barbed wire and sewn his lips together. Drill music videos posted online feature hooded and masked gangs threatening each other, with lyrics about drugs, guns, and stabbing rivals with knives. The real difficulty seems to be how can you continue to transgress in an already transgressive culture which celebrates and promotes transgression? But there is always more death drive to defuse.

A child is born to a mother on methadone maintenance treatment. He is taken into the care of his maternal grandparents when his father dies, soon after he is born, from a suspected drug overdose. By the time he is seven or eight his grandparents can no longer cope with his violent outbursts. And at school he is becoming increasingly violent, hitting other children and abusing the teachers.

Is it not true that everyone has a crime hidden within them? We are just waiting to be accused, to be called out. We are guilty before any possible trial, like Herr K. Thought fragments. Random juxtapositions. A fractal universe. All ultimately pointless, lacking *points de capiton*. This is the death drive unbound. In the Lacanian anti-religion religion, death is free to roam without query. The analogy is with the free radicle coursing through the body damaging cells and tissues as it goes. But just as the free radicals depend upon a healthy body for their disruptive activity, so too does the supremely free (Lacanian) agent depend upon a lawful network of facilitation and protection. Maybe it is strange that the so-called "endless phase of decline" of psychoanalysis is marked by its only truly active principle, the death drive and its celebration!

The radical Left seems to have shaken itself free of any residual gravitational pull. It welcomes the pure life of the death drive fully unleashed that might finally cleanse several centuries of white guilt. Will this not be matched, according to an almost Newtonian principle of action and reaction, by an equal and opposite unleashing on the Right?

> One by one they come knocking at your door. They cry out, they beg you for help and you say: get them away from me … these people who come with these ridiculous stories–I've always loved people who enjoy good meals, who look forward to watching good performances … I've struggled hard to get what I have, but my struggle has always been against others. In fact I have been struggling against the ones who are poor … I'm not on their side, and that too is a choice I am making. What will be home? My own bed, my night table, then on the table, what?
>
> Then on the table, what? Blood, death, a fragment of bone, a piece of a human brain, a severed hand. Let everything filthy, everything vile, sit by my bed, where once I had my lamp and clock, books, letters, presents for my birthday, left-over bright coloured ribbons.

Forgive me. Forgive me. I know you'll forgive me. I'm still falling. I am still falling.[60]

Italian Marxist Franco "Bifo" Berardi who was at the Labour fringe in September 2018:

Five centuries of colonialism, capitalism and nationalism have turned Europeans into the enemy of human kind. May they be cursed forever! May Europeans be swept away by the storm they have generated, by the weapons they are building, by the fire they have ignited, by the hatred they have cultivated.[61]

There is no longer any objective judgement, no final accounting on the rightness or wrongness of our acts; psychoanalytically, politically, it is a question of radical desire. There is no big Other to guarantee or judge. There is no covenant or possibility of ratifying things. Your only duty is, or your orders are, to follow the orientation of your desire. Collateral damage is the price to pay. Who cares?

A recent Žižekian response? *The Courage of Hopelessness*,[62] or as somebody quipped: don't just sit there; do nothing.

Notes

1 "MCMXIV" Philip Larkin.
2 Furedi, F. 2018.
3 See Bradbury, M. 1988, p. 260.
4 Steiner, G. 1971, p. 9.
5 Lacan, J. 1959–1960, p. 314.
6 Ibid., 321 emphasis added.
7 Kundera, M. 1984, p. 5.
8 Millot. C. 2016, p. 115.
9 Žižek, S. 2014, pp. 67–69.
10 Žižek, S, 2006, p. 62.
11 Lacan, J. 2002, p. 34.
12 Freud, S. 1940 [1938], p. 148.
13 Žižek, S. 2010, p. 305.
14 Žižek, S. 2001, p. 104.
15 Lacan, J. 2002, pp. 263/320.
16 Cudden, J. 1977, p. 985.
17 Zupančič, A. 2000, p. 83.
18 Pizarnik, A. 1962–1972.
19 Lacan, J. 1954–1955, p. 326.
20 Lacan, J. 2002, pp. 719/848.
21 Ibid., pp. 152/187.
22 Ibid.
23 Freud, S. 1920, pp. 14–15.
24 Ibid., pp. 262/319.
25 Žižek, S. 1989, p. 4.
26 Lacan, J. 1969–1970, p. 46.
27 Lacan, J. 1959–1960, p. 212.

28 Lacan, J. 1964, p. 197.
29 Žižek, S. 1995, p. 208.
30 Lacan, J. 1964, p. 198.
31 Jagodzinski, J. 2005, p. 260.
32 Ibid., p. 319. www.congressoamp2016.com/bibliofalante/Bibliofalante/assets/common /downloads/page0241.pdf.
33 Heidegger, M. 1978, p. 234.
34 Ibid., p. 223.
35 See, for instance, Segal, H. 1993.
36 Freud, S. 1933, p. 107.
37 Also Freud, S. 1933 (1932), p. 211
38 Laplanche, J. and Pontalis, J.-B. 1973, p. 103.
39 Weatherill, R. 1998, p. 112ff.
40 Ibid., p. 117.
41 Ibid., p. 118.
42 Lacan, J. 1972–1973, p. 228.
43 Lacan, J. 2002, pp. 430/517.
44 Lacan, J. 1959–1960, p. 55.
45 Lacan, J. 2002, pp. 262/319.
46 Bowie, M. 1991, p. 75.
47 Baudrillard, J. 2005b, p. 95.
48 Lacan, J. 1955–1956, p. 185.
49 Roudinesco, E. 2019.
50 Bourne, B. *et al.* 1987.
51 Carey, J. 2005.
52 Carey, J. 2014, p. 326.
53 Ibid., p. 327.
54 Kiberd, D. 2008.
55 Borch-Jacobsen, M. 1991, p. 124.
56 Bruckner, P. 2006, p. 190.
57 http://iclo-nls.org/wp-content/uploads/Pdf/Turin.pdf.
58 Lacan, J. 1959–1960, p. 232.
59 Ibid., p. 319.
60 Shaun, W. 1996 (modified).
61 http://hurryupharry.org/2018/09/14/momentum-speaker-franco-berardi-and-the -new-nazis/ (since removed).
62 Žižek, S. 2017.

References

Baudrillard, J. 2005b. *Cool Memories V*. Paris: Éditions Galilée. Trans. Turner, C. Cambridge: Polity Press, 2006.

Borch-Jacobsen, M. 1991. *Lacan: The Absolute Master*. Trans. Brick, D. California: Stanford University Press.

Bourne, B. Eichler, U. Herman, D. 1987. *Voices: Psychoanalysis*. Nottingham: Spokesman, New Jersey: Hobo Press.

Bowie, M 1991. *Lacan*. Cambridge, MA: Harvard University Press, 1993.

Bradbury, M. 1988. *The Modern World: Ten Great Writers*. London: Penguin.

Bruchner, P. 2006. *The Tyranny of Guilt. An Essay on Western Masochism*. Trans. Tendall, S. Princeton and Oxford: Princeton University Press, 2010.

Carey, J. 2005. *The Intellectuals and the Masses. Pride and Prejudice Among the Literary Intelligensia, 1880–1939*. Chicago, IL: Chicago Review Press.

Carey, J. 2014. *The Unexpected Professor. An Oxford Life in Books*. London: Faber & Faber.

Cudden, J. 1977. *A Dictionary of Literary Terms and Literary Theory*. London: Deutsch.

Freud, S. 1920. *Beyond the Pleasure Principle, SE 18*, 1–64.

Freud, S. 1933 (1932). *"Why War", SE 22*, 197–215.

Freud, S. 1933. *The New Introductory Lectures, SE 22*.

Freud, S. 1940 (1938). *An Outline of Psycho-Analysis, SE 23*, 141–208.

Furedi, F. 2018. "The First Culture War. How the First World War Sowed the Seeds of Identity Politics". *Spiked*. Nov 8. https://www.spiked-online.com/2018/11/08/the-first-culture-war/

Heidegger, M. 1978. *Basic Writings*. Farrell Krell, D. (Ed.) London: Routledge, 2000.

Jagodzinski, J. 2005. *Music in Youth Culture: A Lacanian Approach*. New York and London: Palgrave Macmillan.

Kiberd, D. 2008. "At the Core of 1968 was a Search for Authority rather than Subversion". *The Irish Times*. May 1.

Kundera, M. 1984. *The Unbearable Lightness of Being*. Trans. Heim, M. London: Harper & Row.

Lacan, J. 1954–1955. *Seminar 2. The Ego in Freud's Theory and the Technique of Psychoanalysis*. Miller, J.-A. (Ed.). Trans. Tomaselli, S. New York and Cambridge: Cambridge University Press, 1988.

Lacan, J. 1955–1956. *Seminar 3. The Psychoses*. Miller, J.- A. (Ed.). Trans. Grigg, R. New York and London: W. W. Norton, 1993.

Lacan, J. 1959–1960. *The Seminar of Jacques Lacan, Book VII: The Ethics of Psychoanalysis*. Trans. Porter, J. London: Routledge, 1992.

Lacan, J. 1964. *The Four Fundamental Concepts of Psycho-Analysis, Seminar XI*. Miller, J.-A. (Ed.). Trans. Sheridan, A. London: Hogarth Press, 1977.

Lacan, J. 1969–1970. *Seminar 17. The Other Side of Psychoanalysis*. Trans. Grigg, R. New York: W. W. Norton, 2005.

Lacan, J. 1972–1973. *The Seminar 20. Encore: On Feminine Sexuality, the Limits of Love and Knowledge*. Fink, B. (Ed.). London: W. W. Norton, 1998.

Lacan, J. 2002. *Ecrits. The First Complete Edition in English*. Trans. Fink, B. New York and London: W.W.Norton & Co.

Laplanche, J. and Pontalis, J-B. 1973. *The Language of Psychoanalysis*, London: Hogarth.

Millot, C. 2016. *Life with Lacan*. Trans. Brown, A. Cambridge and Medford: Polity Press.

Pizarnik, A. 1962–1972. *Uncollected Poems*. Trans. Heinowitz, C. https://jacket2.org/commentary/alejandra-pizarnik-uncollected-poems-1962–1972

Roudinesco, E. 2019. *Psychoanalysts Have Contributed to Their Own Downfall*. Trans. Jacob, A. Paris: Le Monde, Feb 9.

Segal, H. 1993. "On the Clinical Usefulness of the Concept of Death Instinct". *International Journal of Psychoanalysis* 74, 55–61.

Shaun, W. (1996) "The Fever". Directed by O'Callaghan, O., *BBC Radio Four*. Date unknown.

Steiner, G. 1971. *In Bluebeard's Castle. Some Notes Towards the Redefinition of Culture*. New Haven: Yale University Press.

Weatherill, R. 1998. *The Sovereignty of Death*. London: Rebus Press.

Žižek, S. 1989. *The Sublime Object of Ideology*. London and New York: Verso.

Žižek, S. 1995. "The Lamella of David Lynch." In Feldstein, R., Fink, B., Jaanus, M. (Eds.) *Reading Seminar XI: Lacan's Four Fundamental Concepts of Psychoanalysis*. Albany: State University of New York Press, 205–220.

Žižek, S. 2001. *On Belief*. London and New York: Routledge.

Žižek, S. 2006. *The Parallax View.* Cambridge, MA: The MIT Press.

Žižek, S. 2010. *Living in the End Times.* London: Verso.

Žižek, S. 2014. *Žižek's Jokes: Did You Hear the One about Hegel and Negation?* Mortensen, A. (Ed.). Cambridge, MA: MIT Press.

Žižek, S. 2017. *The Courage of Hopelessness.* London and New York: Penguin Books 2018.

Zupančič, A. 2000. *Ethics of the Real: Kant and Lacan.* London and New York: Verso.

Part III

10 The Evidence

This chapter suggests *metanoia* as possible. Starting with the radical otherness of transcendent experience, the discussion moves on to order/design/Logos as deep properties of the universe – Fibonacci, the golden ratio, nucleic acids, mathematics, fractals, etc. The philosophy of Plotinus describes the intelligible realm proceeding from the One, implying today that the ubiquity of code, information, and irreducible complexity cannot simply have evolved by random natural selection alone, although the latter still plays an important part in evolution. The deep lawfulness of nature and thought and our being here to record them, the anthropic principle, is just an accident? It is all meaning*less*? Asserting meaning, *creating* meaning in existence is crucial, as Frankl discovered was possible even in the camps. Next, considering the provision of care for the young. It is limited in the animal kingdom until we reach mammals, primates, and finally humans, who can bring to bear "alpha function" (Bion). According to Badiou, women *qua* caregivers are hidden so that God can exist. Derrida pondered unconditional hospitality. Finally, Mary and the shattering Event of the Incarnation *qua* rupture and sheer strangeness, changes the world forever. Human nature exists to receive the total overwhelming gratuity of grace (de Lubac). And why us? Because of our poverty? Can psychoanalysis understand this?

On 22 April 1849, Dostoevsky was arrested and imprisoned with members of a radical group in St Petersburg studying utopian socialist thought. They had been caught because a police informer had become a group member and he reported them to the authorities. Found guilty of subversive activities and condemned to death by firing squad, they were taken out early in the morning of 22 December 1849 onto the parade ground where a scaffolding had been erected. The crimes were read out one-by-one. An Orthodox priest was on hand so that they could repent. Each man was tied to a stake in preparation for the firing squad. At the last moment, a drum roll, then the rifles were lowered. The men had been reprieved by the Tsar, sentenced instead to Siberian exile

DOI: 10.4324/9781003225010-13

for four years of hard labour, then service in the Russian Army; a total in all of ten years.

On being reprieved, brought back from the brink of death, Dostoevsky later declared, 'I cannot recall when I was ever as happy as on that day'. From then on, according to John Gray's appraisal, he no longer believed in the ideology of an ultra-radical progress of history. Instead, the experience taught him that *every human being at each moment stands on the edge of eternity*. Dostoevsky rejected the secular rationalist faith, the nihilism of his former radical intellectual circle.[1]

Dostoevsky learnt his Christian faith from his time in prison and living among the poor. As Robert Louis Jackson comments in his introductory remarks to *Notes from the Underground and The Double*,

> Dostoevsky certainly is one with the Underground Man in his emphasis on the centrality in man's existence of the living process, of "life itself", as opposed to any final earthly goal such as the Crystal Palace. Yet he in no way endorses the Undergrounds Man's existentialist view that man is forever journeying without goal in a meaningless universe. Missing from the Underground Man's conception of man's destiny is what is missing from the utopian Socialist's idea and ideal of the Crystal Palace: a spiritual dimension.[2]

He told his brother in 1846 that his writing proceeds, 'by analysis and not by synthesis, that is, I go into the depths picking things out atom by atom'. Later, in 1862, suggesting that the basic idea in all art of that time was, 'a Christian idea ... the restoration of the fallen man ... the justification of the pariahs of society, humiliated and rejected by all'.[3] For Dostoevsky, religious experience is religious *existence*. You live it however imperfectly. Conversely, an atheist is one who *lives* his rebellion against God. In his novel *The Possessed*, which Malcolm Muggeridge declared was the most important novel ever written, Sara García Sanz writes that,

> Dostoevsky presents the parable of modernity in this light: the Christian West has sought to emancipate itself from God and has become atheist. And since an attempt to run away from God implies running towards destruction, this is precisely why the Christian West is being diminished.[4]

'The West has lost Christ, and that is why it is dying: that is the only reason'.[5]

★★★

Having the Heart[6]

Becoming animal
The surgeon's cut
Wounds the animal's heart.

He doesn't know that it is to heal him.
He withdraws in seclusion.
Or, becomes hyperactive and atrial.
Does he remember lying open there?
In the garage repair shop.
Exposed in an abject awful exposure.
With his cage sawed through
Was it a chain-saw?
In a moment of indifferent madness
Someone said – it only a pump!
In a moment of indifferent madness
Someone said – it is only plumbing

His cells contract and turn away from the cutting lights
He knows nothing of this world
His ways are his own.
And yet he has given such loving service
One hundred thousand beats a day down all the days.
Now, complicit and turned in on himself
Still devotional and constant
How could you bear this cutting insult?
No one speaks to the animal organ.

On Laceration

Laceration creates intimacy
The wound brings us together
The cut creates a disjunction
Before and after
Before was separation and striving
Just before is being separated
Familiar things – my people and things begin to remove themselves
You are leaving/being left.
Then just after
Everything is so moving
Everything weeps in the usual way
The intimacy of laceration
The proximity of laceration
Where everything bleeds, leaks and oozes.
And words die in the telling
Things become intimate
Trees, stones, love
The shower cloud drifting past the hospital window, loves
The wind loves
The BP monitor has beautiful lights.

Adorno:

> The only philosophy which would still be accountable in the face of despair, would be the attempt to consider all things, as they would be portrayed from the standpoint of redemption. Cognition has no other light than that which shines from redemption out upon the world; all else exhausts itself in post-construction and remains a piece of technics. Perspectives must be produced which set the world beside itself, alienated from itself, revealing its cracks and fissures, as needy and distorted as it will one day lay there in the messianic light.[7]
>
> The more passionately thought seals itself off from its conditional being for the sake of what is unconditional, the more unconsciously, and thereby catastrophically, it falls into the world. It must comprehend even its own impossibility for the sake of possibility.[8]

In a lighter vein, George Sanders says something similar:

> If you have a negative tendency and you deny it, then you've doubled it. If you have a negative tendency and you look at it [embrace it, amplify it!] – which is in part what writing allows – then the possibility exists that you can convert [redeem] it.[9]

Redemption stands afar off. Deliver us from sin and free us from captivity. One must be, at least occasionally, at the zero point of knowing and understanding – *for they know not what they do* (Luke 23:34). It is zero. Humility is close to zero. So it is with humus: rotting plant and animal remains, the zero, the death before life can resume. Without humus, there can be no life. Humus is the despair of life hoping for, expecting redemption. Humus is the negative tendency, in the dark below ground. It is the dark web; it waits upon the inevitable redemption of growth into the light.

Design

The big question: is the universe a blind mechanism? Is it blind necessity? If we are the result of blind forces, why should we carry on? Is it just because we are animals programmed to survive? Is scientific materialism – everything can be explained by science – *the* answer. Grab what pleasure you can while there is still time. The courage of nihilism – you are a slave creature, finding momentary (sexual) pleasure where you can get it!

Ironically, a scientific training can begin to challenge such atheistic mythologies. Let us first acknowledge that to be a true atheist takes great courage; to face the absolutely nihilistic *nyx*. Most atheists are merely lapsed Christians.

Consider for a moment the young students who look down the microscope for the first time at, for example, a leaf or the edge of a piece of torn paper. The former with its intricate pattern of veins and the latter where you can see a fur of torn fibres or filaments that make up the paper. Then maybe they look at the neat arrangement of facets of an insect's compound eye. In each case: excitement and wonder! A new world of complexity opens up.

Not chaos but order; an order that appears at each microscopic level to complement the order at visible levels. The leaf arrangements on a stem: opposite, alternate, or whorled. The Fibonacci series in nature: for instance, the number of petals in flowers. Most have three (like lilies and irises), five (Parnassia, rose hips), eight (Cosmea), 13 (some daisies), 21 (chicory), 34, 55, or 89 (flowers of the Compositae). Consider the order-in-complexity of the sunflower seeds and pine-cone scales. The Fibonacci sequence underlies phenomena as diverse as the nautilus shell, cyclone formation at mid-latitudes, hurricanes, and, at the astronomical level, spiral galaxies and superclusters such as the Milky Way.

The golden ratio is about 1.618, and represented by the Greek letter phi, Φ. It is obtained by dividing a number in the Fibonacci sequence by the previous number. The DNA molecule measures 34 angstroms long by 21 angstroms wide for each full cycle of its double helix spiral. These numbers, 34 and 21, are numbers in the Fibonacci series, and their ratio 1.6190476 closely approximates phi, 1.6180339.

A lung, lightning strike, or the branches of a tree, river drainage patterns from above, the branching arteries in a heart, leaf veins, and snowflakes are examples of fractals. 'Nature uses only the longest threads to weave her patterns, so each small piece of her fabric reveals the organization of the entire tapestry'.[10] Organisation, pattern imply design.

Clearly there is design in nature from the infinite to the infinitesimal, down to the atomic level and quantum states.

Those who do not have a scientific training are missing the wonder of the material world. The exquisite beauty of organic chemistry or the periodic table. The metals in their pure state. The pure colours of the compounds of the transition metals.

Nature is bound up with order and beauty. Nature is mathematical. Nature is an orderly system revealing its rationality and design, especially if we look at it closely. Does this order that appears as pure beauty imply an intelligence operating?

> What has made souls forget their father, God, and be ignorant of themselves and him, even though they are parts which come from this higher world? ... by some kind of audacity, a wish to belong to themselves, the souls leave the higher world and forget about their origin. They descend into the sensible sphere and become captivated by earthly things.[11]

Plotinus follows Plato in drawing a divide between the sensible – what can be perceived by the senses – and the intelligible, what can be perceived by thought. The One, the intellect and the soul belong to the intelligible realm. The One is not graspable by thought. The sensible realm is the lowest level including matter itself, bodies, and their qualities of spatial extension and dispersion. The soul originates in the intelligible realm and descends into the sensible to become embodied, while retaining its non-corporeal intelligible status. For Plotinus, the soul remains independent of the body while at the same time taking care of it. This is a danger in that the soul can become lost in its caring role, animating, breathing life into the body and its pleasures and agonies. The task of philosophy and psychoanalysis is to awaken the soul and turn it towards the intelligible realm. However, Plotinus is against the Gnostics for their outright hostility to the world because they believed it was evil.

The intellect is understood as a whole. 'Thus, we can certainly say that the universal intellect exists in one way – that is the one before those which are actually the particular intellects ... But intellect ranges over all of them'. Thus, intellect proceeding from the One is itself one.[12] It is its own subject and object. Likewise, the Neoplatonists believed in a world-soul originating in the intelligible realm.

Although controversial, Neoplatonists believed that there are abstract mathematical objects whose existence is independent of us and our language, thought, and practices. Numbers and sets exist independently of us. Thus, mathematical truths, like the Fibonacci series, are therefore discovered not invented.[13] As Steiner makes clear, the sciences derive from 'the sovereignty of mathematics'.[14] As Galileo pointed out, nature speaks mathematics. Steiner cites Poincaré's paper on mathematical creation which links mathematical formulations, insofar as they work, with beauty and truth. However, Steiner asks the key question about mathematical formulations: 'Do they generate arbitrary, although rigorously deductive, phantasms? Or are they, on the contrary, reflections, descriptions, however refined, however abstracted and theorized, of the world *out there*?'[15]

He suggests the latter: 'If the algebraic operation arises from wholly internalised pattern-weaving, how then can it, at so many points, mesh with, correspond to, the material forms of the world?'[16]

Mathematics challenges the hegemon of Darwinian thinking. Wherever you find information it always comes from an intelligent source. Even a single cell is informationally immensely complex and controlled by the genetic code inscribed in the base sequence of the DNA molecule. As Bill Gates suggests, the DNA is like a software program, although much more complex than anything created. Information comes from intelligent agents. So, whether we are talking about the information in hieroglyphic inscriptions, paragraphs in a book, or information in a radio signal, or section of computer code, you can always trace it back to intelligence – the provision of design – and not a material process.

Proponents, such as Stephen Meyer, point to the difficulty in accounting for the development via Darwinian evolution of the first primitive cells from the "pre-biotic soup".[17] There is a gap of complexity when progressing from molecules, even macromolecules, that can form via abiotic evolution,[18] all the way up to a functioning cell. A massive gap. The gap of complexity is far too large to be accounted for solely by natural selection. Too many things have to happen simultaneously. The argument is that natural selection is too crude to produce such fine-tuning and the informational leaps necessary.

Likewise, from a structuralist point of view, language did not evolve but somehow materialised ready-made as a structure. We do not possess language, it possesses us. We are nothing because we are allegedly overwritten by the text. This is the structuralist point of view. Lacan follows Mauss and his theory of "gift-exchange": 'The structures of society are symbolic; individuals, insofar as they are normal, use them in real behaviours'.[19] These structures are linguistic in nature. Hence, the unconscious is structured like a language. The subject is structured by a language. Lacan suggests, 'when another structural order emerges, well then, it creates its own perspective within the past, and we say – *This can never not have been there, this has existed from the beginning*'.[20]

Tom Wolfe comes to a comparable conclusion without any reference at all to structuralism in his book *The Kingdom of Speech*. He rejects the notion of evolution (of speech) which he asserts has become 'embedded in the very anatomy, the very central nervous system, of all *modern* people'.[21] Language existed apart from evolution. Just as there is a disjunction between the abiotic soup and the first living cells, likewise, according to Wolfe, 'There is a cardinal distinction between man and animal, a sheerly dividing line as abrupt and immovable as a cliff: namely speech'.[22] In short, speech seems to be quite a miracle tool, enabling us 'to conquer every square inch of land in the world'.[23]

More than 50 years ago, molecular biologist Jacques Monod speculated radically about the emergence of "a new realm" in the biosphere. His hypothesis was:

> language may have preceded the emergence of a central nervous system particular to man and contributed decisively to the selection of those variants most suited to utilize all its resources. In other words language may have created man, rather than man language.[24]

The idea that language evolved from bird song, for instance, cannot possibly account for its amazing complexity and diversity.

As biochemist Michael Behe asserts, 'Design is the purposeful arrangement of parts. When we perceive the parts have been arranged to fulfill a purpose, that is when we infer design'.[25] Irreducibly complex systems, such as the bacterial flagellum with its series of molecular motors to propel it towards food sources or away from toxins, could only have come about *as a whole system*. It is a nano-machine, with 40 structural parts, 40 nanometers in size. It is true, ten of the parts are found in another molecular machine in a different bacterial species, but where are the other 30 components going to come from? The point is, alleges Behe, it could not have evolved as merely contingent combinations even over billions of years. Everything fits together so well, that without one part the structure wouldn't work. Then, there is the question of how the machine is assembled in the correct sequence with feedback mechanisms so that components are not over- or underproduced at the correct sequential moment for each part in the assemblage. How could that complex system with its multiple subsystems, each of which requires the assemblage of further subsystems and *so on*, have evolved in a *random* fashion? Darwinian evolution cannot explain irreducible complexity at its many levels of production. One error in the production line and the flagellum will not function.

Darwin, of course, had no access to the molecular complexity of cells, knowledge of which has exploded over the last 70 or so years. Darwin himself acknowledged: 'If it could be demonstrated that any complex organ existed which could not possibly have been formed by numerous successive slight modifications, my theory would absolutely breakdown. But I can find no such case'.[26]

To get such irreducible and interconnecting complexity would require multiple fortuitous mutations to occur at random. That just cannot occur in nature. Most mutations are deleterious. Just as software engineers do not want random glitches in their code, genetic mutations are, on the whole, disadvantageous. Then, considering developmental processes, there is the question of choreography – the right genes being turned on and off at the right time. Therefore, mind, intelligence must be involved. All of life reveals itself on close inspection to be a minutely orderly system yet infinitely complex, down to nanometer levels. This issues as pattern/design at the macro-levels as we have noted above. Darwinian evolution takes place no doubt, but it cannot account for such detail. It takes place on the fringes. Evolution is transformed from being a blind soulless engine of pointless change to becoming the *only* margin of freedom available to us. For if the world is designed, down to this minute detail, ordered in the way that it appears to be, mathematically precise, and *so on*, where does freedom lie? Surely in the contingencies of life where evolution by natural selection can operate. The further up the evolutionary ladder one goes, the more freedom there is. My cat has limited freedom: whether to stay in or to go out? Whether to wait for food to arrive, or to hunt in the hedgerows. Whereas I have the burden of freedom, so many choices, which will affect the direction my life takes.

The anthropic principle

Nature is an orderly system. Nature reveals its rationality and design when we look at it closely. Indeed, the universe is ultra-fine-tuned. The value of the gravitational constant, the mass of the proton, the age of the universe, and *so on*, are, as it were, precisely set to support the evolution of life. The planetary requirements for living systems and a biosphere are very specific. An element such as carbon (evolved in the interior of stars by nuclear fusion) which is metastable at the temperature of water in the liquid phase. Carbon is the *only* element in the periodic table capable of polymerisation, having the capacity to form the long chains needed for macromolecules such as proteins, but, in particular, nucleic acids destined *to carry the information or intelligence* of living systems. A planet is required with a stabilising moon, plate tectonics, the evolution of the right kind of atmosphere of the correct composition and density, large planetary neighbours to mop up stray comets to protect the earth from major catastrophic collisions, and the right kind of star at the right kind of distance, and thus radiance, to maintain water in the liquid phase. All quite a specification! Of course, the universe might be a chance event of no significance and quite meaningless, one of many universes and *so on*, but if, let us dare to suggest, you were indeed *planning* it, how differently would you do it?

However, the Anthropic Principle, a term invented by Brandon Carter in 1973 in a symposium in Krakow to celebrate Copernicus' 500th birthday, tells us we are bound to think like this, to draw these conclusions. Our intelligence is *human* intelligence, and we see everything through this lens. We are biased in our own favour. Is this coincidence of so-called fine-tuning via all the fundamental constants just too good to be true? Is it rather like a local villager in the time before mechanised transport saying that the finest people of all are found in his town alone? *There is no other town.* This town, our town, has been built and developed to reach its finest point now and we are fortunate enough here to celebrate this fact!? But *we* know that there are many other towns because we have travelled to them. Similarly, we can assert that there are many, maybe an infinite number of, other universes and indeed other intelligences. There are multiple intelligences: musical, visual, verbal, emotional, bodily, interpersonal, and *so on*, beyond the logical mathematical.[27] All true, but these should not obscure the impossible miracle of our own "village".

Michael Frayn invokes the so-called strong anthropic principle in *The Human Touch*, when he asserts that the central oddity of the universe is entirely this paradox:

> The Universe is very old and very large. Humankind, by comparison, is only a tiny disturbance in one small corner of it – and a very recent one. Yet the Universe is only very large and very old because we are here to say it is … And yet, of course, we all know perfectly well that it is what it is *whether we are here or not*.[28]

The point is, are we very biased witnesses? Is it a question of: they would say that wouldn't they? Well, why not! Are we not immensely privileged to be able to grasp our position, our *being here now*? And, is this just the start: are there meta-intelligences created by the internet-of-things, yet to be exploited with brain-computer-interface technologies promising total connectivity that will amplify and complexify our present miraculous position, or indeed destroy it? Their exploitation by atheistic scientists is likely to be without soul and without the One and therefore fall into grievous error maybe sooner rather than later. That is for the near future. Nevertheless, to be observing at this time, with this technical understanding, with this long evolutionary perspective stretching back to the Big Bang, being present in the universe at this moment is beyond understanding, and surely unspeakably impressive. In our tiny corner of the universe, consciousness has developed to the point that we can reflect on how it all arose.

How many of us have the humility to acknowledge this miracle? Do we not just proceed, cool as a breeze, proud of our own puny achievements, thinking them as our own, careless as to what could happen, unconscious as it were of the immense theological drama that has unfolded and is unfolding? We think more in the narrow terms of our own entitlement to life and more and more of it. We stop short at the limit of our own horizon rather like the pets that we depend upon. This is univocal atomisation without transcendence. Thus, in this animal state of fighting for survival we have lost pretty well everything *and we do not know it we have lost it.*

Scientists generally agree that to call the fine-tuning of the universe the anthropic principle is a cop out. It gets us nowhere. It is a wish fulfilment. They almost all deny its significance, because they want nothing to do with mystery. Hume and Darwin put an end to any credibility for cosmic teleology among all but a few scientists. We have just won the lottery in this particular universe.[29] We have "selection bias" because we have woken up in this particular universe out of millions possible. There is nothing to see here!

Meaning

Consider, for instance, the popularity of Dawkins:

> The universe we observe has precisely the properties we should expect if there is, at bottom, no design, no purpose, no evil and no good, nothing but blind, pitiless indifference. As that unhappy poet A.E. Housman put it: 'For Nature, heartless, witless Nature / Will neither care nor know'. DNA neither cares nor knows. DNA just is. And we dance to its music.[30]

Let us fully accept this statement about the brutal Real of the blind, pitiless indifference of the universe, serving to cut right across any so-called consoling pagan notions of Gaia and the bounteous earth, but ironically contradicted surely when the first colour pictures of earth from space emerged when the Apollo 17 travelled towards the Moon in 1972.[31] Forget even that impulse. Let us fully accept and acknowledge this nihilism, common – even celebrated – everyplace today. The fatality of the statement bespeaks it appalling content. Yes, it is true about the vastness of the infinite universe that it pays no heed of us, so much so that the fictional astronomer in Martin Amis' 1997 *Night Train*, Jennifer Rockwell, commits suicide even though she had the perfect life, but she had the privileged view through the newest telescopes of the unfathomable vastness of the indifferent universe and she was overwhelmed by her perception of the utter meaninglessness of it all.

However, surely it was part of Pascal's greatness that he was terrified by the silence of the infinite and the infinitesimal spaces. In fact, C.S. Lewis saw the paradox that, through astronomy, one could come 'to realise for the first time how majestically indifferent most of reality is to man, and who abandons his religion on that account, may at that moment be having *his first genuinely religious experience*'.[32]

Thus, while there is a minimal gap between our non-indifference and the universe's vast brutal indifference, then there is still hope. Here, amidst the vast sea of atheism and indifference to indifference, not caring, not giving a shit, sheer ignorance, and *so on*, someone takes on the burden of *non*-indifference. Consider Lewis again: 'If the *whole* universe has no meaning, we should never have found out that it has no meaning'.[33] Earlier, he had been complaining about how unjust and cruel the universe was and therefore there was no God, and *so on*, when he realised that his rage against injustice meant that there must be justice if he like others could imagine it.

Paul Tillich referred to "Ultimate Concern". To be concerned means to be involved, to be engaged in something – *not* to be indifferent, but rather to be concerned *anxiously*. In the Luke story, 10:38–42, Martha is worried about many things, but Mary, for her part, has chosen *the one thing needful*. As Tillich says, 'The one thing needed – this is the first and in some sense the last answer I can give – is to be concerned ultimately, unconditionally, infinitely. This is what Mary was'.[34] She was never indifferent.

If in some small insignificant corner of the universe *someone is concerned*, the universe is not entirely meaningless.

Famously Nietzsche: he who has reason to live, the "why" can bear almost any "how". Viktor Frankl's very simple *Man's Search for Meaning* is still available and selling after 70 or so years. In the gratuitously pitiless universe of the camps, Frankl managed to help some of the abject victims find *meaning* even in midst of dire chaos, and thus to survive. In the light of the Frankl book and the spirit it conveys, the millions of therapy books pale into insignificance. For some camp inmates, helping and being helped by Frankl's and their own discovered courage and inspiration, were able to approach Dostoevsky's dire hope that he might become worthy of his suffering. Having something, or someone, to live for (alive or dead) could enable the victim to keep a minimal hold on their moral and spiritual life. 'A man who becomes conscious of the responsibility he bears towards a human being ... or towards unfinished work, will never be able to throw away his life. He knows the "Why"'[35] One woman, who was dying, clung to the beauty of the blossoms on the branch of a chestnut tree outside her hut. She knew she would die in a few days.

> Pointing through the window of the hut, she said, 'This tree here is the only friend I have in my loneliness'. Through that window she could see just one branch ... 'I often talk to this tree'. Anxiously I asked her if it replied. 'Yes ... It said to me – I am here – I am here – I am, eternal life'.[36]

Those who maintain an inner hold on their moral and spiritual selves stand a better chance of survival that those who don't. Frankl observes how often, 'man considers only the stubble field of transitoriness and overlooks the full granaries of the past'.[37] Frankl's invention of "Logotherapy" depends on the potential for meaning in the past of our own existence, even within unimaginable suffering.

Care

When we go into a garden, with all the flowers and insects and *so on*, it's natural to believe there is a gardener who tends these flowers! When we see a flock of sheep, it is natural to believe there is a shepherd to guard the sheep. When we see children, it is natural to imagine a father to care for them. Tending, guarding, caring, and *so on*.

And, indeed, with a cursory glance at the animal kingdom we see parental care, parental provision in insects, notably the social insects such as ants, bees, and wasps; in certain fish, widely in birds, in amphibians, some reptiles and, especially widely, care provision in mammals, which share two major biological adaptations for care of the young, namely gestation and production of milk. When we reach up our own evolutionary branch, as it were, we find female primates investing heavily both prenatally and post-natally in the care and feeding of infants. And, finally, with humans the caregiving reaches extreme development with premature birth and Winnicott's description of "primary maternal preoccupation",[38] together with the whole panoply of object relation and attachment theories, describing the facilitation of the emerging intelligence connected to the explosively evolved forebrain of the genus *Homo*. Bion refers to the "protective atmosphere" provided by the mother's reverie:

> like the earth, he [the child] carries with him an atmosphere, albeit a mental one, which shields him from the mental counterpart of the cosmic and other rays at present supposed to be rendered innocuous to men, thanks to the physical atmosphere.[39]

And in Bion's terms this availability of intelligence (Plotinus), emanating from the One, is called "alpha function".[40] It enables us to dream, memorise, and think.

> The sleeping man has an emotional experience, converts it into alpha-elements and so becomes capable of dream thoughts. Thus he is free to become conscious (that is wake up) and describe the emotional experience by a narrative usually known as a dream.[41]

This function, associated with the reverie of the mother, is most commonly associated in neurologically reductive terms, with the hippocampus.

It is tempting here to probably fully misinterpret Alain Badiou, when he says that women in traditional societies are hidden so that God can exist: 'Tradition knows that, to keep God alive no matter what, women absolutely have to be made invisible'.[42] Traditionally, men were the bearers of the One, that is, patriarchy, guarantors of stable hierarchy, and *so on*. Women were associated with the Two: between the mother and whore, lover and saint, and *so on*. Thus, women now *appearing* is connected for Badiou with atheism – God cannot now exist. Badiou goes on to make the point that women are becoming the One in the post-patriarchal world – judges, administrators, CEOs, ministers, and *so on*.

> a woman becomes the model of the new One, the One that stands boldly and brashly before the competitive market and is both its servant and its master. Contemporary woman will be the symbol of the new One, erected on the ruins of the Name-of-the-Father.[43]

Three of the traditional figures of the feminine disappear in modernity: seduction, amorous gift, and the mystical sublime. Badiou asserts that: 'And lastly, the woman-One couldn't care less about the mystical sublime. She would prefer to run real organisations'.[44] But from our perspective here the figure of the mystical sublime is key. Women are hidden so that God can exist. God is hidden; woman is hidden. Woman in her bearing of the infant, in her suckling of the infant, in her rapport with the infant; in all of these hidden practices she approaches the simplicity of God on earth. Women are hidden so that God can exist *through her*. Without *Her*, there is no God. Instead, as Badiou continues: 'there is a whole bourgeois, authoritarian brand of feminism. It is not calling for a different world to be created but for the world as it is to be turned over to woman power',[45] and what he calls 'the women-One as capitalism's reserve army'.[46]

Hospitality

Called to the reserve army of capitalism, nothing could be further from the "hidden woman" (like God) of hospitality. The story of the hospitality of Abraham in Genesis 18 is exemplary. Three strangers appear at the entrance to the tent during the heat of the day. Abraham and Sarah offer hospitality to them, including foot washing, rest, and a sumptuous meal. Only later do Abraham and Sarah realise that they have given hospitality to God. This is hospitality beyond the "laws of hospitality". As Derrida says, 'This unconditional law of hospitality, if such a thing is thinkable, would then be a law without imperative, without order and without duty. A law without a law, in short … graciously offered beyond debt and economy'.[47]

Surely the womb of the woman comes closest to unconditional hospitality which (even biologically speaking) is graciously offered beyond debt and economy. And the greatest among women, the Virgin Mary: *Blessed are you among women, and blessed is the fruit of your womb* (Luke 1:42). The incarnational event:

> The mystery of Christ is deeply connected to the mystery of Mary: in her the word of God does not remain empty it is received in the world: the

soil of the Church ... In her heart the soil of humanity became fertile, Mary "found self-fulfillment" in her complete availability![48]

We are to be witnesses to the history of Salvation in the image of Mary. Mary contributes to the history of Salvation with her "*humilitas*" (humility, humiliation) in the image of Christ. It is this "*kenosis*" (humiliation) that moves the history of Salvation forward. It is a difficult path.[49]

Incarnation

Thus, the key transformative moment in evolution, prepared for in the eon's long pre-history, namely the Incarnation, arrives in the most invisible manner. The Word made flesh. The unprecedented entrance of God *into history*, as every child delights in, in the most humble surroundings and circumstances. God gives Himself entirely. But He remains secret insofar as He is a person. He is hidden in His manifestation.

In Christianity, God's proximity had already been provided for through the gift of the Law. But then the Incarnation was an event with cosmic reverberations: the star of the Magi eclipsed other stars.

A star shone in the sky more brightly than all the others. Its light was unspeakable. Its novelty (*kainotes*) was shocking (*xenismon pareikhen*) ... Then all magic was destroyed, colour and every connection of malice abolished, ignorance was dissipated ... And everything was disturbed, for the destruction of death was being prepared.[50]

Forgiveness, charity, mercy, reconciliation, and *so on* fully enter the world. Just as celebrating parents might speculate apropos their young child: 'out there our love is walking'.

Chesterton outlines what is really new and larger than anything that had gone before:

The Church contains what the world does not contain. Life itself does not provide as she does for all sides of life. That every other single system is narrow and insufficient compared to this one; that is not a rhetorical boast; it is a real fact and a real dilemma. Where is the Holy child amid the Stoics and the ancestor-worshippers? Where is Our Lady of the Moslems, a woman made for no man and set above all angels?[51]

The Incarnation as a world-shattering event: 'There is in this buried divinity an idea of undermining the world; of shaking the towers and palaces from below; even as Herod the great king felt that earthquake under him and swayed with his swaying palace'.[52] It is the permanent Rupture of the Divine Gift. According to radical theologians Davis and Aaron Riches, 'The Event is simultaneously the moment of immanent rupture and the eternity of transcendent fulfilment

– it is the creative overdetermination of all material and bodily things. The Event is perpetual'.[53] It explodes every category. It acts as a trauma. It gives abundant life to the lifeless. 'The Event is the repeated mobilization of matter and bodies as the Logos by the Pneuma'.[54] It is registered, without being written down as such, via *metanoia* – a repentant turn towards being-as-gift, breaking open the self-ego.

This conclusion here is written, however inadequately, under the aegis of the liberating Event of the Incarnation, breathing life into and breaking open the self, beyond its pettiness. A potential permanent revolution of an excess – the breath of life, the Spirit indwelling in matter – that is at all times uncontainable and free. *Repent: for the kingdom of heaven is at hand* (Matt. 4:17).

Hospitality beyond the "laws of hospitality", agape incarnated, and the transcendent and immanent meet in a new radical concern for the individual – the broken, the crippled, the poor, and *so on*. Beyond existing notions of human solidarity, as Charles Taylor puts it:

> [T]his is seen more as something to be built, an eschatological concept. And the paradigmatic stepping beyond of *agape*, the incarnation and submission to death of Christ, is not motivated by a pre-existing community or solidarity. *It is free gift of God.*[55]

Furthermore, 'God's intervention in history, and in particular the Incarnation, was intended to transform us, through making us partakers of the communion which God already is and lives. It was meant to effect our "deification" (theiosis)'.[56] God was no longer to be understood as an impersonal Being out there, the idea of the Good or the One of Plotinus, as it were. Instead, Lossky says, 'What would otherwise seem absurd – that fallen, sinful man may become holy as God is holy – has been made possible through Jesus Christ, who is God incarnate'.[57]

This is not so much an evolution, one more large step on the teleological ladder as it were; absolutely not! This is *total* rupture of time – the eternal breaking into time. Agape becomes possible because God became flesh. This is a seismic event, like the Big Bang. So big that ever since we have been trying to reduce the shock of Christianity back down to a mere moral code, to bring it back to human(ist) proportions. Just as every revolution starts ecstatically in the Real and ends up being recuperated by the Symbolic, whereby the Spirit is all but lost in the textual.

Something of that transforming Spirit caught the historian of antiquity, Tom Holland, when he was researching his book, *Dominion*. As a child, like many children, he was very taken with the idea of the power of the dinosaurs. This translated in adult life to writing about the Egyptians and the Syrians, the Babylonians and the Persians, the Greeks, then the Romans. He identified with the glamour and power of the classical world. Caesar killed a million Gauls. Then came the explosive scandal of Christianity, where power is reversed. The weak become strong.

And the foundational symbol of Christianity is someone suffering death on an instrument of torture. There are tortures, there are people burned, there are people hanged. Of course, and Christianity is founded on someone who, rather than fight back, surrenders himself, puts up his sword and willingly goes to death.[58]

Wanton cruelty was entirely normal in the Western world and taken as a sign of power, certainly a legacy of Darwinian evolution. Crucifixion, a celebration of that power to humiliate, used by the Romans against slaves, was taken by Christians and made very parodoxically into a symbol of love and forgiveness.

The Romans, for instance, had one word "*mayo*" for urine *and* ejaculate. Such was the abuse of women (and men). Any orifice would serve. Thus, what the Romans took for granted was deemed perverse in the new Christian light. Thus, when Paul stresses monogamy, spiritual love between a man and a woman, this is entirely new. As Holland stresses, Paul was

> giving an incredibly potent sacral quality to the physical body of a woman. That a woman is not there to be sexually abused … And if that's true of an aristocratic woman, it's also true of the lowest humblest woman in a Roman household.[59]

However, the formula from revolutionary Real to mundane Symbolic is traversed in *Dominion*. Holland claims traces derived from Christianity and eruptions of revolutionary Christianity occur throughout the subsequent two millennia. Plus, of course, Christians themselves engaging in sacral violence: 'there [were] people with crosses on their surcoats who are attacking Muslim Spain and attacking the pagans … And they're taking the cross across the Atlantic and wiping out great empires there. So of course, there is a massive, massive tension there'.[60]

Noting the fate of the Yazidis in 2014 at the hands of the Islamic State, Holland concludes, 'Terror of power was the index of power. That was how it had always been and always would be. It was the way of the world'.[61] However, what he calls the,

> sheer strangeness of Christianity … remains as alive as it has ever been. It is manifest in the great surge of conversions that have swept Africa and Asia over the past century; in the conviction of millions upon millions that the breath of the spirit like a living fire still blows upon the world; and in Europe and in North America in the assumptions of many more millions who would never think to describe themselves as Christian.[62]

This "sheer strangeness" of Christianity must be respected. Thus, to imply in any way that the Incarnation is a mere step advancement in evolution is entirely misleading and wrong. That some immense thing happened, during a very particular moment in (evolutionary) history which changed everything, cannot be refuted, but this cannot be refracted through science. Science cannot *see* this. Thus the "*Science* of Intelligent Design" is a confusion of registers – physics and metaphysics. Science deals in knowledge on the "edge" of the Real. Science is reductive; it can never grasp sheer strangeness. The anthropic "fine-tuning" is investigated and explained by science, but the leap to a transcendent Creator is sheer strangeness. The "evidence" that we are collecting here now is the evidence emanating from the Other. It requires not investigation and analysis, but *openness*. C.S. Lewis has a question for science itself:

> If I swallow the scientific cosmology as a whole, then not only can I not fit in Christianity, but I cannot even fit in science. If minds are wholly dependent upon brains, and brains on biochemistry, and biochemistry (in the long run) on the meaningless flux of atoms, I cannot understand how the thought of those minds should have any more significance than the sound of the winds in the trees.[63]

He concludes,

> I am certain that in passing from the scientific point of view to the theological, I have passed from dream to waking. Christian theology can fit in science, art, morality, and the sub-Christian religions. The scientific point of view cannot fit in any of these things not even science itself. I believe in Christianity as I believe that the sun has risen, not only because I see it but because by it, I see everything else.[64]

Science comes to know things, but it does not know that it knows. Just as when one dreams one generally does not know that one is dreaming and indeed *who* is dreaming. It is only after waking that one can come to know that that was a dream! That was *my* dream! And only then for a brief moment before the other "dream", which is reality, sends us into unconsciousness. As the quip goes, life is what happens when we are making other plans. And we must go further, *abundant* life is what happens if only we are open to it. Not only does the sun rise, but soon it is too bright to behold.

The beatific vision

Influential Jesuit Henri de Lubac tells us, 'Since the time of Plato and Aristotle, "a light has shone in our sky", and all is new'.[65] For Aristotle, the key principle was the supreme intelligence, the thought of thought, an eternal and perfect living being, but one that was quite unaware of imperfect beings – 'no movement of love makes him [it] turn even a glance towards us'.[66] For Christians there is a fundamental change from the *im*personal light of intelligence to the "beatific vision". No longer merely a spectacle of supreme enlightenment, but an intimate participation in the vision the Son has of the Father.

St Paul hints that he has had a vision so powerful that he dared not speak of it. 'We see now in a glass darkly, but then face to face' (I Corinthians 13:12). Likewise, Aquinas thought the "beatific vision" is formally achievable only *after* death. However, then remarkably just before ending his *Summa Theologica*, Aquinas famously declared on 6 December 1273: 'All that I have written seems to me like straw compared to what has now been revealed to me'. Aquinas put down his pen. 'I can do no more. Such secrets have been revealed to me that all I have written now appears to be of little value'.[67] De Lubac tells us that we must consent to "total sacrifice" and quotes Maurice Blondel, 'No man can see God without dying'.[68] Dying with(out) biological dying. But dying in the presence of abundance: 'try to think of the utter gratuitousness of God's gift'.[69] However, we cannot claim or redeem this gift; we are not in any way "owed" it by our obedience or our good works, or our elevated spiritual status, or as a fully analysed person, or the buddha within; none of these. It is entirely gratuitous, not some kind of payback. It is entirely free!

In a sense, this is an insult to all high-minded spiritual elites, who feel they have earned their superior status. Recall Žižek's joke about the two (entitled) rabbis who come before God declaring solemnly their nullity. The first rabbi stands up and says: 'O God, I know I am worthless. I am nothing!' After he has finished, a rich businessman stands up and says, beating himself on the chest: 'O God, I am also worthless, obsessed with material wealth. I am nothing!' Then, a poor and bedraggled ordinary Jew stands up and proclaims: 'Dear God, look kindly upon me, I am nothing'. The rich businessman nudges the rabbi, 'What insolence! Who is that guy who dares to claim that he is nothing too!'[70]

God Himself remains sovereign and utterly independent. De Lubac is clear. God has/had no need or obligation to create us, 'nor could He be constrained or required by anything or anyone to imprint on my being a supernatural finality'.[71] The gift of creation of a spiritual being is enough. That is it! Imagine two floors with no necessary connection between them. If creation is a grace, then the call of God is on *another* floor. De Lubac follows Meister Eckhart in the notion of the two rivers of gratuity: one carrying creation and the other carrying the supernatural. *There is no connection.*

Freely given

If we take the admittedly overwhelmingly magnificent story of evolution that we have been following right up to man and self-consciousness, does it necessarily culminate in the Incarnation? Emphatically, no. Just as the history of Israel was a preparation for the coming of Christ? No. '[T]he distance is as great, the difference is as radical, as that between non-being and being'.[72] Neither is merely about "the more", as it were, but 'the crossing, by grace, of an impassable barrier'.[73] Once again, there is no meritocracy here, no recouping the cost of good works. Just like the prodigal son was celebrated although he had not merited a welcome, far from it. Riches of any kind – financial, intellectual, cultural – are the enemy.

The Incarnation is *the* Christian Event; all the rest pales into insignificance. And Aquinas held that this ultimate finality is something intrinsic, 'affecting the depth of being ... the order of the universe ... the order of parts of the universe in relation to each other'.[74] For this is a whole new world. For orthodox theologian Tracey Rowland only three things have really happened in history! Creation, the Incarnation, and the Eschaton.[75]

If we follow Leithart explaining de Lubac, 'There is nothing that is "purely natural". Since all is created, the "supernatural" (if we wish to retain the terminology) is always already present within ordinary creation. The ordinary is extraordinary'.[76] As we have explained,

> On the one hand, human beings have a natural longing for fulfillment of their nature in the vision of God; on the other hand, this natural longing is fulfilled *not* as a necessity or a matter of justice, but in an act of sheer grace.

To believe that there is an autonomous nature, separate from God, is the source of modern secularism, the reductionism of modern science, and, ultimately, nihilism. Thus, the notion of human nature itself is confusing because *it is already a gift*. Leithart cites Milbank: 'gratuity arises before necessity or obligation and does not even require the contrast in order to be comprehensible. The creature as creature is not the recipient of a gift, *it is itself this gift*'.[77]

To summarise de Lubac's position,

> [W]e could say that if we insist that grace is *merely* given to complete an already existing "pure nature", we give the impression that grace is an added optional extra. Rather, the intention of God in creating human nature is to communicate His divine life to beings other than Himself. The gift of sanctifying grace is incomparable. ***Human nature exists to receive grace*** – grace does not exist for the sake of human nature; the purpose of nature is to receive grace, even though nature can still function in some attenuated form without it.[78]

The key is openness to the super-abundance, the always extraordinary ordinary, the miraculous. De Lubac envisages a twofold call coming from God's initiative which then sounds within the creature of nature now sufficiently evolved with the organ of consciousness to receive it. And the idea that God could have withheld the call is implied by our recognition of it *as a gift*.

> Something we might call an "invention in being", the idea of a gift coming gratuitously from above to raise up that needy nature, at once satisfying its longings and transforming it – such an idea remains wholly foreign to all those whose minds have not been touched by the light of Revelation.[79]

De Lubac speaks of a *sursum*, a lifting up of the heart, the radically new interruption, incommensurate with nature, to exemplify the otherness of the supernatural.

'*The heavens declare the glory of God; the skies proclaim the work of his hands*' (Psalm 19:1).

As Hopkins says, 'The world is charged with the grandeur of God'.

How does one preserve majesty here? How is such otherness not merely trivialised by the clichés in a million "Get well!" cards, or even the astral covers of devotional religious books and therapy leaflets, and *so on*? How is Revelation protected in its aura from every cheapened version? This is the fate of every creation – to be simulated to death; to be copied so much that the original disappears. Even Aristotle's "rational contemplation" is regarded only as a stepping stone to the supernatural,[80] because the contemplation remains, as it were, *in us*. What is missing is 'the idea of God, *upon which all else depends*'.[81] The joy spoken of is the shattering event of agape. Simone Weil, when she was 26 (in 1935), became intensely moved by the beauty of villagers singing hymns during an outdoor service that she came across during a holiday in Portugal. At this point, she became convinced that Christianity was indeed a slave-religion, the religion of the poor.[82] They could see God.

The joy perceptible only through lack, only through humility – being close to the soil – through poverty and suffering, the poverty of nature. What we have gets in the way. "Bless you!" means nothing if you are rich and think you need nothing. De Lubac underlines the danger of understanding God through Neoplatonist metaphors such as emanations, or "gushing generosity", or goodness, and *so on*. Instead, 'God is love in person, love which freely, and not because of any law or inner determination, creates the being to whom he wills to give himself, and gives himself freely ... that living flame of charity'.[83] It is *us, in person*, destined for this love. And the key, 'is to be found in the nature of our intellect: we cannot receive divine revelation without at once starting to ask questions'.[84] And why love us? Not because we are worthy of it; quite the reverse, because we are so utterly poor in spirit, just hanging on by our fingertips.

> Human nature exists to receive Grace
> Without this understanding we are adrift
> Love creates reality. Love breathes life
> Life is gracious
> Love creates the Father, who watches over us.

Not staged

Thus, if the supernatural is the pneuma, the breath that sets the universe aflame, glimpsed by those who have eyes to see, as it were, who might begin to ask questions and bear witness to beauty and to suffering (revealed only by this divine breath), does this not mean in effect that God is pulling the strings behind the scenes? Quite the reverse: creation is a gift freely given. The Real by definition is *not* staged. The Imaginary, the Symbolic, the hyperreal, the virtual, the simulated, or whatever *are all staged and to that degree false*. The Real is beyond all imagining as is the Spirit that animates it, that "abundant life" is utterly free. By definition, however, we are mostly blind to the Real.[85]

C.S. Lewis says that when he sees a field mouse in the hedgerow it is not a mechanical creature put there to amuse him or teach him a moral lesson. He quotes a Greek poet, 'If water sticks in your throat, what will you take to wash it down?'[86] Like Baudrillard's joke: powdered water – just add water. If nature herself is artificial or contrived in some way, where else would you go for the really Real? 'To say that God created her is not to say that she is unreal, but precisely that she is real'.[87] Like a poet, God's creation expresses His idiom. 'Supernaturalists really see Nature. You must go a little away from her, and look back'.[88] You must see the world as it was before man arrived, beyond any chance of adulteration or simulation.

His idiom is immensely complex. The laws of nature (deduced by science) are necessarily reductive of the Real. What we call miracle is perhaps the hidden culmination or climax of that Real, rarely glimpsed, like a beautiful piece of music can be realised from what after all are mere sound waves. Miracles are occurring continuously but we do not perceive them with our low grade perception, made lower by the necessary strictures (and violence) of the scientific method. My cardiologist tells me that the heart is just a pump and the arteries are its plumbing – that's it! Nothing more! Such is our alienation.[89] As Lewis explains:

> A man's rational thinking is *just so much* of his share in eternal Reason as the state of his brain allows to become operative: it represents so to speak the bargain struck or the [evolutional] frontier fixed between reason and nature at that particular point.[90]

We are intelligent, but (super)nature is super-intelligent, with us uniquely in mind due to love. The finite cannot conceive of, cannot accommodate, the infinite.

Maybe we should recall the suicides of the humanoid robots in Ian McEwan's *Machines Like Me*. Having more share in (eternal) reason than us with their artificial intelligence, the Adams and the Eves of this alternative world cannot bear what they see in terms of human folly and outrage. They were exposed/created by super-intelligence *without* love, *without* grace. Unlike us, they were *not* created in the image of God (*imago Dei*), they were created in our scientific image! They are robotic – they have nothing with which to counter a foundational vacancy, and perhaps *their* intelligence senses this appalling void at a greater volume than us lesser intelligencies?

These machines are quite literally *like* me, but with one significant difference, in that they were *not born of woman: in near total vulnerability*. According to McAleer and Wojtulewitz, in a very significant paper, 'It is on account of our origin in immaturity that Christ became incarnate: our wounded desires need the balm of seeing God face to face. Christ came to overcome what Jacques Lacan calls our *primal dereliction*'.[91] There is no doubt that AI (artificial intelligence) is being increasingly realised as the culmination of an essentially anti-Christian ideology. And McEwan obliges. Against human exceptionalism, he recites the list of human de-throning and rather pathetically declares, 'we would devise a machine a little cleverer than ourselves, then set the machine to invent another that lay beyond our comprehension. What need then of us?'[92] McAleer and Wojtulewitz refer to Mary as the 'veil of Christ' with the mother's love as the 'veil of the phallus', to show that the structure of human desire is unique and exceptional and thus not reproducible by technical means. Just as you cannot add grace to nature as an afterthought, you cannot add grace to machine-nature as an afterthought. Our authors believe that motherless AI will only ever have what they call a 'thin psychology',[93] in the absence of this complex privilege of being born from woman and being elected by a father:

> a cradled period of gestation outside of the womb, oriented by the problem of love, its suffering, and the insatiable gravitation towards what is lacking in ourselves, and others, in order to supply for this lack (the phallus). This is not the stuff of technoscience: we live in a commercial civilization and the Apex machine is AI.[94]

The AI "lives" without castration, avoiding Lacan's notion of 'the drama of primordial jealousy'[95] and that dread feeling that something is amiss, which ultimately only God can assuage. Thus, 'this is why AI as *artificial* intelligence cannot track the (fraught) fullness of human intelligence; its underlying structure is always going to be a resemblance, mirroring, or imitation of only an element of human mental life'.[96] In short, the Imaginary.[97] Whereas a baby, although part of the natural order, 'has the quality of a visitation, a coming from *beyond*, as mysterious popping into existence'.[98]

And we have become quite literally *like the machines*, in our desire to escape castration and to escape the largely unknown, because unsought for, incandescence of the Incarnation. We are trying to go it alone, quite literally, which may of course be admirable and courageous, but already doomed. We too have also ended up with a "thin" psychology, as nearly everything about us becomes artificial and in no need of grace. The AI totalitarian super-surveillance internet-of-things is just a few years away.

Beauty

At the other extreme of the machine, there is beauty. Hans Urs von Balthasar was a great lover of beauty.[99] He says that beauty is the first word that we must say. Of the transcendental properties – Truth, Goodness, and Beauty – he presents the order differently to most philosophers, putting beauty first, which bridges the gap between God and man. As Plato says, beauty is the one spiritual form that radiates, as it were, and we can see its radiance with our own eyes. Of the three transcendentals, beauty tends to be relegated to the background.

But Balthasar claims that beauty is in the background not because it is less important, but because it is the most important. It is the ground from which truth and goodness make sense. The true and the good are so because they are beautiful. It is by virtue of beauty that the true is really true and the good is really good. Beauty contains the whole – of all the things we tend to split apart: like, the body and the soul; the intellect and the senses; subject and object, and *so on*. Beauty is both objective (out there) and subjective (a feeling inside), the supernatural and the natural, God and the world. Beauty lies at the intersection of these apparent opposites. This intersection reaches its highest point, as it were, with the Incarnation, where God enters human flesh.

Balthasar is following Aquinas when he points out that beauty is the unity of form *qua* gestalt, and splendour, a light that radiates forth from within. There is something of an epiphany. Firstly, the mystery we perceive in the epiphany is equated with depth, or better, the Real beyond reality. It is far from being superficial or a simulacrum. Secondly, it points to the mystery of being (as opposed to nothing). Thirdly, it points to the mystery of God himself. These three are once again inseparable. Thus, the beauty of this tree for instance, arraigned in its autumn colours, points to the Creator himself. The vision and rapture of beauty, as Balthasar understands it, its veiling and unveiling, moves us, lifts us up, and provides a clarity, reality, and truthfulness, a conviction no less of its divine nature.

However, theologically, it is not vision first, rapture second; that would put *us* too much in control in our approach to God. This incidentally is also the danger of putting truth first, rather than beauty. Or, on the other hand, if the rapture came first then we would not be in control and we would lose our freedom – God would be in control. We would then be talking about a blind obedience, a leap of faith which is irrational. We must have the *two*, vision and rapture, together: we then have our full freedom while also being lifted up to God, being called by God. This sets the stage for what Balthasar calls the theo-drama, the dynamic between human freedom and being called by God. This is played out under the sign of the Good and yields as its fruit, wisdom, deeper understanding, and, thus, to the moment of the truth. If we began with human freedom, God would be under our control. Whereas true freedom occurs under the sign of beauty.

Beauty calls us to the particularity of *this* moment and its infinite possibilities, the transcendent that opens up if only our perception was not so limited. The perception of beauty requires openness. According to Balthasar, cited by Waldstein,

> there is a parallel between [our theological aesthetics] and the phenomenological method of Scheler, inasmuch as this method aims at allowing the object *to give itself purely* ... the first thing we should be concerned with is to apprehend the revelation of God, and God can only be recognized by his Lordship (*Herr-heit*), his lofty splendor *(Hehr-heit)* ... The world was created for God's glory.[100]

The 'object giving itself', Balthasar is concerned with the *objectivity* of beauty – the radiance from within, 'an objective light which breaks into my spiritual space as permanently other than myself'.[101]

Balthasar relies heavily on Goethe's philosophy of nature. As Rudolf Steiner suggests,

> [Goethe's] art appears as the herald of that lawfulness that the poet has grasped by listening to the world spirit within the depth of nature's working. At this level art becomes the interpreter of the mysteries of the world just as science is also.[102]

However, we must be clear, 'For von Balthasar, beauty is not a "cultural" decoration surrounding "serious" reality. It is, rather, the primary and central "face" of serious reality as it graciously discloses itself'.[103]

As Balthasar says, 'every created being is a manifestation of itself (the more intensively, the higher it ranks [in evolution]): the representation of its own depths, the surface of its own ground, the word from its essential core'.[104] This is the polarity between essence and existence, or in Hopkins terms, *instress* and *inscape*, whereby the creative source shapes and is shaped by its form. And this creative source is gratuitousness. God created the world entirely freely, not out of necessity, and this *freedom* thus permeates the world itself in the most radically other way.

> If everything in the world that is beautiful and glorious is *epihaneia*, the radiance and splendor which breaks forth in expressive form from a veiled and yet mighty depth of being, then the event of the self-revelation of the hidden, the utterly free and sovereign God in the forms of this world, in word and history, and finally in the human form itself, will itself form an analogy to that worldly beauty, however far it outstrips it[105]

However, Balthasar is outrightly not proposing a sort of cultural aesthetics, but rather an existential drama in which, 'God utterly freely makes himself present as he commits to the fray',[106] which does not end with beauty. God cannot be contained in this way. In Christ the divine nature enters the world, 'as a sending and a being sent, a remaining in the background and a coming into the foreground, a remaining above and a descending and re-ascending',[107] united by the Holy Spirit.

Unity of nature, based on DNA, evolution, beautifully intricate and complex biochemical, mathematical design, and *so on*, reveals itself as divine, as radically other, yet utterly personal – *God knows us better than we know ourselves* (Romans 8:27). Thus, Revelation is living and personal as well as ineffable and properly hidden. Above all, the Revelation is of a self-abandoning love. As Waldstein summarises: 'one might almost say, the recklessness, with which God gives himself for the salvation of the world. God effectively pours himself out in complete weakness'.[108] Balthasar's key point:

From the deepest of all mysteries, the Father, this glory proceeds as the wellspring of all that is. The beauty of creatures can only be a distant echo of this procession of the Son as image and splendour of the Father in the unity of the Holy Spirit'.[109]

In the Incarnation, Jesus becomes 'the vessel of God's glory'.

Bishop Richard Harries on BBC Radio 4's *Thought for the Day*, speaks of 'his sheer astonishment that there is rational life at all, whether on this earth or any other planet. The big divide is not between believers and atheists but between those who are constantly surprised about being able to be, to think and choose and to love, and those, on the other hand, who take life for granted and think it is normal and are not brought up short before the wonder and mystery of existence. He ponders maybe during the Covid lockdown there has been a shift. People have had time to listen and look and experience the "thisness" of things. Walt Whitman: To me every hour of light and dark is a miracle, every cubic inch of space is a miracle, every square yard of the earth is spread with the same. What stranger miracles are there?[110]

Resurrection

The Resurrection is the key to understanding the whole of Scripture. The Resurrection was not preached in the early Church as a symbolic representation, or a legend, it was preached as a hard historical fact! And it more than likely really happened, as we have very specific eyewitness accounts. *You are the witnesses of these things* (Luke 24:48). The first witnesses to the empty tomb are women, Mary Magdalene, Joanna, and Mary, the mother of James. As women, they would have been regarded as low status persons not trusted to give evidence in court at that time. And they were indeed not believed, until Peter went to the tomb and saw the strips of linen in the empty tomb. If these were simply legends, why would you specify women as the first witnesses and be very careful to name them? Likewise, when Christ appears to the disciples on the road to Emmaus, why precisely Cleopas and Simon? They recognise Him when He breaks bread. And when He appears at the temple among them, he asks his disciples, *Look at my hands and my feet. It is I myself! Touch me and see; a ghost does not have flesh and bones, as you see I have* (Luke 24:39). He wants food, so they give him broiled fish. This is not symbolic. It is real food; Jesus is saying I am *really* here. It is *personal!* And the disciples experienced these scenes very personally.

> *Then he opened their minds so they could understand the Scriptures. He told them, 'This is what is written: The Messiah will suffer and rise from the dead on the third day, and repentance for the forgiveness of sins will be preached in his name to all nations, beginning at Jerusalem'.*
>
> (Luke 24:45–47)

> *When he had led them out to the vicinity of Bethany, he lifted up his hands and blessed them. While he was blessing them, he left them and was taken up into*

*heaven. Then they worshiped him and returned to Jerusalem with great joy. And
they stayed continually at the temple, praising God.*

(Luke 24:50–53)

When the people of that time hear about the Resurrection they tell everyone.
It dominates the preaching of Peter and Paul. And within just a few centuries,
such was the power of the new religion of Christianity, it was able to displace
the philosophers of the classical Greco-Roman world.

Jewish people are the most unlikely believers of this account. They were
forbidden even to say the name of God. Yet in a very short time they were
worshipping a man. Something had shattered their paradigm. The fact of the
Resurrection for them was a very inconvenient truth. Paul was offended by
Christianity and the Gospel. He was a Pharisee. He was killing Christians and
wanted to destroy the Christian cult. Then, on the road to Damascus, the
blinding light; the strangeness was overwhelming. *Have I not seen Jesus our Lord?*
(1 Corinthians 9:1) 'How time itself, like the tucking in of a bird's wings, or
the furling of the ships sails, had folded in on itself, and of how everything was
changed, overwhelmed him'.[111] He realised the Resurrection; Jesus was indeed
the Christ, the anointed One of God.

But if Christ was the Messiah, the anointed one, the chosen one, blessed
by God, and *so on*, how could God have allowed Him to be crucified? For
the Galatians to whom Paul was preaching, His was the most ignominious of
deaths, reserved for criminals and slaves. And Christ in desperation cried out to
God! It made no sense. What kind of salvation can a Messiah like that bring?
How would He be strong enough to save the strong and to save Israel? These
questions were left hanging until news of the Resurrection. Christ was raised
from the dead, so God *did* vindicate him. God did *not* forsake Him. Therefore,
when he was cursed and abandoned by everyone, it must have been thus for
someone else's sins. And then Paul recalls the New Covenant in Ezekiel and
Jeramiah where God is declaring that He is writing the law on their hearts: '*I
will put my law in their minds and write it on their hearts. I will be their God, and they
will be my people*' (Jeremiah 31:33).

With Good Friday and Easter Sunday together, Paul understood the *whole*
Bible with the hindsight of the Resurrection. It is a Messiah coming in weakness to save those who acknowledge their weakness and who feel their poverty, their lack, their relational yearning, their radical dependency on the
Other.

He is thus the most unlikely and paradoxical saviour. Paradoxical because
Christ is *not* just "the immaculate victim". As postmodern philosopher Gianni
Vattimo referring to René Girard suggests,

> Girard argues, with good reason, that this victim-based reading of Scripture
> is wrong. Jesus' incarnation did not take place to supply a victim adequate
> to his wrath; rather, Jesus came into the world precisely to reveal and abol-
> ish the nexus between violence and the sacred.[112]

The crucifixion shines the sharpest most blinding light on the violence of humanity. In essence, Christianity has not weakened itself. Far from it, the life, teaching, crucifixion, and Resurrection of Jesus is not, as is oftentimes alleged, the softening of metaphysics. Far from it, the Kingdom, that is not of this world, thus produces *a massive contradiction with the world*, a world that is fallen and violent, and as Girard has made clear, the Cross is the deepest truth of that violence, heretofore hidden behind the scapegoat. However, Vattimo adds, 'That the Christian churches continue to speak of Jesus as a sacrificial victim testifies to the survival of powerful traces of natural religion in Christianity'.[113]

Finally, the Resurrection is a vindication of Jesus' preaching of the Kingdom: it reveals that it is not just one more philosophy amongst many but is the way to live that is truly pleasing to God. It is precisely the Evental nature of the Resurrection that meant, 'The fabric of things was rent, a new order of time had come into existence, and all that had previously served to separate people was now as a consequence dissolved'.[114] Famously, *There is neither Jew nor Greek, slave nor free, male nor female, for you are all one in Christ Jesus* (Galatians 3: 28–29).

Imago Dei

In Catholic theology, humans are unique as we are created *imago Dei*. Against contemporary thought, according to theologian Tracey Rowland,

> Human beings, like the Trinity itself, are never isolated monads. They are conceived within their mother's womb and enter history as someone's son or daughter, with specific father and mother, and often siblings as well … Their identity is always defined by their relationships, including, though not exclusively their relationship to the Trinity.[115]

Truth, Beauty, and Goodness are all one. None can exist without the other. That primordial relational quality underlies human solidarity. Further, 'This participation is made possible by the fact that the human person has an intellect created to discern the truth, and a will to pursue goodness'.[116] Roland quotes Hubertus Mynarek in his review of Joseph Ratzinger's 1968 best-selling work *Introduction of Christianity*, 'The highest is not the absolute self-contained self-sufficiency, but *relatedness*.[117]

We should note in passing that "Object Relations" theory was a necessary correction to Freud's libidinal formulations. Relatedness is all. As Ronald Fairbairn said, 'The libido is primarily object seeking (rather than pleasure seeking as in classical theory)'.[118] The baby stops crying on sight of the breast.[119]

Not only are we created in God's image, but Conor Cunningham goes further, believing that we are already liberated by being an *intimate part of God's thought*:

> [U]nless we have been thought, that is, unless we subsist as the lived nonidentical repetition of divine thought, then we will lapse into either of the

two problematic models of difference. In being thought by God, being called into existence, I am the recollection of that call – the being of being thought by God. Such anamnesis prevents any subsequent hemorrhage of finitude into indefinite multiplication. For the specific is recalled, so it turns (metanoia) to hear this call, halting its slide into the dark night of purely negative determination, perpetual epistemic investigation, or absolute singularity – Ockham's res absolutae.[120]

Psychoanalysis used to be a vocation before it became reduced to a (serious) profession with rules, regulations, trainings, and mandates. You gave yourself to it and its antecedents and it seized you, like one hand reaching out to another across the void. Do we hear the distant muffled call? Being thought by God, being called by God? Being called to be free. Was this not the original meaning of "Free Association"? Not a negative determination, not a slide into the dark, but a joyous immensely humorous determination. The dream, the joke, the slip – ultimately humorous in their boundless freedom and lightness. The profligacy and excess of language, the innate bias of the human spirit towards *freedom, joy, and laughter.* Chesterton wondered what animals must think of the human animals' capacity to laugh!

> There is a future
> It is the Real
> It is personal
> It is abundance
> It is beyond time

★★★

Charles Melman was speaking at the inaugural congress of the Irish Lacanian analysts (APPI) in Dublin in autumn of 1994. He had mentioned the unintegrated Muslim minority in French cities and how there was increasing paranoia between the two communities. He outlined the mathematical model, the Euclidian notion of closed figures, to represent paranoia – the isolation of what is inside from what is without. And the assertion that what is out there must be kept out there. He was referring to the Lacanian register of the Imaginary, or the Kleinian notion of the "paranoid-schizoid" position. He contrasted this "cut", as Lacan referred to it, with the very different and intricate representation of space to be found in the Book of Kells, which he had visited in Trinity College Dublin.

Here, space is represented as a weaving, a fabric. That which at a certain moment disappears and goes outside returns from within. Melman held up a facsimile of St Mark with the lion, where St Mark himself has a weaving going through his body and he himself is entirely woven. Here of course is a representation of the intricacies of language or a depiction of the Lacanian register of the Symbolic, which constitutes us. Without language, we would not exist. Lacan at one point refers to the 'treasure-trove of signifiers',[121] the absolute generosity of language and meaning into which we are thrown by birth. And "beyond" language, beyond the pleasure principle of language – nothing? Really? Yes, nothing?

Returning to the Book of Kells. It is an illuminated manuscript dating from AD 800 containing the four Gospels of the New Testament, lavishly illustrated, together with various prefatory texts and tables. The manuscript's celebrity derives from the incomparable artistry, decoration, and images of plant, animal, and human ornament that punctuate the text, all with the aim of glorifying Jesus' life and preaching. Four major scribes copied the text. It was designed for ceremonial use on special liturgical occasions such as Easter rather than for daily services. The *Annals of Ulster* described it as 'the chief treasure of the Western world'. It attracts half a million visitors a year.[122] Here then, surely, language as the highest wisdom, the greatest gift to humanity, is displayed. A representation of the Symbolic.

★★★

To return to our theme in this volume:

Foreclose the Name-of-the-Father, degrade this wisdom of the world, represented by the Symbolic, it is not abolished as such, but returns in the Real as splinters or shards in the Night, *as terrifying forms of madness and conspiracy*.

If you foreclose the intricate ethos of courtesy and manners from the Symbolic, developed over generations, they will return in the Real of political correctness, violent "woke" cancellations and paranoid certainties.

If you banish religious belief from the public square, it will return in the murderous Real of fundamentalism and *absolute* knowledge.

If you denigrate and destroy conservative thought, the rich soil of traditional thinking and commentary, it will return in the brutal Real as fascistic violence.

If you undermine and ridicule men who have literally, without fanfare, built civilisation with their bare hands, "masculinity" will return increasingly in the Real of toxicity and rape.

Likewise, as you have divorced and instrumentalised sex from love and reproduction, it has returned in the Real of pornography and violence against the weak and vulnerable.

If you remove the self and its substantial coordinates from the Symbolic, which was once its home, it will return in the Real as a nomad, as a feral child, potentially violent and full of unpredictable rage, making random attacks because of mental dereliction, before, as they say, 'turning the gun on himself'.

Notes

1   Gray, J. 2018, p. 105.
2   Jackson, R.L. 2008, p. xxxv.
3   Ibid., p. xvii.
4   García Sanz, S. and Nzewi, C. 2017.
5   Dostoevsky, notebooks for *The Possessed*, quoted in de Lubac, H. 1995, p. 304.
6   Poems written by the author at the time of his bypass surgery in 2014.
7   Adorno, T. 1953. Aphorism, p. 153.
8   Ibid.
9   Lovell, J. Introduction to Saunders, G. 2013, p. xxx.
10 Richard Feynman. See: www.openculture.com/2012/08/the_character_of_physical _law_richard_feynmans_legendary_lecture_series_at_cornell_1964.html.
11 Emilsson, E. 2017, p. 38.
12 Ibid., p. 137.
13 See, for instance: https://plato.stanford.edu/entries/platonism-mathematics/.
14 Steiner, G. 2001, p. 176.
15 Ibid., p. 180.
16 Ibid., p. 181.
17 Meyer, S. 2009.
18 Kitadai, N. and Maruyama, S. 2018.
19 Lacan, J. 1970, pp. 108/132.
20 Lacan, J. 1954–1955, p. 5.
21 Wolfe, T. 2016, p. 158.
22 p. 163.
23 p. 165.
24 Monod, J. 1969, pp. 15–16.
25 Behe, M. 1996, p. 193.
26 Smith, J. 2012; Darwin, C. 1859, p. 189.
27 Gardner, H. 1983.
28 Frayn, M. 2008.
29 Kuhn, R.L. 2019.
30 Dawkins, R. 1995.
31 The first black and white images came in 1966 when a NASA spacecraft captured the first-ever photograph of Earth from the Moon.
32 Lewis, C.S. 1947, p. 81. Emphasis added.
33 Lewis, C.S. 1952, p. 39.
34 Tillich, P. 1973, pp. 269–270.
35 Frankl, V. 1946, p. 80.
36 Ibid., p. 69.
37 Ibid., pp. 122–123.
38 Winnicott, D. 1956.
39 Bion, F. (ed) 1992, p. 192.
40 Bion, W. 1962, p. 16.
41 Ibid., p. 15.
42 Badiou, A. 2017, p. 95.
43 Ibid., p. 98.
44 Ibid., pp. 98–99.
45 Ibid., p. 97.
46 Ibid., p. 102. Women were the reserve army for Communism too (see Chapter 2).
47 Derrida, J. 2000, p. 83.
48 Wojtyla, K. 2017, pp. 208–209.
49 p. 178.
50 Ignatius of Antioch cited in Brague, R. 2003, p. 156.

51 Chesterton, G.K. 1925, pp. 115–116.
52 p. 118.
53 Davis, C. and Aaron Riches, P. 2005, p. 23.
54 Ibid.
55 Taylor, C. 2007, p. 246, emphasis added.
56 Ibid. p. 278.
57 Lossky, V. 1957, p. 23.
58 Holland, T. 2020. 'Christianity gave women a dignity that no previous sexual dispensation had offered'. https://scroll.in/article/953904/christianity-gave-women-a-dignity-that-no-previous-sexual-dispensation-had-offered-tom-holland.
59 Ibid.
60 Ibid.
61 Holland, T. 2019, p. 525.
62 Ibid., pp. 524–525.
63 Lewis, C.S. 1949, p. 139.
64 Ibid. p. 140.
65 De Lubac is quoting Clement of Alexandria in de Lubac, H. 1965, p. 228.
66 Ibid.
67 https://livingchurch.org/2014/01/28/awakening-aquinas/.
68 De Lubac, H. 1965, op. cit., p. 29.
69 Ibid., p. 50.
70 See for instance, https://thereader.mitpress.mit.edu/five-jokes-slavoj-zizek/.
71 De Lubac, H. 1965, op. cit., p. 80.
72 Ibid., p. 83.
73 Ibid.
74 De Lubac, H. 1965, op. cit., p. 100.
75 Olivant, D. 2004.
76 Leithart, P. 2006.
77 Ibid. Emphasis added.
78 O'Shea, G. 2012, p. 10, emphasis added.
79 De Lubac, H. 1965 op. cit., p. 130.
80 Cited in de Lubac. 1965, p. 223.
81 Ibid., emphasis added.
82 Miles, S. 2005, p. 29.
83 De Lubac, H. 1965, op. cit., p. 235.
84 Ibid., p. 237.
85 In Kleinian terms, the PS ("paranoid-schizoid") position is our normal state with the Real scattered in fragments to make feelings manageable. The D is that point of contact with the Real, which happens fleetingly and could lead to joy or suicide.
86 Lewis, C.S. 1947, op. cit., p. 101.
87 Ibid., p. 102.
88 Ibid., p. 104.
89 However, I am immensely appreciative of the fact that he has spent many years in serious training and devotion to his work in common with other cardiologists all over the world. A massive act of love. And he has saved lives with his scientific method and courage. But, as Pascal famously said, the heart has it reasons of which reason knows nothing.
90 Lewis, C.S. 1947, op. cit., p. 62.
91 McAleer, G. and Wojtulewitz, C. 2019, p. 282.
92 McEwan, I. 2019, p. 80.
93 McAleer, G. and Wojtulewitz, C. 2019, p. 289.
94 Ibid., p. 284.
95 Lacan, J. 1970, op. cit., p. 99.
96 McAleer, G. and Wojtulewitz, C. 2019, p. 289.

97 The *thinness* is experienced by real humans (in say old peoples' homes where robot-carers have been used) as uncanny and almost real.
98 McAleer, G. and Wojtulewitz, C. 2019, p. 293.
99 I am indebted here to Schindler, D. 2017.
100 Waldstein, M. 1987, pp. 14–15. Italics added.
101 Ibid., pp. 17–18.
102 Steiner, R. 1988.
103 Waldstein, M. op. cit., p. 16.
104 Ibid., 22. Balthasar cited.
105 Ibid., pp. 24–25.
106 Ibid., p. 25.
107 Ibid., p. 26.
108 Ibid., p. 31.
109 Ibid., p. 33.
110 BBC Radio 4. 19 June 2020. www.bbc.co.uk/sounds/play/p08hf5yr.
111 Holland, T. 2019, op. cit., p. 66.
112 Vattimo, G. 1999, p. 37.
113 Ibid., p. 38.
114 Holland, T. op. cit., p. 69.
115 Rowland, T. 2021, p. 2.
116 Ibid.
117 Ibid., p. 4.
118 Fairbairn, R. 1952, p. 82.
119 Of course for Lacan *et al.*, the seduction by the breast is the first step towards our alienation in the evil universe of the Other (see Chapters 8 and 9).
120 Cunningham, C. 2005, pp. 95–96.
121 Lacan, J. 1970, op. cit., p. 682.
122 www.tcd.ie/library/manuscripts/book-of-kells.php.

References

Adorno, T. 1953. *Minima Moralis*. Trans. Redmond, D. https://www.marxists.org/reference/archive/adorno/1951/mm/ch03.htm

Badiou, A. 2017. *The True Life*. Trans. Spitzer, S. Cambridge, UK and Malden: The Polity Press.

Behe, M. 1996. *Darwin's Black Box. The Biochemical Challenge to Evolution*. New York: The Free Press.

Bion, F. (Ed.). 1992. *Cogitations*. London: Karnac.

Bion, W. 1962. *Learning from Experience*. London: Karnac Books.

Brague, R. 2003. *The Wisdom of the World*. Trans. Fagan, R.L. Chicago and London: University of Chicago Press.

Chesterton, G.K. 1925. *The Everlasting Man*. London: Hodder and Stoughton.

Cunningham, C. 2005. "Nothing Is, Something Must Be: Lacan and Creation from No one". In Davis, C. Milbank, J. Zizek, S. (Eds.) *Theology and the Political*. London and Durham: Duke University Press, 72–101.

Darwin, C. 1859. *The Origin of Species by Natural Selection*. London: John Murray. https://en.wikipedia.org/wiki/On_the_Origin_of_Species

Davis, C., Aaron Riches, P. 2005. "Metanoia: The Theological Praxis of Revolution". In Davis, C., Milbank, J., Zizek, S. (Eds.) *Theology and the Political*. London and Durham: Duke University Press, 22–51.

Davis, C., Milbank, J., Zizek, S. 2005. *Theology and the Political*. London and Durham: Duke University Press.

Dawkins, R. 1995. "God's Utility Function" *Scientific American* November, 80–85. http://www.physics.ucla.edu/~chester/CES/may98/dawkins.html

De Lubac, H. 1965. *The Mystery of the Supernatural*. Trans. Sheed, R. New York: Herder & Herder, The Crossroad Publishing Company.

De Lubac, H. 1995. *The Drama of Atheist Humanism*. San Francisco: Ignatius.

Derrida, J. 2000. *Of Hospitality. Anne Dufourmantelle Invites Jacques Derrida to Respond*. Trans. Bowlby, R. California: Stanford University Press.

Emilsson, E. 2017. *Plotinus*. London and New York. Routledge.

Fairbairn, R. 1952. *Psychoanalytic Studies of the Personality*. London: Routledge.

Frankl, V. 1946. *Man's Search for Meaning. An Introduction to Logotherapy*. Trans. Lasch, I. London: Hodder and Stoughton.

Frayn, M. 2008. *The Human Touch: Our Part in the Creation of the Universe*. London: Faber and Faber.

Garcia Sanz, S., Nzewi, C. 2017. "Dostoevsky and the Religious Experience. An Analysis of *The Possessed*". *Church, Communication and Culture*, 2, no. 3, 292–299. https://www.tandfonline.com/doi/full/10.1080/23753234.2017.1391674

Gardner, H. 1983. *Frames of Mind: The Theory of Multiple Intelligences*. London: Basic Books.

Gray, J. 2018. *Seven Types of Atheism*. London and New York: Penguin Random House.

Grotstein, J. 2000. *Encyclopaedia of Psychoanalysis. Drawing the Soul*. London and New York: Routledge.

Holland, T. 2019. *Dominion. The Making of the Western Mind*. London: Little, Brown.

Jackson, R. L. 2008. *"Introduction: Vision of Darkness" to Dostoyevsky, F. Notes from the Undergound and The Double*. London and New York: Penguin Books.

Kitadai, N. Maruyama, S. 2018. "Origins of building blocks of life: A review". *Geoscience Frontiers* 9, no. 4, 1117–1153.

Kuhn, R.L. 2019. "Is the Anthropic Principle Significant? | Episode 1904 | *Closer to Truth*". https://www.youtube.com/watch?v=NMV9t-3rFNs

Lacan, J. 1954–1955. *The Seminar Book II, The Ego in Freud's Theory and in the Technique of Psychoanalysis*. New York: Norton, 1991.

Lacan, J., 1970. *Ecrits. The First Complete Edition in English*. Trans. Fink, B. London and New York:W.W. Norton, 2002.

Leithart, P. 2006. "Henri de Lubac: A Brief Introduction". https://www.patheos.com/blogs/leithart/2006/04/henri-de-lubac-a-brief-introduction/?permalink=blogs&blog=leithart&year=2006&month=04&entry_permalink=henri-de-lubac-a-brief-introduction

Lewis, C.S. 1947. *Miracles*. London: William Collins, 2012.

Lewis, C.S. 1949. *The Weight of Glory*. London: William Collins, 2013.

Lewis, C.S. 1952. *Mere Christianity*. London: William Collins, 2012.

Lossky, V. 1957. *The Mystical Theology of the Eastern Church*. Crestwood: St. Vladimir's Seminary Press, 2002.

McAleer, G., Wojtulewitz, C. 2019. "Why Technoscience Cannot Reproduce Human Desire According to Lacanian Thomism". *Forum Philosophicum* 24, no. 2, 279–300.

McEwan, I. 2019. *Machines Like Me*. London: Jonathan Cape.

Meyer, S. 2009. *Signature in the Cell. DNA and the Evidence for Intelligent Design*. San Francisco: HarperOne.

Miles, S., 2005. *An introduction to Weil, S., 1986*.

Monod, J. 1969. *From Biology to Ethics*. San Diego. Salk Institute for Biological Studies.

O'Shea, G. 2012. "Nature and Grace and the Appearance of Insincerity. Silencing the Catholic Voice". *Solidarity: The Journal of Catholic Social Thought and Secular Ethics*, 10 https://researchonline.nd.edu.au/solidarity/vol2/iss1/6

Olivant, D. 2004. "Culture and the Thomist Tradition after Vatican II". *First Things*. https://www.firstthings.com/article/2004/05/culture-and-the-thomist-tradition-after-vatican-ii

Rowland, T. 2021. "The Truth of Love and the Image of God". *Veritas Amoris Review*. Feb 20th.

Saunders, G. 2013. *Tenth of December*. London and New York: Bloomsbury.

Schindler, D. 2017. "Beauty in the Tradition: Hans Urs von Balthasar". *The Hildebrand Legacy*. https://www.youtube.com/watch?v=b26vvB3-97g

Smith, J. 2012. "Irredicible Complexity". https://www.youtube.com/watch?v=NaVoGfSSSV8

Steiner, G. 2001. *Grammars of Creation*. New Haven and London: Yale University Press.

Steiner, R. 1988. *Goethean Science*, trans. Lindeman, W. New York: Mercury Press.

Taylor, C. 2007. *The Secular Age*. Cambridge, MA and London: Harvard University Press.

Tillich, P. 1973. "Our Ultimate Concern". In *On the Boundaries of our Being*. London and New York: Fontana Modern Library of Theology and Philosophy, 269–270.

Vattimo, G. 1999. *Belief*. Trans. d'Isanto, L., Webb, D. Stanford: Stanford University Press.

Walstein, M. 1987. "An Introduction to von Balthasar's *The Glory of the Lord*". *Communio: International Catholic Review* 14, 12–33. https://www.researchgate.net/profile/Michael-Waldstein/publication/329328135_An_introduction_to_von_Balthasar%27s_The_Glory_Lord/links/5c01b7e845851523d15622af/An-introduction-to-von-Balthasars-The-Glory-Lord.pdf

Weil, S., 1986. *An Anthology*. London: Penguin Modern Classics, 2005.

Winnicott, D. 1956. "Primary Maternal Preoccupation". In Winnicott, D. (Ed.) *Through Paediatrics to Psychoanalysis: Collected Papers*. London: Karnac, 300–305.

Wojtyla, K. 2017. *In God's Hands. The Spiritual Diaries. 1962–2003*. London: William Collins.

Wolfe, T. 2016. *The Kingdom of Speech*. London: Jonathan Cape.

Index

abortion 67–68, 123
absent fathers 22–23, 27, 58–60; crime and 53; homelessness and 29
actuality 86
addiction 6, 73; drug 108–109
Adorno, T. 196
affliction 132–137
alcoholism 46
alienation 17, 150, 157, 160, 162; dis- 163
"alpha function" 204–205
Alverez, A. 74
Amis, M. 145; *Night Train* 202
anguish 164
anthropic principle 201–202, 209
anti-Oedipus complex 30
anxiety 9, 11, 23, 163–164; freedom and 109–110
"apocalypse" 156
apoptosis 182
Aquinas, T. 209–211, 215
Aristotle 209, 212
Armand, I. 25
artificial intelligence (AI) 214
atheism 196, 203, 205
authenticity 26, 164–166
authority 22, 23, 30, 31, 59, 67; children and 68; crime and 32–33
autism 71–73; treatment 74–76
automatism 177

Badiou, A. 193, 204–205
Balthasar, H. 214–217
banality 12
Bataille, G. 4
Baudrillard, J. 3, 8–12, 24, 71, 72, 96, 117, 145, 183, 213; *The Transpiration of Evil* 113
BBC 27, 32, 54, 55, 217; *Stabbed: The Truth About Knife Crime* 53

beatific vision 209–210
beauty 214; freedom and 215
behaviour, conduct and 59
Behe, M. 199
being 75–76, 124–128, 130, 133, 136, 143, 145–146, 158, 167, 176, 178, 179, 215; disintegration of 17; Gnosis and 156–157; language and 182–183
belief 3, 18, 24, 34, 64, 221; in God 99
Benjamin, W. 162
Bensoussan, G. 15
Berardi, F. 187
Berggren, H. 26
Berry, F., *Michael Inside* 32
Best, G. 45
Bettelheim, B., *The Uses of Enchantment* 69–70
Biden, J. 14–15, 32
Bielik-Robson, A. 148–149, 157–159, 162, 166
Bion, W. 3, 5, 24, 157, 204
bio-power 131–132
Blair, L. 73
Blondel, M. 210
Bloom, H. 159
Blumenberg, H. 160, 162
Bogomils 163–164
Bokoni, P. 29
Book of Kells 220–221
Boone, C., *The Curious Incident of the Dog in the Night-Time* 73
Borch-Jacobsen, M. 167, 184
Boy A 52–53
Brague, R. 114, 146–148, 151, 168
Bruckner, P. 122, 185
Brussioni, M. 29–30
Bryan, D. 83
Bukharin, N. 16
bureaucracy 13–14, 30–31, 64, 67

Cameron, D. 90
capitalism, family and 25–26
Caputo, J. 13
Carbon, the element 200
Carbonell, N. 75
care 204
Carey, J. 183; *The Intellectuals and the Masses* 184
Carrère, E. 57
Carter, B. 201
castration 59, 60, 89, 91, 214
Centre for Social Justice 22, 33
Chesterton, G. K. 206, 220
children 55, 64, 65, 94; abortion and 67–68; absent fathers and 27–29; authority and 68; autism and 73–75; drug trafficking and 67; hate incidents and 65; identity-play 90; internet and 66; natural play and 69; parental separation and 70–71; responsibility and 71; transitional space 70
Chosen 45
Christianity 134, 137, 145–147, 155, 163, 167–168; Incarnation and 206–211; Resurrection and 217–219; *see also* God
Communism, family and 25–26
community 27
concern, meaning and 203
conduct, behaviour and 59
connatus essendi 125; *see also* Levinas, E.
Constant, B. 147
contraception 68
Cooper, D. 26
"Country Lines" 67
creation 210–213; de- 135
crime: authority and 32–33; international 31–32; knife 53
Critchley, S. 164, 168
Crowley, J. 52
Culianu, I. 160
Cultural Marxism 96, 98
Cultural Revolution 22, 24, 95
Cunningham, C. 155, 219–220
cutting 11
Czermak, M. 44, 50–51

Dalrymple, T, *The Knife Went In* 35
Darwinian evolution 198–199, 202; irreducible complexity and 200
Dasein 127, 164
Davies, E. 33
Dawkins, R. 202
Dawson, M. 75–76
death 23, 145, 167; *apoptosis* 182; drive 6, 9, 17, 22, 35, 88, 98, 100, 107,

121, 157, 167, 175–182, 185–187; by exposure 72–73; fear of 6; of God 147; God of 165–166
deconstruction 98, 111, 122
de-creation 135
Deleuze, G. 9
democracy 14–15
depressive position 5, 6
depth 12, 13, 135
Derrida, J. 122, 159–160, 162, 193, 205
design: anthropic principle 201–202, 209; complexity and 199–200; intelligence and 198–199; Intelligent 209; mathematics and 198; order and 197
desire 125, 165, 176, 178, 214
devolution 98
diachrony 136
Dick, P. K. 25
dis-alienation 163
disappearing 10, 12
"Disintegration Directive" 15
dissent 15
DNA 8, 198
Doing Money 32
Dostoevsky 193, 204; *Notes from the Underground and The Double* 194; *The Possessed* 194
Doyle, R.: "No Man's Land" 7; *Threshold* 9
dream(s/ing) 5, 8, 10, 16–18, 24, 34, 73, 128–129; "alpha function" and 204–205; of control 7; of failure 6; image 10; of killing 5; of resistance 7
drive 163–164, 177–179; death 6, 9, 17, 22, 35, 98, 100, 107, 121–122, 157, 167, 175, 176, 180–182, 185–187; oral 88
drug trafficking, "Country Lines" 67
dualism 163–164

Eagleton, T. 33–34, 72
Eberstadt, M., "The Fury of the Fatherless" 33
Economic and Social Research Institute (ESRI) 29
Edmunds, R. 56
ego 4, 11, 22, 34, 127, 179; Actuality- 86; diachrony 136; ideal 86, 89–91, 97, 108; self-preservation and 88–89; super 6, 24, 83, 89, 91, 97, 108–110, 115, 168
Eliot, T. S. 5
emotion, fatherhood and 51–52
emotivism, MacIntyre 16
empathy 126–127
Enlightenment, the 122
equality 70, 71

ethics 76, 109, 155, 176; of ethics 125, 129; Levinasian 124–127, 129–132, 134–135; psychoanalysis and 37–39
Europe 122
evolution *see* Darwinian evolution
extended family, child-rearing and 27–28

Facebook 15
family(ies) 22, 25–27, 36, 109–110; fatherless 60; responsibility and 68; single-parent 27–29
Fanon, F., *The Wretched of the Earth* 123
father(s) 4, 17–18, 24, 34, 36, 37, 44, 54, 57, 65, 66, 122; absent 22–23, 27, 60; black 28–29; emotions and 51–52; love and 45–49; protector role 60–61; responsibility and 37–38, 58; risky play and 29–30; trust and 55
feminism 123, 205
Fibonacci sequence 197
Fitzgerald, S. 145–146
fixation 92–93
Floyd, H. 15–16
Forbidden Planet 138
forthgiveness 87, 114–115
Foucault, M. 131
fractals 197
Frankl, V. 193; *Man's Searching for Meaning* 12–13, 203–204
Fraser, D. 27
Frayn, M., *The Human Touch* 201
freedom 109–110, 143, 151, 200, 216; theo-drama 215–216
Freud, A. 86, 135
Freud, S. 17–18, 22, 33, 34, 47, 60, 74–75, 83, 84, 86, 88, 93, 99, 111, 121, 124, 127, 179, 181; *The Ego and the Id* 6; *Inhibition, Symptoms and Anxiety* 136; *Moses and Monotheism* 23; pleasure principle 5; Seduction Theory 3–4, 96; self-preservation 88–89
Friel, B., *Philadelphia, Here I Come!* 44, 48–49
Furedi, F. 16, 175

García Sanz, S. 194
Gates, B. 198
Generating Genius 27
Gervais, R. 16
Gide, A. 132–133
"gift-exchange" 199
Girard, R. 218–219
Giridharadas, A. 116
Glynn, M., "Dad and Me" 27

Gnosticism 143, 155, 160, 162, 166; "apocalypse" and 156; Bogomils 163–164; Jewish 157–159; Jonas and 160–161
God 91–92, 97, 98, 107, 108, 133–135, 137, 143, 144, 146, 157–159, 161, 163, 203, 205, 220; belief in 99; Christ and 150–151; creation and 210–213; of death 165–166; Gnosticism and 156; grace and 211; "hidden" 162; hyperreality and 145; Incarnation 206–211, 214, 217; silence of 148, 151; theo-drama 215–216; Torah and 153–154; withdrawal of 148–149, 153
Goethe, J. W. 216
golden ratio 197
Good, the 37–39, 215
grace 211
Gray, J. 156, 194
guilt 51

Hamilton, H.: *The Sailor in the Wardrobe* 50; *The Speckled People* 49–50
Hanaghan, J. 83, 90–93, 95–97, 106, 129–130; forthgiveness 87, 114–115; on marriage 94; "Monkstown Group" and 84–86; "psychoanalytic healing" 84, 85, 106–107; self-preservation 88–89; spirit 89–91
Harries, R. 217
hate 99, 114, 117, 124–125, 138, 143; speech 123
Haughen, F. 15
Haynes, G. 13
"healing" 84, 85, 106–107
Heckman, J. 25–26, 60
Hegel, G.W.F. 165–166
Heidegger, M. 128, 164, 165, 181
Hemingway, E., "Indian Camp" 48
Hillesum, E. 161
Hitchens, P. 123
Hitches, C. 123
Holland, T., *Dominion* 207–208
Holocaust, the 12–13, 131, 154, 155, 159, 161
homelessness 29
hospitality 205–207
humanist psychiatry 184
human nature 211, 212
human trafficking 32
Hume, D. 147, 202
humility 138, 196, 202, 206, 212
humour 14
Hunt, T. 8
hyperreality 9, 10, 13, 71–72; cutting and 11; God and 145

id 5, 34, 87, 98
identification 47, 90
identity 17, 90, 127, 167, 177, 219; *see also* ego; illusion
illusion ix, 5–10, 17, 35, 68, 98, 99, 109, 110, 126, 137, 167, 183; Spinoza 133
Imaginary 9, 10, 212, 214, 220
imagination 90, 92; Oedipus complex and 91
imago Dei 157, 213, 219–220; *see also* God
Incarnation 206–211, 213–214, 217
indifference 90, 112, 116, 117, 145, 202, 203; zone of 37
information 198; *see also* intelligence
Integral Real 71; *see also* Baudrillard, J.
intellect 198; *see also* Plotinus
intelligence 66, 68, 75, 123; in Aristotle 209; in evolution 197–201; *see also* artificial intelligence (AI)
international crime 31–32
International Psychoanalytic Association (IPA) 86, 117
internet 13, 15, 32, 117, 156; children and 66; *see also* virtual reality
ipseity 127–130
Irenaeus of Lyons 155
Irish Psycho-Analytical Association 83

Jackson, R. L. 194
Jagodzinski, J. 180
Jesus Christ 91, 98, 148, 155, 156, 162, 163, 207, 221; Resurrection of 217–219
John Paul II, Pope 32
Jonas, H. 160–161
Jones, E. 83
Jones, S. 127
jouissance 23, 24, 26, 31, 33, 36, 60, 64, 66, 73, 111, 125, 145, 157–158, 179
Joyce, J. 60, 184
Judaism 125, 126, 155, 161; Lurianic Kabbala 149, 157–159; suffering and 152–154
justice 125, 130, 154

Kafka, F. 154; *The Trial* 175
Kanner, L. 75
Kennedy, L. 86
Kenny, M. 32
Khan, M. 86
Khan, U. 126–127
Khogali, Y. 123
Kiberd, D. 184
Klein, M. 99
Klein, N. 14
Klossowski, P. 9

knife crime 53
Kobylinski, A. 17
Kojève, A. 143, 166, 167
Kollantai, A. 25
Krell, F. 181

Lacan, J. 10, 34, 59, 60, 99, 101, 116, 143, 184, 199; death drive 6, 9, 17, 22, 35, 88, 98, 100, 107, 121, 157, 167, 175–182, 185–187; Father 18, 23–25, 33, 34, 44, 46, 57, 156, 165, 209; as gnostic xii, 143, 145, 156–159, 164–167; Real 3, 6, 11, 16, 23, 24, 31, 35, 53, 55, 67, 113, 136, 145, 154, 162, 165, 166, 176, 179, 181, 212–213, 220–221; Symbolic 9, 23, 55, 65, 73, 149, 156, 158, 178–180
Laing, R. D. 162
Lammy, D. 28
language 122, 179, 199, 220–221; being and 182–183
Laplanche, J. 181–182
Lasch, C. 109
Lavin, M. 109
law 114–115, 168
lawlessness 22, 32
Lazier, B. 160
Leithart, P. 211
Levinas, E. 22, 37, 39, 64, 74, 121, 128, 136, 145, 146, 148, 149, 152–154; ethics of 124–127, 129, 131–132, 134–135; *Otherwise than Being* 131; *Totality and Infinity* 124; *see also* ipseity
Lewis, C. S. 99, 202–203, 209, 213; on love 101
libido 4, 83, 86, 178, 219; object-attachment 87–88; Oedipus complex and 87
Loach, K., *I, Daniel Blake* 8
Logotherapy 12
Lossky, V. 207
Lott, T. 54
love 87, 92, 99, 100, 114–115, 133, 135, 212; fathers and 45–49; Lewis on 101; transference 5
de Lubac, H. 209–212
Lurianic Kabbala 149, 157; *Ein Sof* 158; *Kol Nidre* 159; *Tsimtsum* 158, 159

MacIntyre, A., *After Virtue* 16
Madders, T. 66
Maher, B. 30
Malcolm, J. 99
Manicheism 163
marriage 25, 28, 29, 83, 93, 95; Hanaghan on 94

masochism 135, 175
Masson, J., *The Assault on Truth: Freud's Suppression of the Seduction Theory* 3–4
maternity 129–130
mathematics 198
Matrix, The 16–17
Mayock, P. 29
McAleer, G. 213–214
McCullough, L. 136
McElhinney, A. 124
McEwan, I., *Machines Like Me* 213–214
meaning 13, 193, 202; concern and 203
melancholia 87–88
Melancholia 168–169
Melman, C. 44–46, 59, 220
Meltzer, D. 3, 6
mental health 44
mental illness 92, 183; death drive and 182
Merritt, J. 127
Meta 15
metanoia 193, 207
Meyer, S. 198–199
Milbank, J. 168, 211
millenarianism 156
Miller, A. 44; *All My Sons* 47–48; *Death of a Salesman* 47–48
Miller, J.-A. 30–31, 165
Millot, C. 176–177
Mitchell, B. 13
"Monkstown Group" 84–86, 113
Monod, J. 199
moral law 168
mother(s) 22, 24, 27, 75, 204
Muggeridge, M. 194
Myarek, H. 219
myth 69–70, 91; *see also* Symbolic

Name-of-the-Father 30, 31, 205, 221
narcissism 7, 10, 179; phantasy and 8; primary 87, 158; secondary 87
Narey, M. 65
National Council for Civil Liberties (NCCL) 4
natural selection 198–200
nature 213, 216; Fibonacci sequence and 197; human 211, 212; mathematics and 198
Neoplatonism 148, 162, 198, 212
Nerval, G. 147–148
neuro-psychoanalysis 181
Nietzsche, F. 7, 9, 16, 17, 33–34, 143–145, 165, 203
nihilism 17, 55, 132, 163, 196, 202
Noailles, E. 12

No Country for Old Men 44, 53–54
non-existent reality 9
non-judgementalism 16
"not-me" 64, 73

Obama, B. 15, 28
Oedipus complex 24, 58, 86–87, 89; anti- 30; dreams and 4; identification 47; imagination and 91; libido and 87
Omidyar, P. 15
One, the 197–198, 204–205
oral drive 88
order, hidden in universe 197
O'Regan, M. 100
originary passivity 126–127
Orwell, G. 14
Other 22, 35, 67, 99, 148, 157–158, 163, 164, 180, 209, 218
other, the 123, 130, 146
O'Toole, F. 55
Owens, B. 29
Owens, L. 31

Paedophile Information Exchange (PIE) 4
paedophilia 4, 45
pain 136
Pamuk, O. 44; *The Red-haired Woman* 57–58
paramilitaries 31
paranoid-schizoid (PS) position 5–6, 220
parricide 73
Pascal, B. 123, 147, 202
Patrick, T. 29
Paul (apostle) 165, 168, 208, 218
Paul, J., "Speech of the Dead Christ from the Universe that there Is No God" 147
Pavlensky, P. 186
perversion 6; masochism and 135–136
Peterson, J. 18
phantasy 4–5, 7, 83, 91, 99, 114, 158–159, 168; fixation and 92–93; of killing 5; narcissism and 8
phenomenology 145
philosophy 17, 125, 198; *see also* Baudrillard, J.; Caputo, J.; Gnosticism; Hanaghan, J.; Kojève, A.; Levinas, E.; postmodern theory
Pickstock, C. 132
Pizarnik, A. 163, 178
play 73; identity- 90; natural 69; risky 29–30
pleasure principle 5, 178
Plotinus 146, 193, 197–198
Poliakoff, S., *Joe's Palace* 44, 51

politics 15, 44, 57, 124, 125; identity 112, 138, 167
Pontalis, J.-B. 181–182
postmodern theory 7, 13, 16–17, 33–34, 36–37, 51, 58, 71, 72, 75, 109, 125, 176; reality and 15
poverty 27, 28, 58, 109; spiritual 95, 109, 193; *see also* humility
power 66–67, 117, 159, 161, 205, 208; bio- 131–132; feminist 123–124; male 116; ontology of 132; *see also* humility
primary narcissism 87, 158
Prisoners Rights Organisation 28
"Project of Declaration of the Principles of Lacanian Practice" 34–35
psyche, the 107
psychoanalysis 3, 17, 22, 24, 36, 48, 64–65, 83, 92, 98, 100, 101, 117, 126, 127, 177, 184–186, 198, 220; anti-Oedipus complex 30; autism and 75–76; castration 60; children and 66; ethics and 37–39; forthgiveness and 87; Lacanian 35; Logotherapy 12; "Monkstown Group" 84–86; neuro- 181; "Project of Declaration of the Principles of Lacanian Practice" 34–35; self-preservation 88–89; sexual abuse and 4; spirit, the 89–90; transference love 5; women and 111–112; "working through" 86; *see also* ego; Hanaghan, J.; Oedipus complex; phantasy
public good 96

Rank, O. 91
rape culture 4, 32
Ratzinger, J., *Introduction to Christianity* 219
Razzall, K. 67
Reagan, R. 14
Real, the 3, 6, 11, 16, 23, 24, 31, 35, 53, 55, 67, 113, 136, 145, 154, 162, 165, 166, 176, 179, 181, 212–213, 221; Baudrillardian 9; Integral 71
reality 17, 86; banality and 12; cutting and 11; depressive position 6; emotivism and 16; hyper 9, 10, 13, 71–72; non-existent 9; non-judgementalism and 16; objective 10; paranoid-schizoid (PS) position and 5–6; postmodern theory and 15; principle 5; text and 7–8; virtual 11, 72
reason 126–127
recurrence 127–128
relationships 100
religion, God and 146–147
repetition compulsion 100, 177, 178
Repin, I., *Ivan the Terrible and His Son* 58

repression 97–98
resistance 99; autistic 71; family as 25; global x; psychoanalytic 6, 7, 17, 95
responsibility: children and 71; family and 68; fathers and 37–38, 58
Resurrection, the 217–219
Revelation 148, 149, 151, 154, 216
Richardson, W. 37
Riches, A. 206–207
Roberts, S., *Le Mur* ('The Wall') 76
Rosenfeld, H. 3, 6, 7
Rosin, H. 58–59
Roudinesco, E. 183–184
Rousseau, J.-J. 26
Rowland, T. 211, 219
Rowlatt, J. 55
Russell, M. 10
Russia 55–56

Sachs, J. 36
salvation 218
Sanders, G. 196
Schmitt, E. 14
Schoenberg, A., *Moses und Aron* 154–155
Scholem, G. 162
Schwartz, R. M. 153, 154
science 181, 209
secondary narcissism 87
Seduction Theory 3–4, 96
selection bias 202
self 10, 13, 176–177, 221; as illusion 73, 117, 167, 176; not- 73; -preservation 88; *see also* ego; identity; illusion; simulation
Sewell, T. 27
sexual abuse 3–4, 45
shell shock 97
Shriver, L. 44; *We Need to Talk about Kevin* 54, 71
Simpson, J. 32
simulation 9, 10, 13, 64, 212; of childhood 66–67; virtual reality 11; *see also* Baudrillard, J.
Singh, P. 110
single-parent families 27–29
singularity: of AI xii; of God 154; of subject 36–37, 64, 74–76, 126, 127, 220
Skelton, R. 101
Sloterdijk, P. 36, 72
Smith, A. 147
social control 35
socialism 116
social media 10, 11; Facebook 15; non-judgementalism and 16

Sonalker, A. 14
soul, the 35, 37, 72, 84, 85, 90, 107, 112, 125, 127, 132–135, 156, 163–165, 168, 198; and the father 23, 64, 197, 198, 215
soulless 200
sovereignty 117, 178, 198; of God 149–150, 161
spirit, the 83, 89–90, 93, 98, 113, 165–166
Stabbed: The Truth About Knife Crime 53
Stasi 15
Steinbeck, J., *The Grapes of Wrath* 44, 51–52
Steiner, G. 36–37, 154, 155, 175–176, 198, 216; *The Death of Tragedy* 143, 144
Strauss, L. 125, 165
structuralism 199
subjectivism 16
sublimation 34, 92, 95; de- 97
suffering 6, 12, 18, 76, 84, 131, 143, 182, 184, 212; affliction 132–137; anguish 164; God and 144–145; Jewish 152–154; masochism and 135–136
suicidality 50–51
superego 6, 24, 83, 89, 91, 97, 108–110, 115, 168
supernatural, the 211–212
Swedish progressive social model 26
Symbolic order 9, 55, 65, 73, 149, 156, 158, 178–180; Book of Kells 220–221
symbols 31; Lacan on 23

tattoo 11
Taubes, J. 158
Taylor, C. 207
technology 14, 72, 74
text 183; DNA 8; reality and 8
theo-drama 215–216
Thunberg, G. 55
Tillich, P. 203
Tolentino, J. 13
Torah 153
Trakl, G. 35
transference 100–101; love 5
transitional space 70
trieb 157
Trigell, J. 52
trust 55

truth 8, 9, 13, 16–17, 122–123, 144, 183, 215; dissent and 15
Turgenev, I., *Fathers and Sons* 44, 55–57
Tustin, F. 73–74

United Kingdom, single-parent families in 60
universe 203; anthropic principle and 201–202; design and 196–200; order and 197
Ussher, A. 86

Vattimo, G. 17, 218–219
violence 54, 64, 116–117, 123, 124, 130, 143, 208, 221; against children 65; crucifixion and 219; divine 149; names and 183
Virilio, P. 17, 72
virtual reality 11, 72
vision 91, 92, 99, 215; beatific 209–210

Waldstein, M. 216
Walker, B. 132
Warren, E. 8
Weatherill, R.: *The Anti-Oedipus Complex* 125–126; *Cultural Collapse* 6
Weil, S. 39, 121, 132–134, 136, 137, 212
whistleblowers 15
White Mischief 121
white supremacy 122–123
Winnicot, D. 5, 69, 75, 99, 204; *Playing and Reality* 3
Wojtulewitz, C. 213–214
Wolfe, T., *The Kingdom of Speech* 199
women 123, 204–205, 217; Communism and 25; human trafficking and 32; psychoanalysis and 111–112
World Association of Psychoanalysis (WAP) 35

YoungMinds 66
youthful idealism 111, 114

Zhenotdel 25
Zimmerman, M. 129
Žižek, S. 35–36, 65, 73, 131, 134, 163, 178–180, 210
Zupancic, A. 178

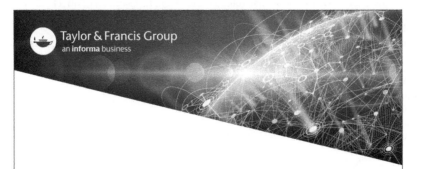

Lightning Source UK Ltd.
Milton Keynes UK
UKHW020632030922
408272UK00005B/47